POPULAR RELIGION AND ASCETIC PRACTICES

New Studies on Mahimā Dharma

Popular Religion and Ascetic Practices

New Studies on Mahimā Dharma

Edited by

ISHITA BANERJEE-DUBE
JOHANNES BELTZ

MANOHAR
2008

First published 2008

ISBN 81-7304-756-1

Published by
Ajay Kumar Jain *for*
Manohar Publishers & Distributors
4753/23 Ansari Road, Daryaganj
New Delhi 110 002

Printed at
Lordson Publishers Pvt Ltd
Delhi 110 007

Contents

Illustrations

Acknowledgements

This book brings to the public new research on Mahimā Dharma, a religious tradition which is still unknown outside Orissa. It is the aim of the editors to draw attention to a religious movement which deserves interest and research. The project goes back to an international seminar on Mahimā Dharma which was held at the Utkal University in Bhubaneswar on 23 February 2002. The seminar was entitled 'Reconsidering Mahima Dharma: New Research Perspectives on Popular Asceticism in Orissa' and was hosted by the University's Department of Anthropology. During the seminar, Indian and German scholars presented their research based on intensive fieldwork and textual research in the recent years. A selection of papers offering multidisciplinary approach, historical, ethnographic as well as literary, is presented here.

We would like to express our gratitude to all staff members for their hospitality and generous invitation. We remember the outstanding guidance of Profs. Prasanna K. Nayak and Kishor K. Basa and the organizational skills of Lidia Guzy who later, unfortunately, had to resign from editing the present volume. We thank them all, again, for their help and encouragement.

As editors we further thank all our colleagues who contributed to this book, sometimes with small notes, sometimes with editorial suggestions. Shinjini Chatterjee undertook the painstaking effort of polishing our text and making it easier to understand. We also thank all the contributors to and participants of the conference, even if their papers are not here. Prasanna Nayak, Rajkishor Mishra and Bhagirathi Nepak who died recently deserve special mention. Their rich comments inspired us and made this volume original.

A publication like this requires funding. We were privileged to get financial support from the German Research Council (DFG) to whom we convey our thanks as well.

Finally we express our thanks to Hermann Kulke, Georg Pfeffer,

Burkhard Schnepel and Heinrich von Stietencron who did not hesitate to integrate our book into the Studies in Orissan Society, Culture and History series. Last but not least we thank Manohar Publishers for the quick and professional production of this book.

New Delhi ISHITA BANERJEE-DUBE
2007 JOHANNES BELTZ

Note on Transliteration and Transcription

We have retained the styles of transliteration and transcription adopted by the individual contributors. Where diacritical marks have been used, the standard academic conventions for Sanskrit have been followed.

Introduction

ISHITA BANERJEE-DUBE
JOHANNES BELTZ

Recent years have seen important developments in the historical study of popular religions in India. Such developments have involved mutual interchanges between history and a variety of disciplines, including anthropology, literary criticism and religious studies. All this has led to nuanced and new understandings of history and religion. This volume builds on such departures by taking up the case of Mahimā Dharma. Bringing together philosophical, theological, ethnological, historical and sociological approaches, it attempts to understand the diverse dimensions of a religious order that emerged in the second half of the nineteenth century and exists even today. Together the essays in this volume raise pertinent questions regarding the nature of 'popular' religion and the way it is perceived and understood by its adherents. They also illustrate the different ways in which scholars approach and examine religion.

Studying Mahimā Dharma

Mahimā Dharma is one of the most fascinating and intriguing religious traditions of contemporary Orissa. Of relatively recent origin, Mahimā Dharma drew upon elements present in Orissa's thought and philosophy for centuries, imbuing them with new meanings and significance. It was propagated in the tributary states of Orissa by a radical, wandering ascetic who has come to be known as Mahimā Svāmī. The new dharma advocated belief in an all-powerful, all-pervasive formless and indescribable Absolute who had created the world out of his *mahimā* (radiance/glory) and who was accessible to all through bhakti (devotion). Mahimā Dharma was open to all; but the vast majority of its adherents came from marginal, mostly untouchable, castes and tribal groups.

Though the movement came to the notice of the colonial state through a dramatic incident in 1881, it was not until the early decades of the twentieth century that scholars began to take an interest in it (Mazumdar 1911; Vasu 1911). However, very few systematic studies were conducted till the time Anncharlott Eschmann embarked on a thorough analysis of the elements and ideas of Mahimā Dharma in the 1970s.[1] As a member of the first Orissa Research Project of German scholars that sought to examine the critical role played by the cult of Jagannātha—the central deity of Hinduism in Orissa—in the growth of the regional tradition of Orissa, Eschmann analysed Mahimā Dharma within the framework of an autochthonous Hindu reform movement that had an anti-Jagannātha character.[2] Her sudden death left her project unfinished. However, the articles she had published and the collection of copied archival material, books and pamphlets in Oriya, photographs and recorded interviews she left behind, inspired younger scholars in India and in Germany to continue the work she had started.

Ishita Banerjee-Dube, who worked independently but in close association with members of the first Orissa Research Project, constructed an anthropological history of Mahimā Dharma on the basis of extensive fieldwork and archival research in Orissa in the early 1990s as well as a thorough study of the Eschmann collection (Banerjee-Dube, 1993). When the second Orissa Research Project was undertaken by German scholars in the late 1990s with a focus on tribal and folk traditions and their impact on the Jagannātha cult, two of its members, Johannes Beltz and Lidia Guzy took up Mahimā Dharma as a project of study. While Johannes Beltz conducted fieldwork in western Orissa and collected Bhima Bhoi's writings, legends and stories about him in order to trace the elevation of Bhima Bhoi to sainthood, Lidia Guzy looked at different centres of Mahimā Dharma in eastern and southern Orissa and analysed the rituals performed there to gauge their impact on the spread of the faith and trace the sect's links with other ascetic traditions (Beltz, 2003 and 2004; Guzy, 2002, 2003 and 2004). Both these researchers used and built on Eschmann's works and the materials she had collected (Beltz, www.mahimadharma.de; Guzy 2001–2).

The last quarter of the twentieth century also saw a surge in dissertations, essays and books on Mahimā Dharma, particularly on its principal advocate, the poet-philosopher Bhima Bhoi, by Oriya researchers. These works, of uneven scholarly merit, have largely remained confined to the boundaries of Orissa. This volume, the result of a conference organized by Beltz and Guzy in Bhubaneswar in 2002, brings together for the first time a range of studies undertaken by Indian, Austrian, and German scholars over the last decade in order to provide a comprehensive account of Mahimā Dharma, underscore its distinct and diverse trajectories and highlight the varied ways in which the faith has been studied. The volume also intends to serve as a basis for further research.

Popular Religion

Mahimā Dharma emerged and gained prominence in the 1860s when Orissa was in the throes of a devastating famine. The unsettled condition of the time probably aided the dissemination of the new dharma, which decried idol-worship and discarded the position of Brāhmaṇs as the mediators between gods and men. It also questioned social hierarchy by bringing the creator of the universe within the reach of all through pure devotion. Moreover, the practices of the sect defied the rules of caste and the norms of commensality. It is not surprising then that the message of Mahimā Svāmī appealed to large sections of marginalized men and women of the *garhjat* (tributary) states.

One still could ask what made Mahimā Dharma a 'popular' religion? We use the word 'popular' here simply to indicate that the social base of the new faith was largely constituted by subordinate groups —members of low and untouchable castes and tribes—and not by elite groups. The overwhelming presence of low-caste men and women among the adherents of Mahimā Dharma was due to the fact that the precepts of Mahimā Svāmī embodied a social ideology opposed to 'the religious and worldly dominance of upper castes' (Lorenzen, 2005: 2). The social critique inherent in the founder's teachings was invigorated and extended in the compositions of Bhima Bhoi, the poet-philosopher and propagator *par excellence* of Mahimā Dharma. Of low birth and without formal education, Bhima Bhoi drew upon the teachings of his master and several religious traditions of Orissa in novel ways to expound a radically new theology. His inspired utterances in the form of *janāṇas* and *bhajanas*, devotional lyrics in praise of the Lord, were sung collectively at gatherings of devotees. This enabled the rapid spread of Mahimā Dharma over a large part of Orissa. Moreover, Bhima Bhoi's compositions lent themselves to appropriations by followers, a fact that accounted for their wide circulation and popularity. Through their own perceptions and practices, the ascetic and lay followers of Mahimā Dharma added force and vitality to the movement.

The unique importance of Bhima Bhoi within Mahimā Dharma has led the historian Chittaranjan Das (1951: 160) to comment: 'although Mahimā Gosain was the founder of Mahimā Dharma, it was really the works of Bhima Bhoi, the blind poet, that brought home to all people the essence and excellence of the new doctrine'. It is not a matter of surprise then that more than one critic has taken Bhima Bhoi to be the actual founder of Mahimā Dharma and that the twentieth century has seen the canonization of Bhima Bhoi. If the force of his message and the accesibility and pliability of his compositions made his works popular among the predominantly non-literate followers, the theology and philosophy contained in them allowed scholars in the twentieth century to discover and uphold Bhima Bhoi as the greatest representative of tribal Orissa. Hence, Mahimā Dharma and Bhima Bhoi have retained their hold and importance among adherents and sympathizers.

Bhakti, Sect and Caste

Since the 1930s, meticulous work by scholars has led to a wide-ranging literature on different traditions of bhakti, sects and *sants*.[3] These studies have improved our understanding of the distinct religious currents in India as they have helped us chalk out the convergence and divergence of new faiths such as Mahimā Dharma with earlier traditions. Broadly speaking, Mahimā Dharma belongs to the trend categorized as bhakti, since devotion to the Absolute constitutes its dominant mode of worship. Although the prevalence of diverse currents of devotion in distinct regions at different times makes it almost impossible to speak of a bhakti movement (Sharma, 1987), works on sects and *sants* have identified two broad streams within bhakti, *nirguṇī* and *saguṇī*. These two currents are distinguished by the way they conceptualize the Absolute who is the object of devotion.

The *nirguṇī* or *sant* movement that arose in north India about the middle of the fifteenth century spoke of devotion to a divine being who is unmanifest, unanthropomorphic and without attributes (*nirguṇa*). It stressed reverence for the saints and gurus of the movement, including their words and songs (Lorenzen, 1996: Introduction). Followers of the *saguṇī* (with atributes) tradition, on the other hand, worship the divine in its anthropomorphic manifestations, usually forms of the gods Viṣṇu, Śiva and the Goddess (Lorenzen, 1995: Introduction). Although they differ in their respective theologies and devotional practices, the two trends are not mutually exclusive and often intermingle to form a complex unity. Protagonists of the *nirguṇī sant* tradition, mainly members of middle or low castes—Kabir, Ravidas, Guru Nanak, Dadu Dayal, Sundardas and Paltusaheb, to name only a few—spoke against the marginalization of certain castes sanctified by the *śāstras* and the practice of idol worship, thereby questioning the ideology upheld by Brahmanical Hinduism. However, their criticism of social discrimination did not amount to an explicit denunciation of the unequal social order perpetrated by Brāhmaṇs or the existence of the caste hierarchy. Their criticism remained confined to religious practices and rarely addressed the society in its totality. The *saguṇī* tradition, which advocated devotion to a god with attributes actually gave a fillip to the worship of idols. This tradition thus seems to have encouraged the dominance of priests and Brāhmaṇs, temple worship and rituals (cf. Lorenzen, 1995: Introduction).

Clearly, Mahimā Dharma belongs to the tradition of *nirguṇa* bhakti, a fact that accounts both for its unorthodox nature and its popularity among subaltern groups. Indeed, the compositions of Bhima Bhoi, the poet-philosopher of Mahimā Dharma, reflect the same mix of a message of pure devotion with an underlying critique of social discrimination, as is characteristic of the *dohās* (couplets) of Kabir. The prevalence of a tradition of devotion to a formless, attributeless Absolute in Orissa has been noted by several Oriya scholars. They have also highlighted the strong impetus given to the trend by medieval mystics, the Panchasakhās, or the five friends (Das, 1951; Pradhan, 1986), and pointed to the contiguity of the tenets of Mahimā Dharma with those of the Panchasakhās. This has helped scholars contextualize the new faith in the long current of *nirguṇī* thought and to understand it in terms of its heritage (Das, 1991). The novelty and uniqueness of Mahimā Dharma has been largely discounted in such understandings.

The myriad studies of sects and *sant* traditions referred to above, particularly the early ones, also attempted to construct genealogies. They focused on the ideas, cosmologies and philosophies of the trends to situtate them within a linear history of religious ideas and philosophies. This often involved detailed textual exegesis (Hess and Singh, 1983; Vaudeville, 1974)[4] to the relative neglect of beliefs and actual practices of the followers. Works that began to appear from the 1980s were marked by a different preoccupation. These studies evaluated and questioned Dumont's (1970) influential model which conceives of the relation between sect and caste as dichotomous, on the basis of the assumed opposition between Brāhmaṇ and renouncer, householder and ascetic, man-in-the-world and individual-outside-the-world. Basing themselves on detailed fieldwork, these anthropological studies questioned the binaries inherent in Dumont's analysis by pointing out that sects do not necessarily recognize any opposition between the renouncer and the householder. Sects, these works argued, adopt different approaches, from total rejection to varying forms of acceptance, towards the rules of caste (Burghart, 1983; Lorenzen, 1987).[5]

The study of religious trends and institutions has been further enriched by the appearance of a large number of detailed analyses on the role and functions of ritual specialists, and the formation and evolution of new religious formations (Appadurai, 1981;

Banerjee-Dube, 2001a; Beetz 2005; Dube, 1998; Fuller, 1991, 2004; Van der Veer, 1989).[6] Combining the methods of history and ethnography, these works have chalked out the varied responses of religious functionaries to changing situations, and underscored the deployment of religious idioms by subordinate groups to cope with their subordination. They have opened a vista of myriad forms of protest and attempts at reform and conversion that have enabled marginal groups to negotiate their subjugation and interrogate the dominance of Brāhmaṇs. By analysing the significance of religion as a mode for the expression of resistance, these studies have taken the discussion beyond the concerns of religious studies and introduced new themes and debates in the study of religion.

The current volume adds to this corpus of academic work. It attempts to understand how members of low castes and tribal peoples registered their protest against oppression and sought to better their lot by becoming members of a radical religious order. The different chapters indicate the manifold ways in which religious reorientation allowed subjected groups to cope with their subordination and gain meaning and dignity in life. At the same time, the contributions do not tell a simple story of dissent and resistance. They highlight the inherent plurality of the tradition of Brahmanical Hinduism, the introspection that characterized it throughout its history, and the elements that Mahimā Dharma drew from this tradition in order to question the dichotomy of orthodoxy and resistance.

Mahimā Dharma in Perspective

The study of Mahimā Dharma was begun by colonial administrators who gradually took on the role of ethnographers. A dramatic incident brought the faith to the notice of colonial officers. On 1 March 1881, a group of ordinary men and women—lay followers of Mahimā Dharma—entered the temple of Jagannātha in Puri with the professed aim of dragging out and burning the idols of the Jagannātha trinity. Although unsuccessful in their attempt, this daring act on the part of the followers of Mahimā Dharma got the new religion inscribed in official records as '[a] sect of Ḥindu dissenters'.[7] *Utkal Deepika*, the only important Oriya newspaper of the time, also carried reports of the incident (*Utkal Deepika*, 1881a, 1881b). However, interest of scholars in Mahimā Dharma dawned only in the early twentieth century with the discovery of the manuscripts of Bhima Bhoi.

N.N. Vasu, the first to chance upon the compositions of Bhima Bhoi and other texts of Mahimā Dharma, began a long debate about the nature of the faith by describing it as 'crypto-Buddhism'. His principal argument was that the notion of the supreme —Śūnya Brahma —advocated by Mahimā Dharma was taken directly from that of *śūnya* or 'emptiness', a key concept in Buddhism. Vasu added that the mode in which ascetics of the Dharma collected alms and their practice of wearing earth-coloured robes were very similar to the practices of Buddhist monks. This theory, which has now been refuted by many scholars, had a great influence on subsequent studies of the faith for decades. Vasu also hailed Bhima Bhoi as the true propagator of Mahimā Dharma. The works of Vasu and others who followed him, and the editing and publication of Bhima Bhoi's works from the 1930s, resulted in the gradual elevation of the status of Bhima Bhoi. He came to be appreciated as a great poet, a radical social reformer, a revolutionary and a versatile genius. This was accompanied by an effort to discover and establish the 'true facts' of the life of Bhima Bhoi. The work of Anncharlott Eschmann in the 1970s turned the focus back on the nature of Mahimā Dharma as a Hindu 'reform movement'.

Eschmann not only outlined the dissimilarities in the notions of *śūnya* propounded by Buddhism and Mahimā Dharma, but also underlined the close resemblance of some key ideas of Mahimā Dharma with those of the Pancasakhās. Comparing the Dharma with other monotheistic reform movements of the time such as the Brāhmo Samāj and the Ārya Samāj, she defined Mahimā Dharma as an 'authochthonous' reform movement which did not arise as a result of the encounter with colonialism or Christianity.

Examination and analysis of Mahimā Dharma was given a further push by the active involvement and participation of one of its leading renouncers Biswanath Baba. An ascetic at the helm of affairs at the headquarters of the Dharma between the 1930s and the 1990s, apart from writing 'authentic' histories and authoritative explications of the Dharma, he took part in seminars and discussions on the nature of the faith. Biswanath Baba clearly differentiated the tenets of Mahimā Dharma from those of Buddhism. At the same time, he aligned the Dharma closely to the Advaita Vedantic tradition of Hinduism. This interpretation has been seen by some as a move away from the original teachings of Bhima Bhoi. It is true that the message of protest against established Brahmanism inherent in Bhima Bhoi's teachings got diffused in the twentieth century. There was a visible shift in the faith's relationship with dominant Hinduism in the course of the century on account of the mutations undergone by it in course of its evolution and because of the influence of Biswanath Baba.

The evolution of Mahimā Dharma has formed the subject of analysis of recent studies. Ishita Banerjee-Dube has tracked the career of Mahimā Dharma and highlighted its institutionalization and its multiple pasts.[8] Works of Johannes Beltz, Lidia Guzy and other scholars associated with the second German Research Project, as well as scholars based in Orissa, have focused attention on new developments within the faith. Lidia Guzy has explored the social diversity of the Mahimā Dharma community by comparing the religiosity of the elites, the *bābās* of the monastic centre in Joranda, and the common lay practitioners in the remote tribal areas. Johannes Beltz, Bettina Bäumer, Sadananda Das and others have gathered legends and stories about Bhima Bhoi and studied his numerous compositions to bring to the fore their distinct dimensions. All this has yielded new and nuanced understandings about Mahima Dharma. The present volume provides a fair representation of this new scholarship and offers a sample of the diverse ways in which Mahimā Dharma has been approached and analysed by academics and scholars who pertain to different disciplines.

Themes and Chapters

As stated before, this volume intends to provide a better understanding of Mahimā Dharma, a multidimensional religious movement, by bringing together analyses of different hues and textures. Together, the chapters in this volume raise several questions. How is the faith, as it stands after almost a century-and-a-half of its existence, to be characterized? Should it be viewed as a new religion or as just another Hindu sect? Is it principally an ascetic tradition? What then is the relation between the monastic and the lay orders? What kind of roles have householders and ascetic leaders played in the evolution of Mahimā Dharma?

The discussion and debate that surround these issues, highlight the different tracks the movement has followed in the course of its existence and the social and regional diversification it has undergone. The present-day Mahimā Dharmīs come from different social classes and castes, though the predominance of lower and middle castes and tribal groups remains. Ritual practices and theological concepts differ in accordance with the social setting. The ritual salutation of the sun and the fire, the veneration of the earth expresssed in the practice of wearing *geru* (earth)-coloured cloth by the followers, the holy hills of the termites worshipped by the devotees from a tribal background, the ascetic practices of the *bābās* as well as the high philosophical speculations of Bhima Bhoi about the Absolute constitute different aspects of the same tradition. Mahimā Dharma is a multifaceted and diverse movement with different centres. The diversity of interpretations and conclusions about the faith formulated by devotees and scholars underscore the same complexity. The chapters in this volume offer insight into the myriad dimensions of Mahimā Dharma and indicate the distinct ways in which it has been perceived. The multiplicity of ideas and interpretations bears testimony to the richness of the Dharma.

Very broadly, the volume highlights three prominent features of Mahimā Dharma. First, it is understood as a radical faith in which elements of reform and protest inhere. Eschmann's contribution places the new faith within 'tradition', emphasizes its indigenous character and tracks the genealogies of its principal tenets. Lidia Guzy draws upon her fieldwork conducted in different centres of Mahimā Dharma to advance a new and a suggestive argument. Examining some of the main rituals of the faith, she concludes that a strong current of asceticism underlies them.

According to her these rituals, which entail a simultaneous acceptance and rejection of features of Vedic and Brahmanical Hinduism, at once strengthen local non-Brahmanical patterns of priesthood and revitalize Brahmanical ritual modes. Guzy points to the wide variance in the practices of the faith across regions, arguing that it is this capacity to adapt that makes it possible for Mahimā Dharma to spread translocally while retaining its basic rituals.

The chapter by Johannes Beltz and Kedar Mishra stresses the challenge posed by Bhima Bhoi to the widely accepted notion of the celibate guru by taking to the life of a householder. In cohabiting with women and according them a prominent position within the faith, Bhima Bhoi, they claim, also countered the effort of male ascetics to control the affairs of Mahimā Dharma after the death of the founder. Till today the position of women within the community of Mahimā Dharmīs remains a central point of distinction between the monastic orders of eastern and western Orissa.

On a related though distinct register, Gourang Charan Dash argues that protest and reform characterized Mahimā Dharma since its inception. His analysis is based on the teachings of Mahimā Svāmī and on secondary literature. Dash suggests that the challenge to the dominant order that underlay these teachings made the new faith attractive to downtrodden people and resulted in the deification of Mahimā Svāmī. Dash also provides a collection of the early reports on Mahimā Dharma, offering primary sources for international scholarship.

The second point this volume underscores is the influence on Mahimā Dharma of a variety of religious and philosophical traditions. This is best reflected in the writings of Bhima Bhoi. Beginning with the unpublished essay by Eschmann, which discusses the influence of the Nāthas and the Panchasakhās on the doctrines of Mahimā Dharma, the contributions of Johannes Beltz, Bettina Bäumer, Sadananda Das and Sanjeeb Nayak highlight an important aspect of Bhima Bhoi's thought that involves the significant presence of one or several traditions. Analysing the eschatology and notion of time in Bhima Bhoi's key compositions, Beltz shows the close connection of these writings with the genre of popular apocalyptic texts known as *mālikās* prevalent in Orissa since the time of the medieval mystics.[9] At the same time, he points out that Bhima Bhoi's writings, interestingly enough, are silent on the new *yuga* (epoch). They speak of the end of the epoch, but not of a new beginning. *Mālikās*, in Beltz's opinion, should not be assesssed only as historical evidence but read as mystical and theological texts.

Bettina Bäumer tries to locate the main elements in Bhima Bhoi's *sādhanā* (prayer). Examining *Ādi-Anta Gītā*, a very difficult text of Bhima Bhoi, she underscores the influence of tantra on the poet. The main principles of tantra—the continuity of the physical, sensual and the divine, sexual symbolism of *cakras*, the association of *cakras* with letters of the alphabet and the integration of opposite but complementary realities—all find a place in the compositions of Bhima Bhoi. Bäumer relates the relative neglect of this dimension of Bhima Bhoi's works to the 'Vedantization' of Mahimā Dharma by Biswanath Baba. This process resulted in the acceptance of some aspects of Bhima Bhoi's spirituality and the marginalization of others.

Sadananda Das elaborates the different connotations of the guru within different religious trends of India, and charts the relationship of the master and disciple as elaborated in Bhima Bhoi's *Stuticintāmaṇi*. The text underlines the complementarity and mutuality of the master and the disciple, an understanding that owes its origin, in Das' opinion, to the intensely personal relation of Bhima Bhoi with Mahimā Svāmī. Despite the fact that Mahimā Dharma does not recognize a guru-*paramparā* (lineage of human masters), the impressive presence and importance of Bhima Bhoi's works among the followers bears testimony to the strong belief and veneration in a human guru within the faith.

Sanjeeb Nayak focuses on the literary style of Bhima Bhoi's compositions in order to outline the elements of rupture and continuity inherent in them. In language and rhythm Bhima Bhoi marked a distinct break with the over-ornamented Sanskritized tradition of medieval Orissa and returned to the earlier traditions of the vernacular. The use of everyday images gave his creations a simplicity and directness that made them accessible, although they contained profound philosophical thoughts.

The third significant point of the volume concerns the mutiplicity of centres and diverse trends within Mahimā Dharma. The papers by Fanindam Deo and Ishita Banerjee-Dube trace the mutations that the sect has undergone over time, resulting in divergent trajectories. Deo's analysis concentrates on Jorandā, the main centre of the faith. Tracing the process by which Jorandā emerged as the headquarters of the faith, he shows how this very process engendered the institutionalization of Mahimā Dharma. Under the aegis of a group of ascetics led by Biswanath Baba, Jorandā evolved as the most important centre through the establishment of permanent structures, and the elaboration on fixed norms, rituals and practices. Banerjee-Dube follows the distinct tracks taken by Mahimā Dharma across the nineteenth and twentieth centuries. Her chapter compares the towering figures of Bhima Bhoi and Biswanath Baba and underscores the differnce in style—of scholarship and leadership—of the two in order to understand the shift in emphasis within the faith. In the course of a century, Mahimā Dharma slowly changed its stance from contestation to conformity with dominant Hindusim, a change that brought a shift in emphasis from the periphery to the centre, from the oral to the written and from dissent to negotiation.

It is in these different ways that the explorations of the careers and incarnations of Mahimā Dharma help to understand the shifting yet salient connections between historical developments and specific local cultural configurations. The story of Mahimā Dharma exemplifies a well-known dilemma: to survive it must change, but in changing it must give up certain essentially charismatic qualities. In fact, it is this phenomena which in the end, is envisioned as an invitation for a broader and interdisciplinary academic debate. The volume seeks to offer a basis for discussion leading to a deeper understanding of religion.

Notes

1. Anncharlott Eschmann, the first daughter of Ernst Wilhelm Eschmann, a renowned professor of philosophy, and Charlott Eschmann was born in Munich, Germany, on 24 September 1941. Anncharlott grew up in Switzerland and studied Protestant theology, comparative religion and Indology at the Universities of Marburg and Heidelberg. In 1969, she completed her doctoral thesis on 'The Idea of History in Aztec Religion'. As a member of the first Orissa Research Project, she came to India in 1970 and met Biswanath Baba, a leading proponent of Mahimā Dharma that same year. She carried on extensive research on Mahimā Dharma till the time of her tragic death in Delhi in 1977.
2. The project was sponsored by the German Research Council and was in effect between 1970 and 1975. Researchers belonging to the project undertook a thorough examination of the cult of Jagannātha and its main centre, the temple town of Puri. Eschmann was the only member of the project who worked on Mahimā Dharma.
3. The literature is indeed vast. A few representative examples are Barthwal (1978); Dasgupta (1946); Gold (1987); Lorenzen (1995); Schomer and Mcleod (1987); and Sen (1930).
4. Several works of W.H. Mcleod on the Sikh tradition provide this kind of linear history of Sikhs.
5. Saurabh Dube's work on the Satnamis of Chhattisgarh has focused on the question of caste and sect from the perspective of a non-twice-born caste, the majority of whose members, gurus and lay followers were householders (cf. Dube, 1998 and 2004).
6. For studies emphasizing the interplay of religion and resistance, see Dube (1992 and 1998); Hardiman (1987).
7. Reports of several colonial officers were summarized and incorporated in the *Proceedings of the Asiatic Society of Bengal 1882*. The account appeared under the title, 'On the Origin and Growth of a Sect of Hindu Dissenters Who Profess to be the Followers of Alekh' (The Asiatic Society of Bengal, 1882). The reports were also included in the Jagannath Temple Correspondence, part VI, 1880–4, Orissa State Archives, Bhubaneswar.
8. For Banerjee-Dube's work in the field, see her texts cited in the References.
9. This is again a theme which had attracted wide interest. See Banerjee-Dube, 2003.

References

Appadurai, Arjun (1981), *Worship and Conflict under Colonial Rule: A South Asian Case*, Cambridge: Cambridge University Press.

Banerjee-Dube, Ishita (1993), 'Religion and Society in Orissa: Mahimā

Dharma in the Nineteenth and Twentieth Centuries', Ph.D. thesis, University of Calcutta.

——— (1999), 'Taming Traditions: Legalities and Histories in Twentieth Century Orissa', in Gautam Bhadra, Gyan Prakash and Susie Tharu (eds.), *Subaltern Studies X: Writings on South Asian History and Society*, New Delhi: Oxford University Press, pp. 98–125.

——— (2001a), *Divine Affairs: Religion, Pilgrimage and the State in Colonial and Postcolonial India*, Simla: Indian Institute of Advanced Study.

——— (2001b), 'Issues of Faith, Enactments of Contest: The Founding of Mahimā Dharma in Twentieth Century Orissa', in Hermann Kulke and Burkhard Schnepel (eds.), *Jagannath Revisited: Studying Society, Religion and the State in Orissa*, New Delhi: Manohar, pp. 149–77.

——— (2003), 'Reading Time: Texts and Pasts in Colonial Eastern India', *Studies in History* (n.s.), vol. 19 (1), pp. 1–17.

——— (2007), *Religion, Law and Power: Tales of Time in Eastern India, 1860-2000*, London: Anthem Press.

Barthwal, P.D. (1978), *Traditions of Indian Mysticism Based Upon Nirguni School of Hindi Poetry*, New Delhi: Heritage.

Beltz, Johannes (2000–1), 'Healing Practices and Mahimā Dharma: A Short Note from Recent Fieldwork in Western Orissa', *Adivasi*, vol. 40 1, pp. 92–102.

——— (2003), 'Bhima Bhoi: The Making of a Modern Saint', in A. Copley (ed.), *Hinduism in Public and Private*, New Delhi: Oxford University Press, pp. 230–53.

——— (2004), 'Devotion, Poetry and Healing: Exploring Bhima Bhoi's Stuti Chintamani', in A. Malinar, J. Beltz and H. Frese (eds.), *Text and Context in Orissa*, New Delhi: Manohar, pp. 143–73.

——— (2005), *Mahar, Buddhist and Dalit: Religious Conversion and Socio-Political Emancipation*, New Delhi: Manohar.

——— (2006), 'Contested Authorities, Disputed Centers, and Rejected Norms: Situating Mahimā Dharma in its Regional Diversity', in G. Pfeffer (ed.), *Periphery and Centre: Studies in Orissan History, Religion and Authsopology*, New Delhi: Manohar, pp. 79-104.

Beltz, Johannes and S. Jondhale (eds.) (2004), *Reconstructing the World: B.R. Ambedkar and Buddhism in India*, New Delhi: Oxford University Press.

Burghart, Richard (1983), 'Renunciation in the Religious Traditions in South Asia', *Man* (n.s.), 18, pp. 635–53.

Das, Chittaranjan (1951), 'Studies in Medieval Religion and Literature of Orissa', *Viswabharati Annals*, vol. IV, pp. 107–94.

——— (1991), *Odisara Mahimā Dharma* (Oriya), 2nd edn., Cuttack: Dharmagrantha Store.

Dasgupta, Sashibhusan (1946), *Obscure Religious Cults*, Calcutta: Firma K.L.M.

Dube, Saurabh (1992), 'Myth, Symbols, and Community: Satnampanth of Chhattisgarh', in Partha Chatterjee and Gyanendra Pandey (eds.), *Subaltern Studies VII: Writings on South Asian History and Society*, New Delhi: Oxford University Press, pp. 121–58.

——— (1998), *Untouchable Pasts: Religion, Identity and Authority among a Central Indian Community 1780-1950*, Albany: State University of New York Press.

——— (2004), 'Entangled Endeavours', in S. Dube (ed.), *Postcolonial Passages: Contemporary History-writing on India*, New Delhi: Oxford University Press, pp. 196–211.

Dumont, Louis (1970), 'World Renunciation in Indian Religions', in L. Dumont, *Religion, Politics and History in India*, Paris/The Hague: Mounton, pp. 33–60.

Fuller, Christopher J. (1991), *Servants of the Goddess: The Priests of a South Indian Temple*, New Delhi: Oxford University Press.

——— (2004), *The Renewal of the Priesthood*, New Delhi: Oxford University Press.

Gold, Daniel (1987), *The Lord as Guru*, New Delhi: Oxford University Press.

Guzy, Lidia (2001–2), 'Voices of Gods: Ecstatic Alekhs and Local Configurations of Mahimā Dharma', *Adivasi*, vols. 40–1, pp. 61–70.

——— (2002), *Baba-s und Alekh-s—Askese und Ekstase einer Religion im Werden*, Berlin: Weissensee Verlag.

——— (2003), 'Mahimā Dharma Ascetics: A Case Study on Popular Asceticism and its Patronage Structure in Rural Orissa', in A. Copley (ed.), *Hinduism in Public and Private*, New Delhi: Oxford University Press, pp. 211–29.

——— (2004), 'Babas and Alekhs—A Religion in its Making', *Journal of Social Sciences, Special Issue, Facets of Orissan Studies*, eds. C. Mallebrein and L. Guzy, pp. 105–11.

Hardiman, David (1987), *Coming of the Devi*, New Delhi: Oxford University Press.

Hess, Linda and Sukhdev Singh (1983), *The Bijak of Kabir*, New Delhi: Oxford University Press.

Lorenzen, David N. (1987), 'Kabirpanth and Social Protest', in K. Schomer and W.H. Mcleod (eds.), *The Sants: Studies in a Devotional Tradition of India*, New Delhi: Motilal Banarsidass, pp. 281–303.

——— (1995), 'Introduction: The Historical Vicissitudes in Bhakti Religion', in L. Lorenzen (ed.), *Bhakti Religion in North India*, Albany, New York: State University of New York Press.

——— (1996), *Praises to a Formless Lord,* Albany: State University of New York Press.

——— (2005), 'Introduction', in L. Lorenzen (ed.), *Religious Movements in South Asia from 600 to 1800*, New Delhi: Oxford University Press, pp. 1–44.

Mazumdar, B.C. (1911), *Sonepur in the Sambalpur Tract*, Calcutta: Brahmo Mission Press.

Pradhan, Nagendranath (1986), *Prachin Oriya Sahityare Nirgun Dhara*, Cuttack: Basanta Kumari Pradhan, Dharmagrantha Store.

Sen, Ksitimohan (1930), *Medieval Mysticism of India*, authorized translation from the Bengali by Manmohan Ghosh, London: Luzac.

Schomer, K. and W.H. Mcleod (eds.) (1987), *The Sants: Studies in a Devotional Tradition of India*, New Delhi: Motilal Banarsidass.

Sharma, Krishna (1987), *Bhakti and the Bhakti Movement: A New Perspective*, New Delhi: Motilal Banarsidass.

van der Veer, Peter (1989), *Gods on Earth: The Management of Religious Experience and Identity in a North Indian Pilgrimage Centre*, New Delhi: Oxford University Press.

Vasu, N.N. (1911), *Modern Buddhism and its Followers in Orissa*, Calcutta: U.N. Bhattacharyya, Hare Press.

Vaudeville, Charlotte (1974), *A Weaver Named Kabir*, Oxford: Oxford University Press.

Weber, Max (1921), *The Theory of Social and Economic Organization*, trs. A.M. Henderson and Talcott Parsons, and intro. by Talcott Parsons, New York: The Free Press.

Journals and Newspapers

'On the Origin and Growth of a Sect of Hindu Dissenters who Profess to be the Followers of Alekh', *Proceedings of the Asiatic Society of Bengal 1882*, Calcutta: The Asiatic Society, 1882.

Utkal Deepika (1881a), vol. 16, no. 11, 12. 3, 1881.

Utkal Deepika (1881b), vol. 16, no. 13, 16. 3, 1881.

CHAPTER 1

Mahimā Dharma and Tradition

ANNCHARLOTT ESCHMANN*

The ideological products of the Age of Reason in modern Europe had, by the early nineteenth century, begun to disseminate to its colonies. Western notions of rationality and reform were to significantly affect the imagination of the intelligentsia in its struggles to come to terms with a colonial identity. In India, one of the areas in which this imagination found actual expression was that of religious and social reform. Some of the greatest and most well-known reform movements, like the Brāhmo Samāj and the Ārya Samāj, were motivated by Christianity and Western thought to initiate critical and self-reflexive actions aimed at purging Hinduism of its archaic customs, like idolatry, ritualism and casteism.

The advent of Mahimā Dharma, a religious movement of this time, can be located in this context. At first sight, it bears the characteristics of other great nineteenth-century movements. Closer study reveals, however, the movement's intimate link with the Oriya tradition. The Brāhmo and Ārya Samāj movements used and reinterpreted the Vedas to make Hinduism more suited to its newly 'modern' and 'rational' adherents.[1] In doing so, they went to some extent against Brahmanical traditions or the traditional commentaries, as they backed their interpretation mainly from contemporary Western philosophy. While Mahimā Dharma too

*This unpublished paper was kept at the South Asia Institute of Heidelberg University. The editors decided to get it published posthumously inserting subtitles and minor changes.

reinterprets the scriptures regarding idolatry and polytheism, a significant departure from the concurrent reform movements was its reference to a peculiar Oriya tradition which had already expressed similar thought centuries before. Mahimā Dharma is paradoxically an anti-traditional movement within the tradition.

Renewals in the History of Religion

Each epoch in history has its distinctive ethos: the nineteenth century was marked by an upsurge of rational consciousness in all spheres of life, and all major religious movements of the time had an agenda of reconciling rationality with religion. Prior to this, it was the sixteenth century which had witnessed major religious renewal all over the world, a renewal which had several common features despite occurring across countries and religions. These were, firstly, the emergence of a new approach towards divinity which denounced cult and ritual worship and stated personal devotion to god to be the highest path to redemption. Secondly, this was a way equally open to all, whatever their social or ritual status. Thirdly, religious doctrines began to be propagated through actually spoken regional languages instead of through sacred or esoteric languages like Sanskrit and Latin, which were by that time no longer understood by the masses. The period is marked by translations of sacred books into regional languages, some of which are read even today, for instance, the German translation of the Bible by Luther, the Hindi *Rāmāyaṇa* by Tulsidas, or the Oriya *Bhāgavata* by Jagannātha Das. Other than the translations, a vast new religious literature in the respective languages also proliferated, like the individual works of the Panchasakhās[2] in Oriya. Of course, I do not mean to say that religious literature in Indian regional languages began at this time; this had been initiated centuries earlier. But this was the period of its glory and the emergence of perhaps one of its greatest exponents.

These three elements: the direct approach to god, the idea of equality of men before God, and the creation of a vast body of religious literature in regional languages is present almost in every religion. Christianity had its Reformation; Hinduism saw an outburst of regionally different theistic schools with their specific literature; and Islam, especially in India under Kabir, produced an accumulation of mystic doctrines denouncing its formal rigidity. Even in Japanese Buddhism, especially in its Pure Land Practice, there was in this period a successful movement which propagated loving surrender to the Buddha Amitabha ('Infinite Radiance', Jap. Amida) as the only means of redemption.

In India, these movements had two more common features: Firstly, they greatly advanced the cause of theism, and most of them were Vaiṣṇava and particularly stressed on the personal communion between the devotee and god. Second, they were primarily directed against archaic tenets of Hinduism. Brāhmaṇic hegemony was seriously questioned, as all souls were considered to be equal before god. Many of the works of this period were written by underprivileged and low-caste people, and a low social condition was even praised as a special boon for devotion.

The Panchasakhās, as mentioned earlier, represented an exceptional form of sixteenth-century renewal very typical of Orissa, the originality of which has only recently been recognized. It is on this special form of Oriya Vaiṣṇavism that Mahimā Dharma relies; therefore, its principal tenets—the worship of *śūnya*, the theory of *Piṇḍa-Brahmāṇḍa*, and the idea of a future redeemer who would come and openly establish what was for the time being a secret doctrine—have been briefly discussed here. Mahimā Dharma derived considerably from all these principles.

The concept of *śūnya* is of Buddhist origin and has caused much scholarly confusion in the interpretation of Mahimā Dharma. Until very recently, it was believed that because of their use of Buddhist terminology, the Panchasakhās' doctrines, as well as the Mahimā Dharma movement, were subaltern forms of Buddhism. The concept of *śūnya* as expounded by the Panchasakhās was, however, by no means identical with the original Buddhist concept of *śūnya* advocated by Nagarjuna.

In Buddhism, as the term implies, *śūnya* originally denoted the negative, non-describable nature of the ultimate reality. But influenced by Hinduism, it gradually came to signify a positive ultimate reality comparable to a certain extent to the idea of the

Brāhmaṇ. Mahāyāna, the theistic form of Buddhism, associated this modified concept of *śūnya* with the nature of the Buddha. Similarly, the concept was taken up by Oriya Vaiṣṇavism. *Śūnya* became the highest abode of Kṛṣṇa, and was even associated with the personal, theist idea of Puruṣa. It was thought by the Panca-sakhās to be the highest, indescribable (*alekha*) ultimate reality, whose glory (*mahimā*) was to be preached. The highest goal of redemption, the union of the soul with the personal god, was called *śūnya samādhi*. And this goal, according to the Panchasakhās, could not be achieved through ceremonies like pilgrimages, sacrifices or worship of images.

I would like to add two more features which have proved to be of some importance for the further development of theism in Orissa: the extraordinary stress which is laid on the idea that the true essence of religious doctrines is secret for the time being, but, though despised by the official religion of the time, would soon be unravelled by a messiah to establish the only religion of a new age.

Karma could therefore be no means to salvation, being on the contrary apt to retain the human being within the bounds of rebirth. True worship, according to the Pancasakhā doctrines, is individual meditation and yoga. The *Piṇḍa-Brahmāṇḍa* theory says that the universe and the human body are interrelated. The true devotee therefore need not travel to distant *tīrthas* (pilgrimages) to offer worship, but should try to attain *tīrtha* within his/her own body by practising meditation. *Piṇḍa-Brahmāṇḍa* states that the devotee should make his/her own mind the forest where true *tapas* (austerities) or *brahmajñāna* (knowledge of Brahman) can be practised in order to attain *śūnya samādhi*. Therefore, traditional scriptures are reinterpreted to imply that beyond the literal meanings of verses, like that of practising *tapas*, which are only for the un-initiated, there is a deeper symbolism in the tenets, which is for the time being a secret doctrine for the chosen.

The third principle, the birth of a messiah, states that a time would come when all non-believers would be killed in an apocalyptical war and only true believers would be left to enjoy the beginning of *satyayuga*.[3] Kalki, the last *avatāra* (incarnation) of Viṣṇu, is considered to be *nirañjana* or *śūnya brāhman*,[4] or Ādi Jagannātha himself. In his wars, he would be assisted by the goddesses of Orissa. He would reveal his glory (*mahimā*) and not spare the non-believers. A special kind of literature, the *mālikās*, deals with these events. Allusions to Kalki and the *satyayuga* are of course common in Vaiṣṇavism, but the intensity with which the advent of this age is repeatedly depicted, and its close relation with the secret doctrines of Oriya Vaiṣṇavism, as well as the extraordinary popularity of this kind of literature in modern-day Orissa seems to me a subject of fascinating study, which requires separate attention. To my knowledge, such an array of apocalyptic literature is not found in other regions of India. The need for such study becomes all the more important in view of the fact that Hindu scriptures are generally considered to have very few instances of this kind of literature.

Mālikās are widely found in Orissa, and their prophecies are prevalent in villages to the present day. The apocalyptic wars described in these have sometimes been identified with political ones, for instance, the fight against the Afghan general Kālāpahār, which thereby appear to have been predicted a long time before the actual incidents took place. The end of the wars signifies the beginning of *satyayuga*, when 'true religion' would reign and there would no longer be caste distinction and temple worship. The *bhaktas* (devotees) who would live to see *satyayuga* are sometimes listed by their names. They are the souls of those who have already converted to the secret doctrine and would be reborn at that time, when the Pancasakhās would also return.

Along with Kalki, and sometimes instead of him, another redeemer/messiah is mentioned. He is simply called Avadhūta and is considered to be a personification of Nārāyaṇa, as well as of Śūnya Śaṅkara. His appearance is said to mark the end of the reign of the Jagannātha *avatāra* and bring the final revelation by gradually disclosing his identity with Śūnya Anākāra (Formless Void). The doctrines of the Pancasakhā were controversial at the time; that is why they were written in an esoteric and secret language. Nevertheless, in course of time, they became widely known and are today generally accepted all over Orissa.

Origin and Growth of Mahimā Dharma

Mahimā Dharma derives from these doctrines to a great extent. It relies on the worship of *śūnya*, which is considered to be the highest reality; its indescribable glory (*alekha mahimā*) is in the origin of everything. But Mahimā Dharma goes a step further in considerably radicalizing these medieval doctrines. What was a secret doctrine for sixteenth-century Oriya Vaiṣṇavism, to be told only to the initiated, became under Mahimā Dharma general religious prescriptions to be openly practised. The idea of the fundamental equality of all souls is also expressed by admitting all castes to the new creed and stressed by taking up and glorifying the ritual of interdining. The encrypted denunciation of Brāhmaṇ supremacy found in medieval scriptures is clearly expressed in Mahimā Dharma, and a general rule has emerged for all Mahimā Dharmīs not to take food from Brāhmaṇs.

The idea of medieval Vaiṣṇavism that true worship is opposed to temple worship and pilgrimage has developed into the prohibition for all Mahimā Dharmīs to worship or even to possess images of gods, or to visit temples. Mahimā Dharma itself has only a few temples, which, following the worship of *śūnya*, are devoid of idols or totems, and rituals are minimal. True to the medieval idea of *Piṇḍa-Brahmāṇḍa*, personal forms of yogic prayer, instead of idol-worship, are considered to be essential for redemption and have to be performed by everybody twice a day.

The founder of Mahimā Dharma, Mahimā Gosāin, is considered to be this very redeemer, as predicted by the Pancasakhās. His followers believe him to be the incarnation of the Śūnya Puruṣa who has come to expose to the world the secrets of religious doctrines. According to the tenets of Mahimā Dharma, he is *ayonisambhūta*, a pure manifestation of the *mahimā* of Śūnya Anādi Brahmā. According to his believers, Mahimā Svāmī came to Orissa in 1826. He first stayed on the Kapilāś near Dhenkanal. There for twelve years he lived as Jalāhārī Gosāin, not taking any food except water. After these twelve years, he accepted his first disciple, Jagannātha, and renamed him Vāsudeva. Mahimā Dharmīs believed that this was Lord Jagannātha himself from Puri, who, gaining knowledge of the advent of the new redeemer, had rushed to his feet. This episode was the fulfilment of a prophecy announced in the medieval *mālikās*, where it was said that the cycle of *avatāras* of the Buddha or Jagannātha would come to an end when the new redeemer emerged.

After having initiated Jagannātha–Vāsudeva, Mahimā Svāmī stayed for another twenty-four years on the Kapilāś. For the first twelve years, he took only fruits and was therefore known as *phalāhārī* (one who lives on fruits) Gosāin, while during the next twelve years, he also took milk, which was sent to him by the mother of the then king of Dhenkanal, Raja Bhagirathi Mahindra Bahadur. After having completed these three stages of secluded life, which in a way marked the process of his incarnation through his gradual acceptance of earthly food, Mahimā Svāmī converted the earth goddess, Annapurna, (to the faith) and accepted a meal of cooked rice from her. Thus, having in a way converted the gods, he set out, accompanied by his disciple Vāsudeva, to convert the men.

One of the first converts was Bhima Bhoi. The story of this conversion is well known and narrated in detail by Bhima Bhoi in his *Nirvedasādhanā*. Bhima Bhoi was found as a blind baby near a palm grove by a Khand (an untouchable caste) couple, who brought him up. But soon his adopted father died, and his mother had to remarry the brother of her deceased husband. After two children were born from the new marriage, Bhima Bhoi suffered stepmotherly treatment, and at the age of twelve became a cowherd of a rich cultivator in the village of Kankanapada near Raidakhol It was there in 1862 that the spectacular conversion took place. Bhima Bhoi had fallen in a well. He refused to be rescued and started arguing with God about his miserable condition. Mahimā Svāmī and Govinda Das Baba appeared at that moment, and he instantly converted into the Mahimā faith. It is even said that Mahimā Svāmī bestowed him his eyesight, but that Bhima Bhoi asked to be blind again in order to be able to see the evils of the world and to be able to concentrate on the propagation of the new faith.

The astonishing success of Mahimā Dharma, which at the end

of the nineteenth century spread across the Mahanadi area from Cuttack to Sambalpur, is due a considerable degree to the works of Bhima Bhoi. Though he lived in the nineteenth century, he may be called the last medieval poet of Orissa, as he took up and continued the tradition of medieval Vaiṣṇavism. Like the Pancasakhās, he wrote *bhajanas* (devotional songs) and dialogues between gods and saints in the style of the Purāṇas. Thus, for instance, in *Nirvedasādhanā* he narrates the dialogue between Mahimā Svāmī and Jagannātha–Vāsudeva, through which the tenets of the new doctrine are explained. Above all, he took up the *mālikā* tradition, composing new ones which are now as well known and famous in rural Orissa as those of the Pancasakhās. It was Bhima Bhoi who depicted Mahimā Svāmī as the coming true of medieval predictions, and this is now widely believed all over Orissa.

But Bhima Bhoi not only described the coming of Mahimā Svāmī in terms of the older scriptures, he also predicted his return in the future. In his *mālikās*, he says that at the definite end of the *kaliyuga*, Mahimā Svāmī will come again, and then only the true *bhaktas*, that is, the followers of Mahimā Dharma—whose names are listed by Bhima—would be saved. The medieval *mālikās* explained the advent of Kālāpahār as a sign of the approaching end of the *kaliyuga*; Bhima Bhoi interpreted British rule and the construction of railways as Kālāpahār. Some of the bazaar-editions of his *mālikās* go further: one may find in these, passages describing the successful struggle for independence as the beginning of a new *satyayuga*. Bhima Bhoi's works rooted the teachings of Mahimā Svāmī within Oriya medieval tradition, thereby changing and influencing this very tradition. Further, in his later years, Bhima Bhoi seems in a certain degree to have outgrown Mahimā Dharma and to have founded a tradition of his own.

Little is known about the decade between his conversion and the end of the worldly life of Mahimā Svāmī. Gosāin, according to his believers, did not die but entered a *samādhi* (a state of intense meditation). This happened at Jorandā in 1876, and soon three temples were built in Jorandā near the place were Mahimā Svāmī attained *samādhi*—temples without any images: the Śūnya Mandira, the Dhuni Mandira and the Gādi Mandira. Jorandā developed into an important centre of Mahimā Dharma, where on Guru Purṇimā, the day of his *samādhi*, thousands of pilgrims gather. After the *samādhi*, a sort of council was held at Jorandā in which Bhima Bhoi seems to have been present. Nevertheless, he took no further interest in Jorandā, but in 1877 established his own *maṭha* (monastery) at Khaliapali near Sonepur, where the Raja of Sonepur, Maharaja Niladhar Singha granted him land.

The *āśrama* (sanctuary) at Khaliapali became a seat of experiment for achieving the synthesis between life spiritual and life temporal. Some of these experiments had a tantric character. Bhima Bhoi had several consorts, temporal and spiritual. Śriyā Mā Annapurnā was his chief spiritual consort, and she must have been a great and impressive spiritual force. Besides, there were two more spiritual consorts and two temporal wives. In 1892, Bhima Bhoi begat a son and a daughter with his wives. The children were considered to be embodiments of the Perfect Man, but soon died. Bhima Bhoi himself died in 1895 at forty-six years of age, and a very impressive Samādhi Mandira was built. After this, Śriyā Mā Annapurnā began governing the *āśrama*, which continued to be a spiritual centre. Her heritage was taken up by Sriyadevi, the daughter of one of the four Brāhmaṇ scribes to whom Bhima Bhoi used to dictate his poetry. Having lost her mother, Śriyā Mā was brought up by Annapurnā and continued her work after her death. Unlike Jorandā, Khaliapali has at present lost much of its spiritual force and appeal. Śriyā Mā, whom I met and who was for many years residing in the *āśrama*, has been driven away by a younger *sannyāsī* (mendicant) who is now occupying the *āśrama* and its lands, while she lives in the village in bitter anger.

The Definite Rift: *Kaupīndhārī* Versus *Balkaldhārī*

In 1912, the Mahimā Dharma movement encountered a split in its ranks. During the lifetime of Mahimā Svāmī, two classes of *sannyāsīs* had been initiated. The first stage was to be *kaupīndhārī*, that is, to wear a saffron loincloth. The sixty-four oldest and wisest *sannyāsīs* were sometimes called *balkaldhārīs* or *kumbhipātias*, and wore loincloths made of the bark (*balkal*) of the *kumbhi* (*Careya arborea*) tree. After the *samādhi* of Mahimā Svāmī, no *kumbhipātias* were initiated up to 1896, when one of the old *siddha sadhus* (wise monks) received a 'Śūnya bāṇī' (command from the void) to do so. Thus, the continuity of the monastic ordination was ensured; but in 1912 a *balkaldhārī* did not pay heed to a second 'Śūnya bāṇī', left the *maṭha* in Jorandā, and established an *āśrama* of his own near the Gādi Mandira. His followers did not initiate any more *balkaldhārīs*. The split in Mahimā Dharma, which probably started with the *samādhi* of its founder, has increased further, and there are now two very different sects in operation. The *balkaldhārī* group has as its core a very strictly organized monastic order. This group is noticeable because of its consistency, and its influence has, due especially to Biswanath Baba's works, spread considerably.

Kaupīndhārī sannyāsīs, in opposition to their bark-wearing brothers, are more free to try individual experiments, and are not subject to such a rigid monastic discipline. So one might find *kaupīndhārī sannyāsīs* settled in different occupations, often disconnected from each other or from any main centre like Jorandā or Khaliapali. But this in no way means that they have become unfaithful to the tenets of Mahimā Dharma.

Both groups still adhere to the basic tenets of the Dharma, and as we have seen, they truly represent the development and fulfilment of the medieval secret doctrines: a development which has by no means reached its end but is full of new possibilities for further interpretations. The different outlooks of the two main groups only assure the vitality of this movement by allowing devotees the chance to accept it in different ways. Whereas the Brāhmo and Ārya Samāj movements have considerably lost their appeal, Mahimā Dharma is continuously spreading. The lasting success of Mahimā Dharma is due to its being rooted within tradition, and this is a singular feature of this tradition. In other religions like Christianity or Islam, such esoteric and radical movements like the Pancasakhā school or Mahimā Dharma would create deep and lasting schisms, a total separation of the new movements from the traditional churches. In Hinduism, such movements are also questioned, discussed and perhaps cause clashes, as for instance in some villages with a small group of Mahimā Dharmīs. But such movements nevertheless generally stay within the folds of tradition and thereby facilitate the growth of new and even more radical movements, thereby enabling Hinduism continuously to be reformed and renewed out of its own tradition.

Notes

1. For instance, the leaders of these movements stated that the Vedas do not support idol-worship and that they contain descriptions of a higher, civilized form of life with great technological and scientific advancements which had been lost to succeeding generations.
2. The Pancasakhās or the 'five friends' were Achyutananda Dās, Balarama Dās, Jagannātha Dās, Ananta Dās and Yasovanta Dās—the pioneers of this sixteenth-century renewal in Orissa.
3. *Satyayuga* means here 'the age of truth', the new age.
4. The absolute Brahman is 'emptiness', without form, name and qualities.

References

Eschmann, Anncharlott (1978), 'Mahimā Dharma: An Autochtonous Hindu Reform Movement', in A. Eschmann, H. Kulke and G.C. Tripathi (eds.), *The Cult of Jagannath and the Regional Tradition of Orissa*, New Delhi: Manohar, pp. 375–410.

——— (1975), 'Spread, Organization and Cult of Mahimā Dharma', in Nilamani Senapati (ed.), *Mahimā Dharma*, Cuttack: Dharma-grantha Store, pp. 9–22.

Sahu, Nabin Kumar and Nilamani Senapati (eds.) (1968), *Orissa District Gazetteers, Bolangir*, Cuttack: Orissa Government Press.

CHAPTER 2

Translocal Rituals of Mahimā Dharma: The Fire and the Prayer

LIDIA GUZY

Introduction: Mahimā Dharma—A Religion between Monks and Shamans, Abstention and Ecstasy

Monks and laymen represent the ascetic religion Mahimā Dharma, which literally means 'the glorious dharma'.[1] The main features of this new religion are asceticism, in terms of a strict discipline of body and mind, a vegetarian diet, and a denial of caste. Mahimā Dharmīs worship Mahimā Alekha as the highest, unwritten (*alekha*),[2] indescribable god. Mahimā Alekha is conceived to be *śūnya*—the void—all and nothing. This god can only be approached through meditation, an ascetic lifestyle and ritual practices mainly consisting of: (a) fire rituals performed only by the ascetics, and (b) individual prayer practised by ascetics as well as by laymen. The religious concepts and values go back to the founder of the religion Mahimā Goswāmī, who lived at the beginning of the nineteenth century. His origin is unknown, but for his devotees Mahimā Goswāmī is the incarnation of Mahimā Alekha.

As a monastic organization, Mahimā Dharma is structured by two brotherhoods of monks dispersed throughout central Orissa (Dhenkanal): the *balkaldhārīs* and the *kaupīndhārīs*. The monastic centre of Mahimā Dharma is the holy city of Jorandā (in Dhenkanal). Hindu rural folk—and in recent times, the tribal population as well—in southern Orissa comprise most of Mahimā Dharma's lay members (Eschmann, 1975: 9–22; Eschmann, 1978: 386–7, Guzy, 2000–1; TRB, 1968 9).

Transgressing and adopting local religious configurations, Mahimā Dharma has assimilated diverse local religious features within its ascetic doctrine. In central Orissa, Mahimā Dharma has grown from being a subaltern reform movement (Banerjee-Dube, 1999 and 2001) to a powerful landowning ascetic group (*sampradāya*).[3] In central Orissa, the group often maintains good associations with local ruling elites who provide for the ascetics (*bābās*). Thus, in Dhenkanal, the asceticism of Mahimā Dharma reflects the system of patronage between local leaders and ascetics. Rural politics in central Orissa operates within the system of patrons in relation to ascetics. By sponsoring holy men and rituals, as well as places of worship, worldly patrons gain religious benefits and the moral sanction of being good rulers (Guzy, 2003: 211–29).[4]

In western Orissa (Beltz, 2006), Mahimā Dharma has developed its own religiosity which is centred on Bhima Bhoi and the Sambalpuri literature. According to the legends, Bhima Bhoi, a Khond in origin, was a mythical blind poet who is regarded as the first enthusiastic propagator and devotee of the religion. Despite being a layman, he was surrounded by followers in the nineteenth century. His popularity was especially widespread in the former Redhakhol (Rairakhol) state, where his sanctuary—Khaliapali near Sonepur—had risen to great prominence. Bhima Bhoi's devotion to Mahimā Goswāmī resulted in the creation of impressive masterpieces of Oriya literature (Mahapatra, 1983). His literary creations are assembled in collections called *Stuticintāmaṇi* and *Bhajanamālā*. In the theology of the Mahimā Dharma, these poetic compositions have gained the status of holy, prescriptive texts. Moreover, Bhima Bhoi's tradition displays an ambivalent character. Since the followers do not respect the authority of Jorandā and its ascetics, but consider Bhima Bhoi as their guru, the community of Bhima Bhoi represents a separate tradition within Mahimā Dharma.[5]

In southern Orissa (Koraput), Mahimā Dharma displays its locally specific tribal profile of asceticism. In Koraput, professional ascetics are rare, appearing once a year from Dhenkanal to initiate new devotees (*dikhyā*). The new teachings have become ever more popular due to ecstatic vocal rituals of the *alekha gurumai*, the local ritual specialists of the new religion. The ethics of these ascetics find their expression in the local shamanic tradition of ecstatic dialogues with the Divine. These ecstatic musical séances of *alekha gurumai* are considered holy healing sessions and play a crucial role in propagating the ascetic doctrines (Guzy, 2002 and 2004).

Since religious meanings are locally contested and always dependent on the speaker's interpretation and his/her social context, ritual practice remains the most crucial feature of the ascetic religion. It is not theological or religious concepts which define who is a Mahimā Dharma ascetic or layman and who is not, but the ascetic practice. On the one hand, the practice of ascetic ritual is external and translocal, moving beyond the specifically local configurations of concepts and ideas. On the other hand, ritual practice is internalized in the form of an ascetic lifestyle. As such, the ascetic ethic also overcomes localities and follows a translocal way of life.

Theological speculations on Mahimā Dharma are diverse and rich, especially within the laymen groups. Institutionalization processes in terms of a canonization of religious concepts and scripts into a standardized Mahimā Dharma theology, with the *Stuticintāmaṇi* and *Bhajanamālā* as its holy books, can be observed in Jorandā, the monastic centre of the organization (Beltz, 2006; Guzy, 2002). Until now, the process of institution-alization is still under development and the bifurcation of the brotherhood due to internal disputes has not yet been resolved.

This chapter will focus on external and internalized ritual practices followed by the Mahimā Dharma monks and laity in central Orissa (Dhenkanal), as these ritual practices create the translocal character of the religion. I will limit my description to ritual features mainly practised by ascetics.[6]

The Rituals of Ascetics: Fire Ritual

For the ascetics within the monk organization in central Orissa, religious practice means 'ritual reduction'. This expression implies that only one ritual pattern is used for all religious ceremonies.

For all family and village ceremonies, fire rituals (*jagia*) of diverse intensity and duration (see below) are performed by ascetics (*bābās*). Only the *bābās* are allowed to carry out the religious duties connected to the sacrificial fire. The *bābās* mainly perform for their patrons, who gain spiritual prosperity by sponsoring the ritual event. Dependent upon their social and religious contexts, *jagias* are named as follows:

(a) *ghiopura*, which is a small fire ritual, mostly performed for private occasions;
(b) *catordośi*, the official monthly fire ritual on the day before full moon. It is celebrated in all holy places (*tīrtha*) of the Mahimā Dharma religion; and
(c) *jagia*, the biggest fire ritual, which is mostly performed in Jorandā.

The Ritual of ghiopura

The ritual of *ghiopura*, which literally means the pouring of *ghī* (clarified butter) upon the fire, takes place at the name-giving ceremony on the twenty-first day of a baby's life. *Ghiopura* is also a purification ritual for the baby. Subsequent to *ghiopura*, and twenty-one days of ritual seclusion, the newborn, with its mother, re-enters the social community with a new name and religious identity. After the name-giving ceremony, *ghiopura* is conducted annually on the child's birthday. It thus commemorates the biological and the social birth of the child, marked by the fire ritual. In non-Mahimā Dharma folk traditions of rural Orissa, the name-giving ceremony and the purification ritual after birth are called *ekuisya* (twenty-one).

Ghiopura is also celebrated twenty-one days after the death of a Mahimā Dharma devotee. It marks the end of the impure period after the death, characterized by ritual seclusion and mourning of twenty-one days. Furthermore, the ritual can be performed in the following situations: (a) as a sign of repentance in case of an involuntary killing of a cow; (b) for benedictions against barrenness or against too many female children; and (c) as part of the celebration of any joyous family occasion.

The Ritual of Catordośi

The ritual of *catordośi*, which literally means the fourteenth day of the lunar cycle, takes place one day before full moon at all mythical places (*tīrthas*) of the religion. It lasts the whole night until early morning and includes sequences of *ghiopura* and *balelila*, which will be described later.

The Ritual of Jagia

Jagia is the generic term for the sacrificial fire ritual. It represents a large fire ritual in Jorandā performed daily by the oldest ascetics. During *Māgha Catordośi* and *Māgha Pūrnimā*, one day before full moon and on the full moon day of February or early March, the fire ritual is performed for up to seven days. Although occasions for the rituals and their sizes are different, substantial similarities in their structure can be observed: the phase of *ghiopura*, the pouring of *ghī* into the ritual fire; and the phase of *balelila* (literally, the 'joy of children') occur in all types of fire rituals—*ghiopura*, *catordośi* and *jagia*.

The Phase of Ghiopura

The patron of the ritual (*poriposako*) provides food and new clothes to the ascetics and the ritual ingredients and utensils for the fire ritual. The necessary ingredients for the ritual are *ghī,* food and donations of money. After an elaborate bath, a small afternoon meal and the evening prayer, the ascetics start to construct the fire altar. The scale of the preparations depends on the occasion and on the category of the fire ritual. Preparations are dependent on whether it is a *ghiopura* ritual, which is of a more private character; or a *catordośi* ritual, which is performed officially for the well-being of the village; or a *jagia* ritual, which is performed for the well-being of the whole cosmos at all official holy places of the religion.

The fire altar: Each *tīrtha* has its permanent fire altar (*dhuni-mandira*), which consists of a quadrangular sacred space, made originally out of clay and these days out of cement. This altar may only be entered by the ascetics. It usually remains closed and is opened solely for the ritual of *catordośi* or *jagia*. In the case of all private rituals of *ghiopura*, if a fire altar does not exist, it has to be constructed first. The construction of the fire altar starts after the ritual patron has drawn a quadrangular form, which is then sprinkled with cow dung. In the middle of the quadrangular form, the trunk of an inverted banana tree (*kondho*) is put into the earth. A small clay pot with *ghī* and a cotton thread are placed near the *kondho*. This small *ghī* lamp is lit at the beginning of the fire ritual. A canopy of mango and banana leaves is constructed for the altar with the help of *bhaktas*. The sacred place of the altar is then cordoned off by ropes. The fire ritual can start soon after the altar is built and after the sun has risen.

The start of the fire ritual: The blowing of a conch shell (*śaṅkha*) by an assistant marks the beginning of the ritual, and the fire is lit immediately by an ascetic. At the moment of the lighting of the fire, all surrounding ascetics and devotees start invoking, '*Alekh mahimā, alekh! Alekh, mahimā alekh!*'. The chanting is accompanied by the heavy playing of the *gini*, or metal gongs. All devotees stretch their arms towards heaven, call the name of the god and lie prostrate with arms outstretched in front of the fire altar and the ascetics. Through their posture, they show respect to the ascetics as well as to the God Alekha, represented by the fire.

After the fire is lit, ascetics pour *ghī* upon the fire. Shortly after the pouring of *ghī*, the 'seven nectars' (*soptamurto*) are symbolically offered to the fire. The nectars given to the fire by the ritual patron are held in a brass bowl in front of the fire. The *soptamurto* consists of *ghī*; milk (*khiro*) and curd (*dohi*); coconut (*nuria*) and bananas; molasses (*guro*) and honey; rice flakes (*chenna*); sandal paste; and camphor.

With the beginning of the first pouring of the volatile camphor into the bowl of the *soptamurto*, God Alekha is loudly praised by ascetics and devotees. As soon as the fire is lit, an ascetic takes one spark of the fire to the altar of the banana trunk to light the small *ghī* lamp (*akhonda batti*).

The first to lie down on earth in front of the fire altar and in front of the *ghī* lamp are the patron of the ritual and his wife. They first pay their respects to God Alekha, to the fire and then to the ascetics. After they light the incense sticks (*agarbatti*), all other devotees start their ritual prostrations.

The singing of bhajanas: While one ascetic pours *ghī* upon the fire, another starts to sing *bhajanas*—the religious songs and poetical creations of Bhima Bhoi, assembled in the book *Bhajanamālā* and then memorized by the devotees through the acts of listening and repeating.

In due course of time, other ascetics and devoted laity begin to participate in the performance. Only ascetics use a *khanjoni*, a small membranophone made out of wood and stretched with lizard leather. This small tambourine-like instrument is held with the left hand and hit with the right in keeping with the rhythm of the music. In a counter-rhythm to the *khanjoni*, the devotees play *gini* (metal gongs) as they passionately express their devotion to Mahimā Alekha. Ascetics and lay disciples dance around the *dhuni-mandira*, the temporary or permanent quadrangular fire altar; and passionately sing the *bhajanas* of Bhima Bhoi in different choral groups. After this event, lay devotees continue singing devotional songs and reciting from Bhima Bhoi's verses. A new ritual sequence, involving ecstatic dancing and singing by laymen—mostly young men—begins. Some men imitate women's voices and movements. This part of performed devotion can last a whole night and has a boisterous and joyous character. During the night, other young men from the village, irrespective of caste, also join the devoted chorus and the circle of singers and dancers. In many villages, musical performances of devotional songs take place, wherein musicians play *gini* and local drums and sing the *bhajanas* of Bhima Bhoi.

The devotion to Mahimā Alekha has a performative, sensual character and is expressed through physical movements and one's voice. Alternating song leaders introduce new rhythms and melodies to the chorus. They enter the chorus circle and start to dance ecstatically. The rhythms and ecstatic movements are accompanied by exalted cries for Mahimā Alekha. This physical display of devotion makes the ritual a passionate and intense religious performance.

These sequences of *ghiopura*, *catordośi* or *jagia* display the performative aspects of the ritual, involving all adherents. All can participate in the ritual, expressing with their obeisance through songs and dances. Anyone who creates his own variations of *bhajanas* and participates in the chorus can become a song leader. This performative character of the fire ritual showcases its egalitarian values: through the devotion to God Mahimā Alekha everyone becomes equal. After the events of the night, which include the most important performative practices for all participants, the *balelila* which takes place the next morning completes the fire ritual.

The Balelila

The final morning of the ritual starts with the usual ritual ablution and physical purification by ascetics and devotees (at about 3 a.m.). After sunrise, the morning prayer is performed seven times and then all start to sing *bhajanas* in praise of Mahimā Alekha.

The 'seven nectars' of the day before are mixed in a clay pot by an assistant and held upward towards heaven. All devotees and ascetics chant the name of god, and ascetics and laymen then throw themselves down on the ground in veneration. Afterwards, the *soptamurto* is poured from the *clay* pot into another brass pot and the clay pot is thrown away. Then, in the brass pot, the seven nectars are mixed with flattened rice (*lia*) and distributed as *balelila* among the children of the village. This ritual and sacred food, which is very sweet and nourishing, is meant only for children.

After the *balelila* is given to the children, the adult participants and ascetics drink a sweet juice (*limbo pani*), and a rice meal with vegetables is consumed together (*satsanga*) by all Mahimā Dharma devotees and ascetics, without caste restrictions. In fact, all villagers might join the collective meal and thus celebrate the ritual of commensality. This is a very important symbolic practice. The food is served either by ascetics or by laymen and expresses the egalitarian and reformist character of the religion. The most rigid caste boundaries, usually expressed by commensality restrictions between different castes, are consciously neglected by Mahimā Dharma ascetics and devotees. Everyone can participate, eat and drink together and can thus express their equality within a new ritual community. After the collective meal, the participants discuss religious issues and the gathering slowly disperses.

Characteristics of the Fire Ritual

The fire rituals has reformist and egalitarian characteristics: ritual commensality and ascetic practices create a community of equals and neglect the hierarchy of castes, which is usually expressed through commensality restrictions. Additionally, the performative practices within the rituals create a sense of togetherness through the ritualized acting out of solidarity and devotion. The gradation in the brotherhood is nevertheless clearly observable during the performance of the fire ritual itself. The laymen participate as musicians, dancers or ritual assistants, but a hierarchical demarcation between ascetics and laymen can be noted: without the ascetics the fire ritual cannot take place. Ascetics are the ritual fire specialists; their devotees are only their assistants.

Fire Ritual as Opposition to Classical Asceticism

The fire ritual as the centre of Mahimā Dharma rituals therefore moves away from the classical depiction of the ascetic as *anagni*, 'one without a fire', seen in opposition to the Brāhmaṇ priest (who handles fire rituals) and householder (Michaels, 1998: 355). Classical asceticism thus presents a critique of the life of a Brāhmaṇ householder (Olivelle, 1992). The ritual practice of Mahimā Dharma ascetics then seems to be based on a different attitude towards the fire. The emphasis laid on the fire ritual also reminds one of Vedic ritual patterns.

Vedic rituals[7] venerated the fire god, Agni, and were centred on the fire. The priestly specialization in relation to the fire was exclusively connected with the caste of Brāhmaṇs. Buddhism for instance, as a strong critique of the Vedic ritual, denounced Brāhmaṇ authority and allowed the admission of all castes into the ranks of monkhood. In Buddhism, new ceremonies were created by the incorporation of Vedic fire rituals as part of tradition (Staal, 1989: 67). In Mahimā Dharma as well, ascetics of non-Brāhmaṇ origin express their opposition to Hindu customs in two ways: (a) against the conception of asceticism which excludes the fire ritual of the householder from the ascetic principle represented by the itinerant ascetic and the eremite; and (b) against the Brahmaṇ, since the faith of Mahimā Dharma rests upon non-Brahmanical principles. Empirically, no Mahimā Dharma ascetic was of Brāhmaṇ origin.

In classical Hinduism, fire rituals are connected with the daily duty of a Brāhmaṇ householder and with his specialization as a priest. While Mahimā Dharma ascetics place fire in the centre of their ritual activities, they act in opposition to the Hindu ideal, where only the Brāhmaṇ householder is associated with the fire and can only leave his domestic fire in old age to renounce the world as a hermit (Madan, 1997). When non-Brāhmaṇ ascetics of Mahimā Dharma perform the fire ritual, they ideologically position themselves against this principle of exclusiveness. Incorporation and rejection of the Vedic and Hinduistic tradition is thus visible in the ritual and ascetic practices of Mahimā Dharma.

Incorporation and Rejection of Brahmanical and Vedic Elements in the Rituals of Mahimā Dharma

Brahmanical and Vedic elements are at once rejected and accepted within the rituals of Mahimā Dharma.

1. Vedic rituals consist, on the one hand, of 'public' *śrauta* rituals performed for a ritual patron (*yajamāna*) and sometimes for a king. On the other hand, there are private *gṛhya*-rituals, which belong to a householder's daily routine (Staal, 1989: 66–7). In Mahimā Dharma rituals, we find the same distinction. Here, public rituals are *catordośi* and *jagia*, which are performed for the patrons of the rituals, mostly

powerful village leaders. The private *ghiopura* rituals can be seen as equivalent to Vedic *gṛhya* rituals performed for the family.

2. During *śrauta* rituals, ritual incantations of Vedic verses (*mantras*) are crucial. The Vedas, however, do not play any role in Mahimā Dharma ritual practices. The only *mantra* used during the fire rituals of Mahimā Dharma is the Alekha Mahimā *mantra*, which consists of chanting the name of God Mahimā Alekha. As in Vedic rituals, where ritual singing (*stotra*) from the *Sāmaveda* and the reciting (*śāstra*) from the *Ṛgveda* are important during several sequences of the Vedic ritual (Staal, 1989: 81–3), so also in Mahimā Dharma, singing and recitation of devotional songs form a very important part of ritual practice. The *bhajanas* from Bhima Bhoi's *Bhajanamālā* or *Stuticintāmaṇi* are sung as a crucial part of the expression of ritual devotion.
3. Contrary to the drinking of *soma* (juice of a plant with hallucinogenic effects) in Vedic rituals, no narcotics are consumed during Mahimā Dharma rituals. Ritual conviviality is reduced to the drinking of *limbo pāṇi* in the morning following the fire ritual.
4. The singing and loud recitation of the name of the God Mahimā Alekha reminds one of the ritual incantation in the Vedic rituals where the sound of the chants has the capacity to attract the gods to the place of the altar. The sound of the *śaṅkha* in the initial phase of the fire ritual played in Vedic and Mahimā Dharma rituals indicate priestly specialization in both Brahmanical and Mahimā Dharma traditions.
5. As in Brahmanical rituals, the construction of the fire altar, where only vegetarian offerings are made, plays a crucial role in Mahimā Dharma rituals.
6. An evident rejection of the Vedic tradition lies in the insistence of the non-Brāhmaṇ origins of the ascetic priests in Mahimā Dharma.

The fact that ascetics of Mahimā Dharma are also musicians

might show a relation with the ritual activities of local non-Brāhmaṇ priests in rural Orissa. These priests perform diverse ritual duties by playing specific musical instruments. They are the ritual specialists for the non-Brāhmaṇ population in tribal or semi-tribal rural regions. Rituals for the remembrance of the dead in particular consist of music performances by these non-Brāhmaṇ priests. Their instruments are occasionally made of animal skin. In the local context, the instrument and the player become the representatives of the intangible (untouchable) power of the divine. In the hierarchy of purity–pollution in Brahmanism, the use of musical instruments made with hides classifies the musicians and priests as untouchables, thereby ascribing them the most polluted status.[8] There seems to be a direct connection between the activities of Mahimā Dharma ascetics and those of the local non-Brāhmaṇ priests. The ritual activities of the former reflect the continuity of traditional local structures of non-Brāhmaṇ priesthood very common in rural Orissa.

Local Brāhmaṇs are contemptuous of the activities of Mahimā Dharma ascetics, while the latter too do not care about Brāhmaṇ categorizations. They declare: 'We are ascetics and as such we do not need to be Brahmans. As ascetics we already are!' Self-definitions of this kind are very common among Mahimā Dharma ascetics. They illustrate the centrality of local concepts as well as of their ritual efficiency and power in the local arena. Within the context of the Mahimā Dharma religion, not the Brāhmaṇs but the ascetics act as the central ritual specialists for their devotees and patrons. As such, the local socio-religious autarchy of Brāhmaṇs is displaced by ascetics who contest the exclusive categories of Brahmanical Hinduism.

Rituals of Internalization

The Sociology of Prayer[9]

Besides the fire ritual, the prayer called *darśana* plays a main role in the everyday ritual practice of Mahimā Dharma ascetics and devotees. The prayer consists of physical exercises. For *bābās* as well as *bhaktas*, religious devotion (*bhakti*) to Mahimā Alekha is especially expressed through the language of the body. The sequences of the prayer are performed along with invocations of the name of the god and yogic postures. Before sunrise, ascetics and devotees prostrate themselves seven times on the earth; before sunset they worship five times. Stretching out on the ground during prayer is always accompanied by complex bodily exercises. The performances of *darśana* ritual represent for *bābās* as well as laymen a public demonstration of the obeisance to the rules of religious conduct. The proper form of bodily prayer is synonymous with practising the 'right' ideas of Mahimā Dharma. An accurate practice—the orthopractice—of the sequences of the prayer provides credibility and discipline —the 'right' rule—within one's own life conduct. In this sense, asceticism in Mahimā Dharma requires adherence to the rules of the founder of the religion. The prayer is considered a medicine for the body and mind. As such, performance of the prayer leads to an internalized 'moral' purity with individual steps towards salvation. Thus, practices of prayer reveal the ancient Greek use of *askesis* for 'exercise', crucial for the internalization processes of ascetic ethics in Mahimā Dharma.

In practices of asceticism within Mahimā Dharma, the body is the medium of *darśana*—of looking at the divine. The human physique is the actual embodiment of ascetic principles: through the everyday performance of prayer, the Mahimā Dharma doctrine is inscribed on to the body of ascetics and devotees. Therefore, the body is both the medium of worship, and its result.[10] In opposition to the classical concept of *darśana*, where the images of gods and goddesses serve as a medium for 'seeing the divine',[11] ascetic bodies themselves represent the image of divinity.

Conclusion

The paper illustrates the principal rituals of the new ascetic religion, Mahimā Dharma. The translocal rituals transgress and connect localities. Ritual practices operate through a negative identification with the Vedic and Brahmanical traditions, both incorporating and rejecting elements of the dominant tradition. Asceticism in Mahimā Dharma hence proves its ritual efficiency through the local autonomy of the fire and the prayer. On the one hand, the ritual practice of ascetics strongly revitalizes the Brahmanical ritual model; on the other, the rituals of ascetics and laymen maintain the local non-Brahmanical patterns of priesthood. The important role of the body during prayer displays processes of religious internalization. Religious internalization consists in a transformation from the external fire ritual into the internal 'fire' of the ascetic ethic. While the fire rituals are accompanied by performative devotion of the wider religious community, the ascetic doctrine engraves its values on the bodies of ascetics and devotees through the bodily prayer. Ascetic body discipline creates a new way of life and conduct. Therefore, external fire rituals seem to transform the ascetics of Mahimā Dharma into new moralists of asceticism. Those who have internalized the external fire ritual in their own body discipline shape a new ascetic ethic. Therefore, external fire rituals seem to transform the ascetics of Mahimā Dharma into new moralists.

Notes

1. Dharma is a polysemic socio-religious concept in South Asia. It can be translated as 'religious code'. For a discussion, see O' Flaherty and Derrett (1978).
2. *Alekha* was explained to me as 'not to write/unwritten', referring to everyday usage. In Sanskrit, the term means 'without writing', having a pejorative connotation.
3. The *New Indian Express* (Bhubaneswar, 4 December 2003) carried a report on the judicial disputes between the *balkaldhārīs* and the *kaupīndhārīs* concerning land properties.
4. For a broad discussion on the topic of patronage and kinship in South Asia, see Quigley (1999 [1993]).
5. See the article by Johannes Beltz in this volume.
6. To study the structure and forms of the Mahimā Dharma ascetic tradition, I stayed six months in Jaka, a *tīrtha* of Mahimā Dharma near Dhenkanal town. For the great help in my research I thank Prof. Prasanna Kumar Nayak, the family of Jagmohan Sahu and the respected Mahimā Dharma ascetics, Promod Das and Vira Das from the Jaka *tīrtha*, for their constant help and assistance. I thank the Deutsche Forschungsgemeinschaft (DFG, German Research Council) for the generous research grant without which the study could

not have been conducted. For comparative studies in the tribal context of Mahimā Dharma, see Guzy (2000–1: 61–70, and 2004: 105–11).

7. In using the term Vedic rituals, I mean rituals which were practised between 1000–500 BC by Brāhmaṇs, who were ritual specialists venerating the fire as the representation of the fire god Agni (Staal, 1989: 65–70).
8. By referring to the music of the non-Brāhmaṇ priests, I use my own ethnographic devices from western Orissa, where I conducted research on local music and dance traditions.
9. Using this term I refer to the work of Mauss (1968: 357–477).
10. By using the metaphor of inscription on the body through physical exercises and techniques, I refer to B. Schnepel's (2000: 156–71) research on local theatre in Orissa and the use of physical expressions.
11. In the context of Mahimā Dharma, *darśana* does not refer to the common visual devotion (Eck, 1981) to the deity, but to the physical exercise performed by the devotees in order to praise God Alekha.

References

Banerjee-Dube, Ishita (1999), 'Taming Traditions: Legalities and Histories in Twentieth-Century Orissa', in G. Bhadra, G. Prakash and S. Tharu (eds.), *Subaltern Studies X: Writing on South Asian History and Society*, New Delhi: Oxford University Press, pp. 98–125.

——— (2001), 'Issues of Faith, Enactments of Contest: The Founding of Mahimā Dharma in Nineteenth-Century Orissa', in H. Kulke and B. Schnepel (eds.), *Jagannath Revisited: Studying Society, Religion and the State in Orissa*, New Delhi: Manohar, pp. 149–78.

Beltz, Johannes (2000–1), 'Healing Practices and Mahima Dharma: A Short Note on Recent Fieldwork in Western Orissa', in *Adivasi*, vols. 40–1, pp. 92–102.

——— (2006), 'Contested Authorities, Disputed Centres and Rejected Norms: Situating Mahimā Dharma in its Regional Diversity', in G. Pfeffer (ed.), *Periphery and Centre: Studies in Orissan History, Religion and Anthropology*, New Delhi: Manohar, pp. 79-104.

Eck, D.L. (1981), *Darshan: Seeing the Divine Image in India*, Chamberburg: Anima.

Eschmann, A. (1975), 'Spread, Organisation and Cult of Mahimā Dharma', in S.N. Senapati (ed.), *Satya Mahimā Dharma*, Cuttack: Dharmagrantha Store, pp. 9–22.

——— (1978), 'Mahimā Dharma: An Autochthonous Hindu Reform Movement', in A. Eschmann, H. Kulke and G.E. Tripathi (eds.), *The Cult of Jagannath and the Regional Tradition of Orissa*, New Delhi: Manohar, pp. 374–410.

O'Flaherty, W.D., J. Duncan and M. Derrett (eds.) (1978), *The Concept of Duty in South Asia*, New Delhi: Vikas Publishing House.

Guzy, L. (2000–1), 'Voices of Gods: Ecstatic Alekhs and Local Configurations of Mahimā Dharma', in *Adivasi*, vols. 40–1, pp. 61–70.

——— (2002), *Baba-s und Alekh-s—Askese und Ekstase einer Religion im Werden. Vergleichende Untersuchungen der asketischen Tradition Mahimā Dharma in Orissa/östliches Indien*, Berlin: Weissensee Verlag.

——— (2003), 'Mahima Dharma Ascetics: A Case Study on Popular Asceticism and its Patronage Structure in Rural Orissa/India', in A. Copley (ed.), *Hinduism in Public and Private,* New Delhi: Oxford University Press, pp. 211–29.

——— (2004), '*Babas* and *Alekhs*—A Religion in its Making', in *Journal of Social Sciences,* Special Issue, *Facets of Orissan Studies,* eds. C. Mallebrein and L. Guzy, pp. 105–11.

Madan, T.N. 1997 (1987). *Ā l'Opposṛ du Renoncement. Perplexitṛs de la Vie Quotidienne Hindoue*, Paris: Éditions de la Maison des Sciences de l'Homme.

Mahapatra, S. (1983), *Bhima Bhoi: Makers of Indian Literature,* New Delhi: Sahitya Akademi.

Mauss, M. (1968), 'La prière et les rites oraux', in M. Mauss, *Œuvres I. Les fonctions sociales du sacre*, Paris: Les Éditions de Minuit, pp. 357–477.

Michaels, A. (1998), *Der Hinduismus: Geschichte und Gegenwart,* Munich: C.H. Beck.

Olivelle, P. (1992), *Samnyasa Upanishads: Hindu Scriptures on Asceticism and Renunciation*, Oxford: Oxford University Press.

Quigley, D. (1993), *The Interpretation of Caste,* New Delhi: Oxford University Press.

Schnepel, Burkhard (2000), 'Der Körper im "Tanz der Strafe" in Orissa', in Klaus-Peter Köpping and Ursula Rao (eds.), *Im Rausch des Rituals,* Hamburg: Lit. Verlag, pp. 156–71.

Staal, F. (1989), *Rules without Meaning: Ritual, Mantras and the Human Sciences*, New York: Peter Lang, pp. 65–70.

Tribal Research Bureau (TRB) (1968–9), 'Impact of Satya Mahimā Dharma on Scheduled Castes & Scheduled Tribes in Orissa', *Adivasi*, vol. 10 (1), pp. 43–76.

CHAPTER 3

Mahimā Gosāin: Compiling a Hagiography

GOURANG CHARAN DASH

In the mid-nineteenth century, the *garhjats* (tributary states under Oriya rulers) and British Orissa witnessed the presence of a few dynamic personalities who were well ahead of their contemporaries in many respects. Among them was Mahimā Gosāin, held by many as the incarnation of the absolute Brahman, who enlightened the hearts of large sections of Orissa's subaltern population. Mahimā Gosāin has been deified by his enthusiastic followers on account of the lack of reliable sources. What confounds the researcher most is that the testimonies do not provide enough evidence to sustain clear conclusions about Mahimā Gosāin, or the founding of the Mahimā Dharma 'sect'. To my mind, the life he lived was so humble and humane that he appealed to thousands of downtrodden, miserable people. This may be the cause of his canonization as saint by the masses and the growth of a large number of legends around him. Through a survey of stories and records, this paper attempts to arrive at a better understanding of the significance of Mahimā Gosāin, the founder of Mahimā Dharma. Though the stories may sometimes be full of exaggeration and praise, they still evoke the extraordinary charisma of this outstanding leader.

Legends about the Guru

It is said that there was a time when the earth was in terrible pain because of the misrule of King Kali. There was chaos everywhere.

Mother Earth prayed to the Almighty incarnate himself to relieve her of the unendurable misery. The Absolute willingly accepted Mother Earth's invocation and manifested himself as Mahimā Gosāin in the mountains of the Himalaya, held by the Hindus as the abode of the gods.

In the year 1828, Gosāin left for Sriksetra, Puri. At that time, he wore only a loincloth and smeared his body with dust, his intention being to identify himself with the destitutes. They called him 'Dhulia Baba'. After spending some time in Puri, he wandered from place to place for the next twelve years in the regions around Puri—Khurda, Dhauli, Khandagiri, Banki and Dhenkanal. In the year 1838, he arrived at the Kapilāś hill where he spent the next twenty-four years of his life as an ascetic. He is believed to have lived the first twelve years exclusively on fruits and roots (*phalāhāra*), the next twelve years on milk and water (*jalāhāra*), and finally on air (*pabanāhāra*). An aborigine named Sadananda is said to have looked after him during his long stay at Kapilāś. Maharaja Brahmarobara Bhagirathi Mahendra Bahadur, the king of Dhenkanal, and his queen were among Gosāin's admirers and took care of the *sannyāsī* by supplying him with milk everyday, which Sadananda took to the Svāmī. In the end, after a long meditation spread over several years, Mahimā Gosāin was endowed with supernatural powers. During his stay at Kapilāś, the ascetic, an *achari Boishnab* (practising Vaishnava) who believed in and worshipped Hindu gods, became a devout worshipper of Candraśekhar-Śiva. He lived near a Śiva temple and took pains to improve the place by clearing the jungle, creating gardens, looking after the *bhog* or food offering of the idol and taking care of pilgrims who periodically visited the hills.[1]

The *phalāhārī* Gosāin took great care of the ailing and gradually succeeded in earning the respect of the people of surrounding villages. The belief became popular that he was in secret communion with the gods and could successfully intercede with them on behalf of the votaries. Living for several years at Kapilāś, Mahimā Svāmī left the place when he found that he had established his reputation and secured the respect of the people. He openly stated that Mahādev and other idols worshipped by Hindus were nothing but objects of stone and wood and that the worship of these perishable objects was useless.

Mahimā Gosāin then returned to Puri and remained for some time in the vicinity of the temple of Lokanāth Mahādev.[2] He next went to Daruthenga which is near Khurda and Puri, where he built a place of worship and began to propagate the new doctrine. It was here that Mukunda Das, as he had been called before, became deified. From now on, he was addressed as Mahimā Gosāin. He is said to have had two disciples, Govinda Das and Narasingha Das.[3]

In the course of his sojourn, Mahimā Gosāin travelled through most of the *garhjats*, namely Ganjam, Koraput, Phulbani, Banki, Sonepur, Sambalpur, Chhattisgarh, Sundargarh, Keonjhar, Rairakhol, Sukinda, Talcher, Angul, Hindol, Dhenkanal and many other places of *Mogalbandi* (regions earlier ruled by Mughals and under British rule at the time). His magnanimity and charisma soon drew devotees from all walks of life, many of whom left their homes to join his *āśrama.* They actively participated in spreading the message of Mahimā Gosāin among the country-folk, as also stories of the manifestation of his supernatural abilities: that he could walk through floods and on air, create new fountains, revive corpses, grant motherhood to barren women and cows, and cure the sick using only cow dung and cow urine as medicine (Biswanath Baba 1991: 55–62, 89–105).

The success of the Guru was reflected in a different incident. In 1857, on a full-moon day in the month of *Kārttika* (October–November), a fair was held at Jakka in Dhenkanal where a large number of followers of Mahimā Gosāin assembled with rich presents including valuable clothes and silver utensils. It was said that the Babaji, or 'Svamī' as he was also addressed, offered those presents to the Maharaja of Dhenkanal. When the raja declined to accept, the gifts were openly burnt in the sacred fire of the *dhuni.*[4]

Bhima Bhoi, the founder poet and direct disciple of Mahimā Gosāin, envisaged his Guru as a holy fire without smoke, which with its warmth could liberate the human being from mundane environs and grant him ultimate relief from sufferings. In *Mahimā Vinod,* a work about the life and philosophy of Mahimā Svāmī, Bhima Bhoi metaphorically narrated the *Dharma Yātrā* (journey on the path of dharma) of the divine soul, which began in the Himalayas and ended at Kapilāś. During his *yātrā*, the Svāmī is said to have visited the following places: Badrika, Naimisaranya, Dwaraka, Prayaga, Kashi, Brindaban, Mathura, Puri and Navadwipa. Though it might be a legend, he is believed to have done it in order to witness and experience the social and religious life of his people.

The stories tell that everywhere except Puri, the abode of Lord Jagannātha, he received warm welcome from the gods, goddesses and monks. What annoyed him at Puri were the evil and irrational practices of religion and the exploitation of common men in the name of faith. This was being carried out under the stewardship of the king in connivance with the priests and pundits. With a determination to purge Puruṣottama-Jagannātha's land of its depravity, Mahimā Gosāin searched for a place to begin his work, and the forests of the Kapilāś suited his purpose. Such stories make the Svāmī an enigma for all time to come. Mahimā Gosāin died in the year 1876, on the tenth day of the second fortnight of *Phālguna* (February–March). For the followers, his death was not a worldly death. Their master had transformed himself to be united with the 'non-entity', the *Paramabrahma*.

The Puri Incident

Oriya intellectuals and Westernized elites did not accept Mahimā Svāmī as the spiritual leader of the masses. In their eyes, he was in no way superior to a village *bābā* who could only impress simple, uncivilized tribes (*adivāsīs*) and the people of the lower strata of society. Five years after his death in 1876, news reports appeared in the *Utkala Deepika* (1881a, 1881b, 1888c; also cf. ibid.: 1883, 1926), following an incident which occurred in the temple complex of Lord Jagannātha at Puri on the noon of 1 March 1881.

It is reported that a group of sixteen 'half-savage', 'nearly naked', 'barbarous' and 'fanatic followers' of the Svāmī (twelve men and four women), whose bodies were smeared with ash, who were shouting the name of *Alekha*, forcibly entered the *garbhagṛha* (inner sanctum) of the temple of Jagannātha, with the intention of dragging the idols down from their throne and burning them.[5] This led to a combat between the intruders and the servants of the temple, in which the leader of the group Dasaram died or was killed. This unexpected incident became a law and order problem for the British administration and angered the Hindus. In view of this incident, Gouri Shankar Ray, the editor of *Utkala Deepika*, was among those who began to investigate the rise of the enigmatic Mahimā Gosāin, the founder of the Mahimā sect, and Bhima Kandha, the preacher. This investigation led to the publication of the news item in the *Deepika*.

Thus, the journey of the Gosāin and Bhima Bhoi from the jungles to the 'civilized' world and activities with regard to the dissemination of a new religious order came to be known after two-and-half decades of the emergence of the sect. Newspapers and journals like *Sambada Bahika, Sambalpur Hitaisini, Mukura,* and *Sahakara* devoted pages to Mahimā Dharma, but did not provide balanced accounts, simply stories based on slim facts (cf. Mohanty, 1907–8; Roy, 1914; Sahoo, 1934).

Consent and Dissent

The British government in Orissa was not a silent observer of the incident of 1881. The Commissioner of the Orissa Division issued orders to the tahsildars of Banki and Angul and the manager of Dhenkanal to furnish detailed reports on the sect after due investigation. In 1882 several significant reports were published in the *Proceedings of the Asiatic Society of Bengal* and the *Calcutta Gazette* (Asiatic Society of Bengal, 1882; *Bengal District Gazeteer*, 1882). Scholars like Nagendranath Basu and Bijay Chandra Mazumdar also began conducting research to trace the roots of the Mahimā faith and philosophy and their relationship with other branches of the Hindu way of life (Basu, 1911; Mazumdar, 1911 and 1925).

But the scholars and the persons to whom we are most indebted today are Biswanath Baba (1931, 1935), an exponent of Mahimā Dharma and one of the gurus of the faith; Artaballabh Mohanty (1925), who has edited most of the writings of Bhima Bhoi;

Chittaranjan Das (1951), a researcher of repute; Nabin Kumar Sahoo (1972), an eminent historian; Satrughna Nath (1970), an educationist-scholar and an adherent of the faith; Bhagirathi Nepak (1987), Pabitra Mohan Nayak (2001), Ghanasyama Das (1953), Siddharth Das (1997) and many others. Without doubt, the works of these scholars have helped in the understanding of the sect and its principles. But on careful scrutiny, the writings of Artaballabh Mohanty and Biswanath Baba reveal a certain bias. *Satya Mahimā Dharmara Itihāsa* (*The History of Mahimā Dharma*), written by Biswanath Baba and published in 1935, attempts to establish the orthodox, 'classical' origin of Mahimā Dharma. Biswanath Baba has also authored many stories on the life of the Svāmī, which are replete with legends and which underplay or ignore Bhima Bhoi's contribution to the movement and glorify its founder.

On the other hand, Rama Chandra Nanda's *Dhenkanal Itihāsa* (1929) provides a fair account of the life of Mahimā Svāmī. Though it was written under the direction of the patron, Raja Sri Shankar Prasad Mahendra Bahadur, and was based on the documents available in the archive of the palace, the text merits attention as being the work of a serious scholar. The narratives on the life and philosophy of Mahimā Gosāin, a homeless *sādhu*, are not tinged with exaggeration. The author states that Gosāin was a man with a saint-like personality, a rebel who dreamt of a society full of love, compassion and brotherhood among people from all walks of life. But it was also the same society, which, affected by age-old superstitions and upper-caste hegemony, forced the *sannyāsī* to escape to a safe place where he would not be persecuted. It is thus that he died of pneumonia in the distant village of Madhi, far from Dhenkanal and close to the border of the state of Keonjhar (Nanda, 1929).[6]

Biswanath Baba has done a disservice to the Dharma by neglecting the contribution of Bhima Bhoi. What Gosāin had experienced in life could not have touched the hearts of the numerous poor people had there been no genius like Bhima Bhoi to propagate Mahimā philosophy with missionary zeal. Indeed, it is both the guru and his disciple—Mahimā Gosāin and Bhima Bhoi—who are held in equally high esteem by their followers and who have legends written about them. The two inspired their followers over a large region stretching from western and southern Orissa to the present Chhattisgarh.[7]

Mahimā Gosāin's Deification

An analysis of the reports relating to Mahimā Gosāin's long stay at the hills of Kapilāś reveals him as an ascetic. He spent the early phase of his life as a worshipper of Sri Nilakantheswar (Śiva), free from worldly attachment, a practising *hatha yogi*. But this description of the guru was not enough for his followers. They adorned him with two more epithets, 'Lord Jagannātha' and 'Prabuddha Svāmī'. However, Biswanath Baba (1991) declared Mahimā Svāmī as superior to Lord Jagannātha. In addition, according to legends Sadananda, the Sabara, had the first vision of Mahimā Svāmī at Kapilāś. These legends, incorporated by Biswanath Baba in his *Itihāsa*, gave more importance to the tribes than to the local kings. One has to keep in mind that Jagannātha was a tribal *sabara devatā* before he was taken over by the kings and transformed into a *rāṣtra devatā*, shifting from the forest to a settled space. In the story told by Biswanath Baba (1931), the Sabara becomes more important than the king, an inversion which Ishita Banerjee-Dube (2001: 157) calls 'poetic justice'.[8]

In telling the story of Mahimā Gosāin, it is very difficult to separate reality from myth. The reports and stories narrate how he survived with only one meal a day, how he wore only a piece of bark of the Kumbhi tree around his waist and slept on bare ground, sometimes on the village road under the open sky or in a small thatched hut (*tungi*). Stories also abound of his healing skills, particularly his ability to heal using ordinary cow-dung and cow-urine. He was also said to be able to cover miles walking barefoot through rocky hillocks and wild forests and to befriend outcastes and ferocious animals. If one believes in these stories, can one dismiss the Gosāin as an ordinary man?

The Svāmī started his divine journey from Puri in the year 1865. It is repeatedly reported that the beauty of his soul was such that hundreds of village-folk spontaneously joined him with love and devotion. Persons like Govinda Das, Narasingha Das, Bhima Bhoi, Madhabananda, Achyutananda, Bhagirathi and others accepted him as their spiritual leader.[9] They left their homes and spent the rest of their lives spreading his message. But the Svāmī never advised his followers to leave their homes and to disregard their duties as householders.

Social Evils and Suffering

The death of Gajapati Mukunda Dev of Bhoi dynasty in 1568 created a vacuum in central leadership. This resulted in the division of what was then Orissa. Under the Afghan, Mughals and Marathas, who conquered Orissa after Mukunda Dev's reign, the state fell into misrule.[10] Then followed the British rulers who were even more indifferent to the well-being of their subjects. The chiefs of the tributary states who did not come under direct British administration tried to safeguard their own rights by paying annual revenues to the East India Company's government. Drunk with power, they claimed to be the representatives of god and treated their subjects as slaves. They also engaged in war with each other in an effort to expand their territories.

Let me add another point. As Kulke (1978: 199–208) has rightly observed, the construction of temples of Lord Jagannātha and royal palaces by the rulers of the feudatory states in the mid-nineteenth century was an expression of their newly found confidence and their protest against the cultural hegemony that the *Gajapati*—the king of Puri and the first servant of the state-deity Jagannātha—had tried to exercise by restricting the spread of the cult of Jagannātha.

The conflicts among these small kings and the indifference of the British made the people suffer. Moreover, the subjects of the tributary states were forced to serve the lords with unpaid forced labour, offer gifts and presents, supply rations for the army and other such help during the time of war, official visits and natural calamities. They were also forced to serve the king in many other different abominable ways.[11] At times, young women had to be sent to the rulers. There were very few institutions to impart formal education, and people shouldered the burden of many 'feudal' practices. According to the *muali pratha*,[12] the property of a family automatically passed on to the king if the head of the family died without any biological heir.

The princes exploited their subjects in inhuman ways. It was not that the British rulers were unaware of these atrocities. But in order to extract their share of the booty and keep the tributary kings in good humour, they turned a blind eye to these, and therefore indirectly played an important role in the ruin of the subjects. Of course, the people of Keonjhar, Nayagarh, Dasapalla, Ghumusar and Sambalpur protested against such exploitation and economic harassment by the kings. But they never got justice from the colonial masters.

The Reformer

Mahimā Gosāin was moved by the suffering of the people. Through a simple message of faith, he tried to urge them out of the fear and helplessness that had gripped them. Advocating belief in the formless Absolute who was accessible to all through devotion, he tried to infuse into these people a sense of confidence and dignity. His philosophy was thus not very different from the monotheism that Rammohun Roy was preaching through his Brāhmo Samāj around the same time. The Gosāin's disregard for idol-worship drew the attention of the Christian missionaries. They acknowledged him as the leader of an 'extensive religious movement' in the *garhjats* since he attracted thousands of disciples. The missionaries believed that the 'movement' was destined to have an important bearing on the spread of Christianity in the *garhjats*. Reverend Miller commended Mahimā Gosāin as 'an abstemious man ... he has one meal a day, drinks only water or milk, never indulges in any narcotics'.[13]

Sometimes Mahimā Gosāin is described as a worshipper of the sun—the symbol of truth, energy, equality and righteousness. The religious practices performed by the devotees of Mahimā Dharma, like the offering of *praṇāma* by prostrating on the ground facing the sun at sunrise and sunset, and not taking food at night, suggested the conclusion that they were sun-worshippers (Nanda, 1929: 318–24). Laxminarayan Sahoo, on the other hand, refuted these suggestions and argued that Mahimā Gosāin was a devotee of Mother Earth (Sahoo, 1934: 727–32). I would like to argue that Mahimā Svāmī cautiously adhered to some Hindu rituals only to avoid arousing the anger and resistance of kings and priests and be able to carry on preaching his radical message.

Let me elaborate. Mahimā Svāmī did not believe in the worship of idols and considered it foolish to build a house for god. The construction of an empty temple in Jorandā, a *Śūnya Mandira*, without any idol inside, may be the outcome of this. He appreciated monotheism and accepted it as the essence of Hindu philosophy. Besides, he also regarded the *Śrīmad Bhāgavata Mahāpurāṇa* with respect. He further saw the cow as a sacred animal; we have seen that he healed sick people with cow dung and cow urine. These might lead some to believe that the Svāmī perpetrated the 'traditional' beliefs of the people in the name of religion. To my reckoning, things are a bit more complicated. It was precisely his simple message and practices that made him appeal to the uneducated lower classes of society.

Mahimā Svāmī and his followers also held the fire to be sacred. In this, the Svāmī probably acknowledged the popular belief that all gods and goddesses receive the offerings made to them through fire. The importance of fire is emphasized in Mahimā Dharma by an ever-burning fire that is kept lit in front of the *Śūnya Mandira*. Through this show of respect for the fire associated with the *yajña*, Vedic sacrifices and the cow—also held to be sacred in Hinduism—the Svāmī was probably trying to ward off the anger of the Brahmaṇs as he set about challenging other norms of Brāhmanic Hinduism. But the Brāhmaṇs understood the threat posed by Mahimā Svāmī and tried to enlist the support of rulers and feudal lords in challenging him.

Mahimā Gosāin openly expressed reservations against kings, Brāhmaṇs, prostitutes and priests. He believed that these people earned their wealth by exploiting the emotion and religious faith of ordinary people. Yet, some rulers supported the missionary activities of Mahimā Svāmī and his followers. Apart from helping him set-up *brahmāgni* (holy fire) in places like Daruthenga, Malabiharpur, Tangi, Khuntuni, Jorandā and Khaliapali, they had also made offerings to the Gosāin. In fact, the kings had plans of their own. By helping Mahimā Gosāin, they desired to increase their popularity among his followers, and keep the attention of the subjects away from the hardship they imposed on them. The Brāhmaṇs, of course, did not like the royal patronage of Mahimā Dharma and thoroughly opposed it.

After all, it is possible that the kings and the Brāhmaṇs were somehow involved in a disastrous incident connected to Mahimā Dharma in Malabiharpur. Stories steeped in mystery say that there was some kind of religious celebration in Malabiharpur, by the side of Lake Ansupa, where more than 10,000 disciples had assembled for an annual convocation on a full-moon day. That day, it is said that there were 1,38,000 (80 *kahana*) earthen pots filled with cooked *prasāda*. When this *prasāda* was about to be served, there were shouts of *āna, āna* (bring, bring) by some members of the crowd who were probably asking for the *prasāda* to be served to them. The story goes that most of the large crowd misheard the shouts as *hāna hāna*, meaning 'behead, behead'. This created confusion and the crowd started attacking each other out of fear and rage, leading to the death of many. It seems, however, that many had gone armed to the convocation ground with the intention of causing damage. The story is still narrated and commemorated by Mahimā Dharmīs today, as I came to understand while conducting several interviews. The question here arises whether this was a plot of the local elites, Brāhmaṇs or rulers who intended to arrest the popularity of Mahimā Gosāin? Though a definite answer might not be possible, I wonder whether this event was not provoked to counter the uplift of the untouchables, who had already started revolting against their discrimination.

In 1873, another unfortunate incident took place in a village named Kalibira, adjacent to Malabiharpur. Baba Achyutananda Das, an ardent follower of the Gosāin, became enraged, committed homicide and was transported for life. Narasingha Baba, who was in-charge of the *āśrama* of Malabiharpur, was accused of abetting the offence and imprisoned for a year in Cuttack Jail.[14] The 'victims' were the chief of the village and a few of his associates. The act was said to be the result of unpalatable abuses the victims showered upon the innocent Baba and the Gosāin. The followers of Mahimā Dharma became frightened by the severe punishment given to their fellow-believers. They prayed to Mahimā Gosāin for an end to their suffering, hoping that he might punish those culprits by supernatural power, but the saint advised them to accept this woeful occurrence as the will of Almighty.

In the same year, some persons submitted representations before T.E. Ravenshaw, the then Commissioner of Orissa, complaining that Mahimā Gosāin was seducing women of respectable families and forcing them to become nuns of the Mahimā faith. This provided sufficient ground for Ravenshaw to send Rai Bahadur Harekrishna Das, the Assistant Superintendent of Police to arrest the ascetic. Rai Bahadur came to Dhenkanal with police enforcement. Mahimā Gosāin proceeded to Keonjhar in order to evade government action against him (Sahoo, 1972: 18).

The Brāhmaṇs were truly frightened by the fact that many people of their own caste and Kṣatriyas of the Sukinda area had adopted Mahimā religion. As reported in *Utkal Deepika* (1873), they convinced the king of Haripur to order the Babaji and his followers to leave the kingdom. They also warned the king that the subjects were preparing to rebel against him and the British rulers. In a previous article in the *Utkal Deepika* (1871), the sender of a letter to the editor suggested that the Baba and his large number of disciples might create disturbance in society. The writer also abused the Baba, calling him an 'ignorant and uncivilized' person.

In propagating his message, Mahimā Gosāin not only denounced caste discrimination, but also insisted that the people of every village feast together. Moreover, he tried to bring about a radical change in the prevalent system of marriage, proposing that the bride and the groom be married by a mere exchange of garlands and with the invocation of the name of Mahimā Alekha. He asked men not to have illicit relationships with others' wives and steal others' property and in general abhorred a life of deceit and lies. He considered the killing and eating of animals to be a sin. He struggled for benevolence and longed for a new world of moral values. Most of all, he preached to his followers to practice a life of purity and holiness, while leading domestic lives and being part of society. One did not have to renounce the world and retire to the forests to mediate; to lead a life of purity while being a householder, one had to be devoted and faithful to one single entity. For Mahimā Svāmī's followers, this entity was Alekha. Mahimā Svāmī also stressed that for one's economic well-being, one had to carry on his age-old occupation with sincerity and piety. Preaching his new dharma till the end of his life, Mahimā Gosāin breathed his last in 1876.

Conclusion

When Mahimā Gosāin began propagating his dharma of love and compassion as an itinerant *bābā*, upper-class Hindus, feudal lords and rulers became apprehensive that his message might inspire some to rebel against them. It would be wrong to say that Mahimā Gosāin attracted such a large following because he was endowed with supernatural powers: he was just an extraordinary man blessed with great wisdom. He might have studied the scriptures and imbibed their spirit. It is clear that Kapilāś hill was the place where he devoted his time in pursuing his thirst for knowledge. It is also certain that he was concerned with the economic, political and social life of the people and succeeded to a great extent in his mission to ameliorate the conditions of the common man. Like many religious movements, Mahimā Dharma suffered a rift, which ultimately ended in its fragmentation into several 'sects'. Differences in opinion exist in all movements, so do dissidents, and Mahimā Dharma is no exception in this regard.

Finally, it needs to be underlined that Mahimā Gosāin was an eminent saint-reformer who dedicated his life to the cause of the suffering humanity, and this at a time when India was ruled by foreign powers. His greatest contribution was the creation of a new awareness among the common people, laymen, women and the downtrodden segments of society. The need for uprising should be considered as central in the processes of the routinization of charisma.

Notes

1. Report of the Commissioner of the Orissa Division, Board Document No. 445/1, Orissa State Archives, Bhubaneswar.
2. Several sources mention a man named Mukunda Das or Mokund Das, who was probably born somewhere in the vast *garhjats* in the beginning of nineteenth century. But it is difficult to establish how and when this man transformed himself into Mahimā Svāmī or was renamed by his followers as such. He is said to have originally come from the Kapilāś hill in Dhenkanal. See for example the report of the Tahsildar, Banki to the Commissioner of the Orissa Division, Jagannath Temple Correspondence, p. 1339.
3. Report of the Secretary to Government, Judicial Department, Jagannath Temple Correspondence, 1 November 1881, pp. 1339–45.
4. Second Report of Banamali Singh, Manager of Dhenkanal State, to the Superintendent of Tributary Mahals of Orissa, Jagannath Temple Correspondence, 4 October 1881, p. 1334.
5. Report of J.S. Armstrong, Esquire C.S., Magistrate, Puri, to the Commissioner of Orissa Division, Cuttack, 15 March 1881, Jagannath Temple Correspondence, p. 1328.
6. This book was written as per the wish of the king of Dhenkanal, drawing upon the documents available at the palace. The author has devoted seven pages (318–24) of his book to portray the life of Mahimā Gosāin, the dharma he preached and the reasons responsible for its decadence, which seems closer to the reality.
7. In contrast to this popularity, the founders and adherents of Mahimā Dharma were also vehemently criticized. According to the Tahsildar of Banki: 'They have almost lost their faith in it and have only kept up some forms of it as they have not the moral courage to relinquish it entirely and return to their former religion. In fact, they never learnt and understood what it really was but adopted it and had blind faith in it in ignorance' (Jagannath Temple Correspondence (1 November 1881, p. 1327). According to Banamali Singh, Manager, Dhenkanal State, the founder of the religion, who was believed to be immortal died at last and the *tungi*, together with the goods it contained, were sold and most of the followers found out that Mahimā Gosāin was no more immortal than any ordinary man. They therefore began disbelieving what he had taught and reverted to Hinduism. The disciples and followers who had left their homes and been outcasted could not go back to their families, and were obliged to continue with their newly adopted life (Jagannath Temple Correspondence, p. 1337).
8. 'What is clear, however, is that the staging of Mahimā Svāmī's encounter with the Savar and the raja helped establish the contestatory credentials of Mahimā Dharma. This was poetic justice' (Banerjee-Dube, 2001: 157).
9. According to the report of the Tahsildar of Banki, it was at Daruthenga where he was first deified and came to be known as Mahimā Gosāin. His disciples Narasingha Das of Killah Boud, Bhagaban Das of Brahmanbasti in Cuttack,

and Krishna Das and Bhogi Das of Andharua and Madhab Das, Krupasindhu Das and Achhyutananda Das of Daruthenga in Killah Khorda propagated the religion in different parts of Orissa. Numerous persons were kumbhipatias (living) in the *dhuni* houses following the orders of Mahimā Dharma. They went to several parts of Orissa and to the Sambalpur and Ganjam districts to propagate the creed (Jagannath Temple Correspondence, 6 August 1881, pp. 1324–5).

10. 'But wretched as the State of Orissa had been under the Mughals, a half century deeper misery remained for it under the Maratthas. The memory of these fifty years haunted the whole population like a nightmare, long after it passed under British rule.... The result is a scene of extortion, desolation, and rapine, which even at this distance cannot be read without indignation and horror' (Sahu, 1980: 175).
11. For a discussion of the history of *garhjats*, see Mazumdar 1911 and 1925; Mohanty, 1997 and several issues of *Utkal Deepika, Hitaishini, Sambada Bahika* and *Utkal Darpan*.
12. Regarding the *garhjats* of Orissa, cf. also: *Utkal Deepika*, 1872, 1873; see Appendix 3, historic documents. *Utkal Darpan*, 1873.
13. See the Indian Report of the Orissa Baptist Mission for 1873–4, quoted by Ishita Banerjee-Dube (2001: 159).
14. Report of the Tahsildar of Banki to the Commissioner of Orissa Division (Jagannath Temple Correspondence, 6 August 1881, p. 1326); see also *Utkal Putra*, 1873.

References

Banerjee-Dube, Ishita (2001), 'Issues of Faith, Enactments of Contest: The Founding of Mahimā Dharma in Nineteenth-century Orissa', in H. Kulke and B. Schnepel (eds.), *Jagannath Revisited: Studying Society, Religion and State of Orissa*, New Delhi: Manohar, pp. 149–77.

Basu, Nagendranath (1911), *The Modern Buddhism and its Followers in Orissa*, Calcutta: U.N. Bhattacharyya, Hare Press.

Bhima Bhoi (n.d.), 'Mahimā Vinod', unpublished manuscript.

Biswanath Baba (1931), *Satya Mahima Dharma Pratipadaka*, Bhubaneswar: Utkal University.

——— (1935), *Satya Mahimā Dharmara Itihāsa*, revised edn. Mahimagadi, Dhenkanal: Mahimadharma Granthakosa Samiti (1991).

Das, Chittaranjan (1951), *Odisare Mahimā Dharma*, Shantiniketan: Viswa Bharati.

Das, Ghanasyama (1953), *Alekha Lila,* Cuttack: Dharmagrantha Store.

Das, Siddharta (1997), *Mahima Dharma: A Cultural Dissent*, Cuttack: Arya Prakashan.

Dhal, Braja Kishore (1980), *Bhulibu Nahin (We Won't Forget)*, Bhubaneswar: Book Land International.

Kulke, Hermann (1978), 'Jagannath as the State Deity under the Gajapatis of Orissa', in Anncharlott Eschmann, Hermann Kulke and Gaya Charan Tripathi (eds.), *The Cult of Jagannath and the Regional Tradition of Orissa*, New Delhi: Manohar, pp. 199–208.

Mazumdar, B.C. (1911), *Sonepur in Sambalpur Tract*, Calcutta: Brahmo Mission Press.

——— (1925), *Orissa in the Making*, Calcutta: U. Ray & Sons.

Mohanty, Artaballabh (ed.) (1925), *Bhima Bhoi's Stuti Chintamani*, Bhubaneshwar: Utkal University.

Mohanty, Damodar (1907–8), 'Bhima Bhoi and Legend', *Mukura*, December.

Mohanty, Gobinda Chandra (1997), *Dhenkanal Gana Bidroha (Mass Uprising in Dhenkanal)*, Cuttack: Naba Yuga Granthalay.

Nanda, Rama Chandra (1929), *Dhenkanal Itihāsa,* Dhenkanal: Sura Pratap Machine Press.

Nath, Satrughna (1970), *Bhakta Kabi Bhīmabhoi* (Oriya), Cuttack: Mahima Dharmalocana Parishad.

Nayak, P.M. (2001), *The Voice of Silence: Sonepur Durbar and Indian Cultural Traditions,* Bhubanswar: Orissa Sahitya Akademi.

Nepak, Bhagirathi (1987), *Bhima Bhoi: The Adivasi Poet Philosopher*, Bhubaneswar: Bhagirathi Prakashan.

Roy, Sachidananda (1914), 'Mahimā Dharma', *Mukura*, vol. 9, pp. 4–5.

Sahoo, N.K. (1972), 'Bhima Bhoi', in Daitari Panda (ed.), *Mahimā Dharma and Darshan*, Koraput: D.A.V. College, Shankar Philosophy Education, pp. 17–18.

Sahoo, Laxminarayan (1934), 'Joronda Gadi and Mahimā Dharma', *Nava Bharat*, March, pp. 727–32.

Sahu, N.K. (ed.) (1980), *A History of Orissa by W.W. Hunter, Andrew Sterling, John Beams and N.K Sahu*, vol. 2, New Delhi: Bharatiya Publishing House.

Journals and Newspapers

Asiatic Society of Bengal (1882), 'Origin and Growth of the Sect of the Hindu Dissenters Who Profess to be the Followers of Alekh', *Proceedings of the Asiatic Society of Bengal*, Calcutta.

Bengal District Gazetteer Sambalpur, 1882, Calcutta.
Utkal Darpan, August 1873.
Utkal Deepika, 26 August 1871; 26 October 1872; 13 March 1873; 3 April 1873; 17 April 1873; 12 June 1873; 4 September 1873; 'Mahimā Babaji', 6 September 1873; 'Mahimā Dharma', 12 March 1881; 'An Attack to Jagannath Temple', 26 March 1881; 'Kumbhipatia Babaji', 19 November 1881; 'A Letter to the Editor by Damodar Pattanaik, Dhenkanal', 17 March 1883; 'Alekha Dharma', 5 November 1926.
Utkal Putra, 3 September 1873.

CHAPTER 4

Apocalyptic Predictions, Prophecies, and a New Beginning: Mahimā Dharma and the Arrival of the Satyayuga

JOHANNES BELTZ

Introduction

In the past decade or so, we have come to know quite a few things about Mahimā Dharma, the religious reform movement of nineteenth-century Orissa, through ethnographic fieldwork and the publication of research articles on the subject.[1] There still remain, however, a number of important and crucial questions that have not been addressed in detail by scholars, one of them concerning the eschatology of Mahimā Dharma, especially with regard to the notion of time, in particular that of sacred/cosmological time. The term 'eschatology', originating from Greek *eschatos* (last), designates the 'doctrine of last things' and remains, despite its strong Christian connotation, appropriate for comparative religious research. It should serve here as comparative term for any religious belief or philosophical speculation regarding the end of time. Let me add that the idea for this paper originated when I was investigating the Orissa Archive of Heidelberg's South Asia Institute. Looking extensively into the material—notes, photographs and publications collected by Anncharlott Eschmann—I discovered a number of important *mālikās*, a literary genre discussed later, some of them translated into English. From her field notes, I also developed a strong interest in this particular theme, that is, 'predictions of the future', 'apocalyptic' and 'esoteric' writings. On account of her premature death, her research was never completed or published. Since I became inspired to continue her investigations, I dedicate my paper to her.

Sacred Time in Hindu Cosmology

In order to understand the nature of speculations about time and space within the Mahimā Dharma tradition, a few crucial notions and concepts have to be established briefly. Since they can be found in many mythological, cosmological, as well as ritualistic texts, I will limit myself to very general observations.

The first notion to mention is that of *yuga* (age) which, according to Heinrich von Stietencron, was elaborated for the first time in the *Mahābhārata* and the Purāṇas, and probably originated between the fourth century BC and the third century AD (von Stietencron, 1986: 136). Once established, this notion became part of several philosophical and religious movements, and even went to be a fundamental part of what became Hindu cosmology. But there are different types of *yugas*. How long are they and how do they differ? Let us recall that one day of Brahma consists of one *kalpa* (eon); and each *kalpa* goes on for 1,000 *mahāyugas*, which are grouped into the four *yugas* (Michaels, 1998: 331): *kṛtayuga*, *tretāyuga*, *dvāparayuga* and *kaliyuga*. It is commonly accepted that we live today in the *kaliyuga*, which started on 18 February 3102 BC (von Stietencron, 1986: 141). Though there are differing modes to count the beginning of this age, there is no doubt that it is the worst of all ages.[2] It is the age of *tamas* (darkness). The particularity of the *yuga* concept is that time is conceptualized as cyclical. Ages come, go and return. Creation and destruction are part of the divine play (*līlā*). In other words, since these periods are recurrent, there is no end and no beginning. In this sense, the terms 'apocalyptic' and 'eschatological' must be redefined. When one talks about the end of the *kaliyuga*, one does not take it to mean an absolute ending. There is not only a new beginning but also another end. The idea exists of an ongoing process of creation and destruction, action and inaction, birth and death.

The second, equally important, notion is that of *avatāra* (divine descent),[3] which links god with man. A possibility of bridging the distance between the divine and the human is through the ascending progression of human beings to degrees of godliness; notions of *siddha* or *guru* are examples of this ascent. The other way is descent from the divine to the human. The Supreme God is therefore an *avatārin*, the source of *avatāras*. Lord Kṛṣṇa—probably the most popular *avatāra*—is immortalized as the incarnation of Viṣṇu in the *Bhagavadgītā*. He came to the earth in order to destroy the wicked and to restore the dharma.[4]

The third notion may be less known, but is no less important for our purpose. It is *mālikā*, a literary genre of predictions.[5] Let me just indicate here that Bhima Bhoi, as well as the other authors of Mahimā Dharma literature, quote from a rich and old tradition of 'apocalyptic' writing in Orissa consisting in particular of the literature of the so-called Pancasakhās (Five Friends): Jagannātha Dās, Balarāma Dās, Yaśobanta Dās, Ananta Dās, and Achyutānanda Dās, who lived in the fifteenth and sixteenth centuries. They are known to have been social reformers who are also accredited as the pioneers of Oriya literature. In this regard, they can be compared to the *bhakti* tradition that pushed the *sants* to write in vernacular languages. The first, Jagannātha Dās, is famous for composing the *Bhāgavata Purāṇa* in Oriya, which is recited, listened to, and read in every household in present-day Orissa. Balarāma Dās wrote the *Rāmāyaṇa* in Oriya, while Achyutānanda Dās was perhaps the most radical among them. Witnessing the instabilities and political turmoil of his time, he engaged himself in predicting the future, and was probably the most famous composer of *mālikās* (Chaini, 1998: 55; Das, 1951: 136). According to him, people should follow the way of dharma to avoid being slaughtered by Kalki's sword.

For our purpose, it is important to note that, despite all differences and the gap of time (several centuries lie between the origins of the two traditions), the Pancasakhā literature and Mahimā Dharma are very similar in several aspects, particularly in their extensive production of *mālikās* and insistence on the concept of *śūnya*.

Bhima Bhoi's Predictions

What is the peculiarity of the *mālikās* written by Mahimā Dharmīs? Let me first present the sources of my investigation (cf. Banerjee-Dube, 2003). The most important text is Bhima Bhoi's *Stuticintāmaṇi*. Though I have already discussed the multiple dimensions of this work elsewhere, let me repeat a few facts here about this piece of poetry (Beltz, 2004).

Stuticintāmaṇi (*The Jewel of Spiritual Hymns*) is probably one of the most significant but also difficult works of Bhima Bhoi. Unfortunately, we possess neither a critical edition nor a good English translation of this major text. The widely circulated edition by Vidyadhara Sahu is considered to be a distortion. The first edition published by the king of Sonepur during the early days of the twentieth century remains lost, and the still-existing palm-leaf manuscripts await proper editing.[6] *Stuticintāmaṇi* reveals a theology similar to other medieval devotional *nirguṇa-bhakti* movements. Bhima Bhoi advocates a god without form (*arūpa*), one who cannot be described (*alekha*), one without a name (*anāma*), without attributes (*nirguṇa*), who is unlimited, shapeless, without desire, void (*śūnya*). Still he is the source of everything and *is*, in fact, dharma (*Stuticintāmaṇi* 1.10, 2.14, 6.7, 6.8, 6.12, 14.17). Composed in 100 *bolis* (chapters) of 20 verses, each with two lines, the text contains 4,000 lines of cosmological speculations and hymns about Brahma, the lord of void, the one without form. Yet, the main theme is the miserable situation of the world (*duḥkha*). The suffering of the world due to sin and guilt is characteristic of *kaliyuga*.

The second text is *Padmakalpa* (*The Lotus Age*), also attributed to Bhima Bhoi. However, there is serious doubt that the work as it exists today was written entirely by him. The language and style of this book and his other works are quite different, and the interpolations can easily be traced. Even a reading of its English translation leads one to the same conclusion.[7] Most scholars think that the original in Oriya was written as late as the 1930s, and that like the *Brahmācalaka,* it was attributed to Bhima Bhoi. I have to add here that though Vidyadhar Sahu edited the *Padmakalpa* from his Dharmagrantha Store in Cuttack, he published it as a separate text, rather than including it in Bhima Bhoi's collected works.

However, contested authorship does not really matter for my purpose here. My point of interrogation is not who composed the text; the important consideration is rather that *Padmakalpa* is a source of inspiration and a reference for Mahimā Dharmīs. As such, it has incontestable value. Though it may be of recent origin, it proves how the *mālikā* tradition still lives. I will come back to the questions of creativity and innovation. The text is composed of 37 chapters (*adhyāya*) that contain no uniform number of verses. Sometimes, the verṣes are numbered, sometimes not. The content of this collection is a continuing stream of predictions for the future. The messages are, however, sometimes abstruse and hidden. Multiple allusions are found to mythical and actual political events, kings and gods, recent politicians like Jawaharlal Nehru, and mythical heroes. Their tone portends doom.

There are many more texts to quote, for example, *Nirveda-sādhanā*, in which Bhima Bhoi narrates the conversation between the Lord Alekha and Govinda Baba, the reincarnation of Lord Jagannātha; or his popular collection of devotional songs, *Bhajanamālā* (cf. song 241). All deal more or less with the question of when and how the present age would come to an end. Though their authenticity is questionable, *mālikās* were and still are widely circulated and read. The tahasildar of Angul wrote as early as 1881 to the Commissioner of Orissa that disciples of Mahimā Svāmī had a *mālikā,* and he explains that this is '. . . a book of predictions which treats the incarnation of Alekh in the shape of Mahimā Svāmī to save the world from the burden of sin and to show the way towards salvation'.[8]

Apocalyptic Topics

The basic assumption is that we live in *kaliyuga* and that it is going to end soon. As mentioned before, it is not only the last of the four ages, but also the worst. It is the age of diseases, wars and moral decline. The *Padmakalpa* expresses in detail the terror of being in this world that will end very soon. Bhima Bhoi laments:

Where shall I go? What shall I do? I feel so helpless. I am apprehensive that people will indulge in wicked acts. The Brahmins will first commit sinful acts and will give up the Vedas. They will drink liquor, go to others' women and lose their ways. . . . They will forget the Gayatri mantra[9] and instead sing tantric chants, giving up the practice of trisandhya. . . . They will eat dried fish and will carry loads on their shoulders. (*Padmakalpa*, Chapter 2: 1–3)

The political situation would be no better:

Hear me, oh Surabhī:[10] Here is an account of the kings and their reign. The British will rule for 13 generations that will extend to 495 years. They will utter truths but will secretly oppress their subjects. They will behave like the water of coconuts which, when poured on a plant, destroys the wood. Thus, the British will reign over this continent. As the white ants eat away the wood even though there is water at the root, so the British rule will destroy the people. Attending the calls of nature, they will not use water. Dirty as they are, they will eat the flesh of cows, buffaloes and goats, and they will drink liquor everyday. (*Padmakalpa*, Chapter 2: 4–8)

But not only is the human world affected by this decline; the gods will suffer too:

Gods and goddesses will feel ill at ease to see their (the human beings') wicked deeds. Pṛthivī devī[11] will lose her beauty and fortunes, and she will cry day and night. The earth will tremble and break down in both the south and the Himalayas. The head of Vāsuki will also tremble, and tears will flow from his eyes. There will be droughts and famines, and Lakṣmī[12] will go away from the earth in fear. The kings will meet with their destruction when she (Lakṣmī) would get no food and cry incessantly. (*Padmakalpa*, Chapter 2: 9–11)

In this narrative, Vāsuki, the snake, carries the earth on his head. Because of sin and immorality, the burden (*bhāra*) would become so heavy that Vāsuki would start shaking and the earth would be in trouble. Again and again, Bhima Bhoi warns that the earth cannot bear the burden of wicked people and that the snake is humbly praying to the Lord (*Stuticintāmaṇi*, 13: 7). In response to its pitiful prayers, the Lord has come to its rescue (*Padmakalpa*, Chapter 1: 3 and Chapter 2: 11). Mahimā Svāmī comes to help. The heaviness of the earth and its burden on the snake's head are common mythological motifs in Orissa (Dash, 1991: 193). This is also how earthquakes are said to occur: when Vāsuki shakes its head, the earth vibrates.

The quoted paragraphs from the *Padmakalpa* reveal a number of topics that can be extrapolated systematically. To my knowledge, they recur in several of these 'apocalyptic' texts.

Sin and Diseases

During *kaliyuga*, sin (*pāpa*) increases. Interestingly, diseases (*roga*) are seen as an indicator of fallen humanity. Bhima Bhoi writes:

> Diseases will attack the limbs and cause worry and sorrow. People will die. Some will live with diseases, having no physical strength. All will be subjected to diseases, and their bodies will shiver. All the living beings of the houses will have tears rolling from their eyes. (*Stuticintāmaṇi*, 24: 6–7)
>
> Pox[13] will take a heavy toll of cows, buffaloes, goats, and sheep. All will die. (*Stuticintāmaṇi*, 24: 15–16)

I emphasize here that diseases and epidemics affecting human beings or animals are signs of the increasingly sinful state of the world. Bhima Bhoi is quite clear on this matter: 'Oh Gurudeva, kindly consider in what way you will lighten the burden of sin. The *kaliyuga* is beginning to end. What will happen?' (*Stuticintāmaṇi*, 70: 16). 'In this great *kaliyuga*, there is untruth everywhere. So how can I pass my days?' (ibid., Chapter 42: 12).

One can easily observe that these texts are loaded with theological notions of sin (*pāpa*) and its varied forms, such as untruth (*asatya*), amoral behaviour (*anyāya* or *anīti*), prostitution and consumption of alcohol. Bhima Bhoi believes that mankind's immorality is responsible for decline, devastation and disease. If one follows the cyclical logic of decline, destruction, and a new beginning, one could argue that time itself disintegrates and causes the decline. But Bhima Bhoi thinks that a collective (bad) *karma* (or, to use Halbfass' expression, 'a combined individual *karma*') causes the degeneration (Halbfass, 2000: 235). What Bhima Bhoi proffers is very similar to statements in ayurvedic texts, like the *Carakasaṃhitā*. He follows an established tradition here. Like the *Carakasaṃhitā,* he remains general with his diagnostics, not giving details about what kind of sin would cause which disease. In relating the sins and diseases of the age with the advent of Mahimā Svāmī, the curing of diseases becomes far more than a mere metaphor in the religious practices of Mahimā Dharmīs. From historical reports as well from my fieldwork in western Orissa, one can conclude that healing was and still is a central ritual practice (Beltz, 2001).

Ignorance

Like lust, greed and hatred, ignorance too is immoral and sinful, and the *kaliyuga* breeds ignorance through creating illusions. 'The illusion of the great *kaliyuga* is coming with a great roaring sound and has spread throughout the entire world. Oh Lord, kindly give protection to the beings living under your banner' (*Stuticintāmaṇi*, 31: 16).

The notion of *māyā* (illusion) permits further theological speculations. The manifest world is nothing but an illusion, and god is above all manifestations. But human beings are part of the perceptual world, and thereby, imperfect. They must also be criticized:

> They are involved in injustice, bad conduct, corruption, crookedness, etc. What dharma should they adopt? And how will they get salvation? (ibid., 24: 4)
>
> In the bodies of the entire 56 crores of creatures, there is now the mire of sins. Due to the influence of kaliyuga all have become ignorant. What more I will say? (ibid., 54: 10)
>
> They (the ignorant people) discourage the company of the pious and the sages and utter jocular sounds out of mockery. . . . They have given up the truth. They have trodden on the undesirable track. They are full of crookedness. There will be bazaars and markets where falsehood is the article for marketing. They don't know dharma. They do not have the taste of nectar. They are drinking poison by giving up the company of the sages and pious who are like sweet juice. (ibid., 14: 9–11)

In this *kaliyuga*, men have become voracious and intoxicated (*Stuticintāmaṇi*, 70: 6). A characteristic of the *mūrkha* (ignorant or stupid) people is that they do not recognize the Guru. Bhima Bhoi is preaching the way out of this terrible situation, but they remain ignorant and blind.

> We are considered as unwise, as we are worshipping the Guru. The people of the *kaliyuga* say that we are ignorant and that they are counting our mistakes. The people of the *kaliyuga* consider that person ignorant who had brought divine knowledge from the void. . . . (*Stuticintāmaṇi*, 66: 14–15)
>
> Oh Lord, publicise your name in the ten directions and let the *kaliyuga* end. Let Jambudvīpa be initiated into the Mahimā religion, which does not believe in the Vedas. I explained it to all, but they did not believe it. I have no hope. All the people of the world have lost their senses and have become insensitive like earth and stones. (ibid., 26: 11–12)

This is again a common motif in hagiographic narratives. Also think about the statements of Old Testament prophets. The prophet has received the message of God, but the people prefer to ignore him. Even worse, they often attack him. Quite a few similar events occur in Bhima Bhoi's life when he becomes a victim of ignorant people.

This blindness could also help us reconsider the often suggested blindness of the author himself. It is indeed claimed that Bhima Bhoi was blind (*andha*) from his birth. Though he never clearly said that he himself could not see, this story persists. His blindness should perhaps not be understood in literal terms and might be traced to a misinterpretation of his poetry, for example, when he calls himself ignorant and blind in the face of the Almighty void. Apart from this self-characterization, there is no reason to think that he was really blind.

Disasters and Death

It is striking that sin and ignorance are not the only common motifs comparable to the biblical prophets. The narrative on *kaliyuga* also contains prophesies of diseases, epidemics and natural catastrophes:

Due to delusion and illusion, the three worlds will be destroyed. The affairs of the earth will also end. . . . The food meant for eating will assume bad colour, (as if) dust has been thrown on it. (*Stuticintāmaṇi*, 14: 6–7)

The earth will be destroyed, and nobody will survive. Come all of you. Let us utter His name. Bhima Bhoi, the disciple of Anādi Guru, invites all of the world and composes this song. (ibid., 23: 20)

In *Nirvedasādhanā*, Bhima Bhoi gives another explanation how terrible this will be. He predicts that there will be a chaotic condition. A war will break out, and a comet will fall on the earth (in the translation by A. Das, 105). In the *Padmakalpa*, one reads:

The Creator of the universe speaks about the anantayuga[14]. . . . The three worlds will be shaken. . . . The floodwater will rise everywhere. Meteorites will fall from the northern sky, and many thunderous sounds will be heard ceaselessly. The earth will be severely shaken. . . . Floods will rush towards the north. Huge waves will rise in the sea and rush towards the land. (*Padmakalpa*, Chapter 34)

It is perhaps this motif which is the most known. Its popularity is based on Bhima Bhoi's prediction of the 'super cyclone'. His *Padmakalpa* is often quoted: 'All of a sudden a cyclone will come and swallow all villages, towns and countries' (cf. Sahu, 1999: 21–2). These narratives about natural disasters are often reiterated, as Bishnu Mohapatra has mentioned at a conference in Salzau (Mohapatra, 2000). The terrible prophecies of these texts, predicting corruption, disease, floods, cyclones, hunger and poverty in Orissa, remain as appropriate today.

How will you save us from *kaliyuga*? We have all fallen into the mire of sin. It is now destroying the bodies and the world by means of giving premature death. If you kill the death god and remove the illusion, there is the remedy. All the creatures of the three worlds have lost their prestige. (*Stuticintāmaṇi*, 43: 14–15)

All the idiotic wise men, the heretics, the *pāpīs* (sinners) will die first. Nobody has to be blamed for this, as they would die for their sins and would be devoured by the ghosts and spirits. The *mlecchas*,[15] the villains, the irreligious, and those who are crooked will lose their heads. They will be cut-off and roll on the ground. (ibid., 26: 2–3)

At the end there is mass-scale death and destruction. The ignorant people, the people who refuse to follow the path indicated by Bhima Bhoi, will vanish in the mud (*panka*) of sin. Sinners are inevitably punished for their faults. The end of the *kaliyuga* is synonymous with death (*mṛtyu* or *maraṇa*). Analysing the present age with the eyes of Bhima Bhoi, *karma* is understood as the reason for the ongoing cycle of existence (*saṃsāra*). As in so-called classical Brahmanical texts, Bhima Bhoi attributes the decline to human ignorance and greed, that is, karmic misdeeds.

A New Eschatology: The Juncture of Personal and Cosmological Time

Bhima Bhoi's apocalyptic narratives are not impersonal. He suffers too, and his report of what will happen is not really detached. He feels terrified because he is part of the decline. He experienced the decline of the world as personal suffering (*duḥkha*).

> I made truth as my religious commodity by uttering, *śūnya, śūnya*. The world is unbearable to me, and tears are rolling from my eyes. (*Stuticintāmaṇi*, 31: 14)
>
> . . . I'm weeping daily to find the vices and corruption in the world that are the principles of the *kaliyuga*. (ibid., 35: 11)

Still, one could argue that the prophet's personal suffering is also a literary motif. Is it not standardized rhetoric when Bhima Bhoi says that while mediating at the feet of his guru, he predicts great difficulties for the world? (ibid., 43: 20). This kind of text incorporates traditional 'prophetic' elements. Bhima Bhoi uses well-known themes of prophecy and remodels them to make them his personal testimony.

After all, Bhima Bhoi's message not only announces the end of the *kaliyuga*; it also opens a new terrain for speculation about the future and evokes the beginning of a new era. The appearance of the Guru on earth marks the new beginning. In other words, neither the *Stuticintāmaṇi* nor the *Padmakalpa* are pessimistic texts, but offer hope. Though the present situation is terrible, they predict better times. But one must be prepared; one has to take refuge in the Lord, one must recognize him and pray to him. In this sense, the texts are alarmist, but not pathetic.

In this *kaliyuga*, all should take shelter under the name of God and recite it. If they do so, it is likely that some will survive and be the seeds for the future generation. (*Stuticintāmaṇi*, 97: 10)

I said that if they would recite the name of Mahimā from the very beginning, they would be able to live in the world and get over the *kaliyuga* and enter the *satyayuga*. (ibid., 68: 19)

Compared to this terrible and dangerous *kaliyuga*, which is like the ocean of sin, Mahimā Dharma is like an ocean of greatness. . . . (ibid., 89: 9)

The new age is *satyayuga* and Bhima Bhoi knows it:

. . . Oh pious and wise men, please hear this. The *satyayuga* is coming. (*Stuticintāmaṇi*, 89: 2)

There will not be any trace of pride, blaming others or obstinacy. The females will import knowledge to the males, and then the *satyayuga* will return. Those who utter the name of the Lord and follow the truth will survive. . . . (ibid., 24: 18–19)

Despite religious affiliation, there is only one escape. Being Vaiṣṇava or Śaiva, there is no difference. Everybody has to take refuge in Mahimā Dharma:

There are also giants and demons. See, the *kaliyuga* is ending, so all of you should call Mahimā. There are mendicants, sages, Nāganthīs, Vedantīs, Yogantīs, Siddhantīs. All be mindful of Mahimā. (ibid., 100: 3–4)

There is a definite sense of exclusivity. It means that Mahimā Gosāin is mightier then everyone else. All sects of the Vedantīs or Yogantīs have to submit themselves to the Lord. He will persist till the end of all. He has been always here. Linear and cyclic concepts of time intersect in these narratives. It is stated that Lord Alekha was born in every *yuga* as an *avatāra*. It is not clear whether he became incarnate as the sage Markanda, the Buddha Vaiṣṇava, or the Guru Śūnya Brahmā (*Padmakalpa*, 1: 19), but it seems very likely. Nevertheless, there is little doubt that he personified all incarnations of Viṣṇu: he was the dwarf Vāmana (Bāmana) who had asked King Bali to give him as much of his land as he could cover in three steps. Once the latter agreed, Vāmana grew to a gigantic height and walked to the sky. From that point, Bali was only allowed to reign in the underworld (*pātāla*).

In the *satyayuga*, oh Hari, you assumed the incarnation of Vāmana and converted yourself into the gigantic figure, took a gift from King Bali and deprived him of all his riches. (*Stuticintāmaṇi*, 10: 6)

The Guru was Kṛṣṇa in the *dvāparayuga*:

In the *dvāpara* age you took birth in the house of Vasudeva and resided in Gaya. You are known as Kṛṣṇa in this location. You killed the wicked Kaṃsa and lightened the burden of the earth. (ibid., 10: 8)

Bhima Bhoi is amazed: how can the Master appear in this *kaliyuga* in a human body despite being formless (ibid., 41: 18)? Bhima Bhoi understands that in all four ages the Guru has relieved the distress of the earth (ibid., 15: 13). He was Kṛṣṇa, who enjoyed the *gopīs* (maidens); he was also the Buddha. Similar passages can be found in Bhima Bhoi's other writings. In *Nirvedasādhanā*, the Lord of the Void is described as having appeared in this *kaliyuga* in order to establish the sacred fire in Jambudvīpa as well as the Nirveda dharma.

Where or Who is Kalki?

According to traditional Hindu mythology, Kalki is the last *avatāra*. Conceptualized as a saviour, he is supposed to descend to earth to mark the end of *kaliyuga*. According to the Pancasakhā tradition, he will ride on a horse, holding his sword high in order to destroy evil. Looking at the illustrations, one always comes across the same imagery and iconography. Let us ask what happened to Kalki in Mahimā Dharma mythology. At first, there is a significant absence of Kalki. Was he replaced by another hero? But who is he according to Mahimā Dharma eschatology? The Lord himself? Let us look into the texts. Bhima Bhoi writes:

Much of injustice and evil has spread in the three worlds, and the four dharmas have been destroyed. So the Kalki incarnation has come out in the garb of a mendicant. (*Stuticintāmaṇi*, 10: 10)

He will destroy the wicked, save the pious, and maintain the people. At the end of *kaliyuga*, *satyayuga* will be ushered in, and Anādi[16] will be the Rāja. (*Stuticintāmaṇi*, 10: 14)

There is no mention of a white horse or a sword. Eschmann has noted that the Lord is prophesied to come in the form of an old ascetic (Eschmann, 1978: 391). Indeed, Mahimā Gosāin is identified as the Lord in the form of a mendicant.

> From the day that the *dhūni*[17] was lightened on the earth . . . I could understand with apprehension that the *kaliyuga* will come to an end. I asked myself what will happen to the world and what the creator has been doing. Things, which would occur rarely are now happening. . . . The Lord of the world, who has no end, has taken the garb of the naked sage. The shapeless (*anākāra*) has given up clothes and a place to sit. He has no respite for a moment, and he is always busy. . . . (*Stuticintāmaṇi*, 14: 1–4)

Is this why Bhima Bhoi identifies Mahimā Gosāin as Kalki? Eschmann observed that the description of the *sannyāsī*, who wanders the earth as a manifestation of Nārāyaṇa, goes back to the *mālikās* of the Pancasakhās. Or is he the sage Markanda? Eschmann thinks that mentions of the *sannyāsī* in the Pancasakhās are interpolations. According to the Pancasakhās, the ascetic will first hide in the Himalayas; then practise *brahmajñāna* under the guidance of Śiva at Kapilāś, and roam through the country to gather *bhaktas* around himself (Eschmann, 1978: 391). Let us pause here. Some more irritating—or should I say 'heterodox'?—stories circulate about the incarnations of the Lord. An 1883 newspaper report claimed that the Lord Mahimā

> takes up different incarnations in different *yugas*. He delightfully travels in the human world. . . . First in a fair-complexioned body, bearing matted hair on his head, hanging on his chest a necklace of *akshyas*.[18] He wears a bark with four hands round his waist. He holds a water pot in one of the four hands. This is the form of god that all sadhus worship. (*Utkal Deepika*, 1883: 267)

So far, the story seems to confirm that the Lord took birth as a mendicant. It is a characteristic of the Lord to reduce gods in their importance. Even the royal deity of Orissa, Lord Jagannātha, has lost significance as the Lord of the Universe. Interestingly, the Lord of the Void did not become incarnated as Jagannātha, but as Mahimā Gosāin. Anncharlott Eschmann (1978: 376) advanced the idea that Mahimā Dharma functions as a succession movement, where the source of authority shifted from Jagannātha to Mahimā Svāmī. Indeed, Jagannātha is de-legitimized. The wooden idol in

Puri is dead; it has lost its divine presence. Jagannātha finds place in Mahimā Dhạrma as Govinda Bābā, Mahimā Gosāin's first disciple (Pal, 1997: 77–85). In fact, Jagannātha is the link between the new eschatological claims of Mahimā Dharma and the older tradition.

What Happened after Bhima Bhoi's Disappearance?

Two literary texts have been the centre of our interrogation up to this point. One should not forget that there are further references in other texts or documents not attributed to Bhima Bhoi, as well as a rich oral tradition. The most interesting question is, what happened after the Guru and his early disciples died? How did their absence influence the eschatological expectations of devotees? It is fascinating to observe that new themes were added, while eschatological claims were reshaped and adapted to the situation.

Let us go back in history and look into some news reports made at the end of the nineteenth century. They interrogate Bhima Bhoi's progeny that he begot after settling down in the *āśrama* in Khaliapali.[19] However, according to most orally transmitted texts, Bhīma Bhoi was not supposed to have had any children. As a holy man, he was thought of as a kind of asexual being. But Bhima Bhoi did in fact have a sexual life: three women lived with him at one time in the *āśrama*, and there are indications that he had a few children with at least two of them. Interestingly, one part of the hagiographic tradition perceives them as eschatological divine figures. This may go back to Bhima Bhoi himself. When people interrogated him about the fact that his 'spiritual' companions were pregnant, he explained that he would give birth to a boy who would remove the evil of the world.[20] It is said that he would root out all unbelievers. When the expected boy turned out to be a girl, his prediction was not affected. Unfortunately, the girl died. But a few of his children achieved high status, at least in the *āśrama*, and are noted as having performed numerous miracles. Interestingly, Kapileswar, the only surviving son, is depicted as riding a horse and holding weapons. Do I over-interpret this imagery as a mythological motif referring to Kalki?

Let me turn now to what I would call an 'adaptation' to the present context. I should mention my surprise when I discovered stories about Mahatma Gandhi being the incarnation of Govinda Bābā.[21] The *Alekha Purāṇa* (Pal, 1997: 233) narrates the story of Lord Alekha, informing us that his disciple Govinda will be incarnated as Gandhi in the middle of *kaliyuga*. Being the reincarnation of Jagannātha, he will come to establish *satyayuga* (ibid., 77). Gandhi is not the only politician who figures in these narratives. There are references to Jawaharlal Nehru in the *Padmakalpa* which are certainly interpolations showing the dynamic nature of this tradition, lending itself to continuous renewal. Equally interesting is the fact that references to natural disasters are either added or reinterpreted. The already mentioned 'super cyclone' of 1999 that devastated large areas of Orissa is the perfect illustration of such reinterpretation. These re-readings allow *mālikās* to be reprinted and they sell like hot cakes to this day. Calamities are commented upon by a large body of *mālikās*, all referring to the end of *kaliyuga*.

The following incidence illustrates that the writing and reading of *mālikās* is a dynamic exercise. During my fieldwork, I was twice confronted by a narrative stating that my arrival from Germany had already been predicted by Lord Mahimā. Of course, I tried to retrace this statement, but was unable to get any written proof. I got only vague answers when I asked where this was written.[22] I realized that this would be part and parcel of the interaction between the ethnologist and 'his subject'.

A New Era has Started: The Juncture of Linear and Cosmological Time

This holy or cosmological time is accompanied by or contrasted to the existence of linear time. The new era starts with the appearance of the Guru and the Mahimā Dharmīs of Jorandā, the main monastic institution. The beginning of the Mahimā *abda*[23] is 1826, which corresponds to the appearance of Mahimā Gosāin in Puri, and carried forward by Biswanāth Baba (1987: iv). However, this new era is marked by publications of Biswanath Baba and his disciples, whether in Jorandā or in Cuttack, through the Dharmagrantha Store. I did not come across claims to the contrary. More important is that this Mahimā *abda* is not the only era used by Mahimā Dharmīs.

The most fascinating variety of conceptualizing the beginning of the new era comes from the Mahimā Dharmīs of Kardula, representing perhaps the most interesting of the unorthodox and independent branch of today's Mahimā Dharma (Beltz, 2006). It is known that Satya Nārāyaṇa Bābā, the founder of the sect, is considered to be an incarnation of Bhima Bhoi. After his death in 1988, the ultimate authority passed to his wife, who is considered to be Annapūrṇā, Bhima Bhoi's spiritual consort. What I would like to stress here is that his appearance and initiation into Mahimā Dharma heralds a new era here—one different from its counterpart in Jorandā. According to the new calendar of the sect in Kardula, the *kaliyuga* ended in 1965. In an interview conducted in Kardula, Rukadev Das, the younger son of Satya Nārāyaṇa Bābā, narrates:

> There were four yugas earlier: *krtayuga*, *tretayayuga*, *dvāparayuga* and *kaliyuga*. The *kaliyuga* was over on 13 April 1965. It was the first day of *meṣa*.[24] From the next day began the Srī Svādhin Satya Bhogayuga. Since we have left *kaliyuga* behind us, we chant, 'Haraye Anant'.

In this new *yuga*, the name of the Brahmā redeems the world: 'Haraye Anant, Haraye Anant, Anant Anant Haraye, Haraye Alekh, Haraye Alekh, Alekh Alekh Haraye'. The name of the new era indicates the presence of both *satya* (truth) and *bhoga* (enjoyment). I should add that I have personally seen many letters sent by Das to different religious and political institutions in Orissa in order to get the new era recognized by Puri's religious authorities, to which he never received any reply.

There are other similar examples. I was told that a certain Ananta Bābā, also belonging to the Gaṇḍā Pāṇa caste, is venerated by his followers as *kalika avatāra*, which probably goes back to Kalki. It is also told that he was born 60 years after Mahimā Gosāin's death and was his reincarnation, being blind and healing people.[25]

The Mahimā Dharma eschatology attained a conceptual closure when the gurus disappeared. One notices that this tradition is not codified or canonized but is permanently reshaped and reformulated. New elements and items of speculations are added. In the end, speculations about the future, sacred ages and final liberation remain full of contradictions and mystical references, and are often deliberately cryptic and dense.

Conclusion

I shall end with a few concluding observations and a number of questions. Throughout my investigation, I have tried to show how Bhima Bhoi integrated the tradition of *mālikā* into his poetic writings and how he accorded it a far more important place than often admitted. The ending of the *kaliyuga* and the beginning of a new era are central to his *Stuticintāmaṇi*, *Nirvedasādhanā,* and *Bhajanamālā*. Interestingly, there is no 'positive' passage that could be read as a description of an imaginary paradise. These texts do not even discuss the *satyayuga* in any detail. How will the new age be? It is the age of Mahimā Dharma, but what does it mean? What is also striking is the absence of any reference to the start of a new cycle. In other words, no mention appears that another decline will bring an end to the *kaliyuga*. It is said that the Guru has been incarnated in all the *yugas*. But will this cycle continue? I'm not certain about a definite conclusion. There are small hints—notions like *anantayuga*—which could be read as indicating a state of endlessness, of no beginning and no end. But they are rare. Let me come to another point: the *mālikās*.

Among scholars, there is a certain tendency to take historic circumstances as explanation. Ratnakar Chaini (1998: 55) thinks that the incessant invasion of the Muslims, political instability and social disorder had compelled the Pancasakhās to write *mālikās*.[25] Is Chaini right when he reads the *mālikās* as testimonies of an antagonism between the invading Muslims and the Oriyas (ibid.: 29)? Are Bhima Bhoi's passages about hunger to be understood as references to the great famine of 1866–7? Are his passages about diseases to be read as references to historical occurrences of epidemics? This is rather unlikely. I am not ignoring the fact that these texts usually address the society in which they live; but they have a mystic and hidden dimension which is sacred, and additionally, they are cryptic and not to be read by the public at large. In fact, I would underline this hidden meaning.

But apart from this, I would like to address the theological and rhetoric dimensions: *mālikās* are items of moral and religious advice; they are prophetic calls for change. But they also reformulate religious doctrines. New theological programmes are promoted and legitimized. Eschmann (1978: 91) stated that the *mālikās* can be read as a criticism of orthodoxy. Indeed, there is explicit criticism of Vedas (cf. *Stuticintāmaṇi*, 100: 17). Heinrich von Stietencron (1986: 145) concluded that the doctrine of *yugas* permitted religious movements to legitimise their birth and existence. Every new beginning, every new era, is connected with a new *dharma*. In our case, Mahimā Dharma fulfils predictions of the Pancasakhās but inaugurates a new area at the same time.

However, a general question should be asked, which I am unable to answer for the time being. *Mālikās* are still composed in Orissa. After the super cyclone, a massive production of pamphlets started, all predicting the end of the *kaliyuga*. The books refer to biblical apocalyptic texts as well as to Nostradamus, a phenomenon that could be understood as the globalization of esoteric literature (Sahu, 1999). I ask whether *mālikās* are a peculiarity of Orissa, because I could not find parallels in either Maharashtrian mysticism or in the Hindi *sant* tradition.[26] Neither Tukaram nor Kabir speculate elaborately about future *yugas*. Neither the *Bhaviṣya Purāṇa* (Hiltebeitel, 1999), nor Hajari's recently published *Pingala Devāyaṇa Brahma Kalpa*[27] can compare to the kind of literature produced by Mahimā Dharma and the Pañcasakhās.

There are two possible answers to my question. The first is that *mālikās* are specific to Orissa. If this is so, one must explore the reasons. The second answer indicates the existence of parallel texts and similar traditions in other parts of India. In this case, further investigation of these other currents is necessary to define similarities and differences.

Notes

1. See, for example, the articles of Ishita Banerjee-Dube (2001 and 2003) and Beltz (2001, 2003 and 2006).
2. This significance is indicated by the literal meaning of the word. *Kali* means 'trouble' or 'quarrel'. *Kali, kaliyuga,* or *kalikāla* are terms used to designate the present 'bad age'.
3. It comes from the Sanskrit root *ava* + *ṭṛ*, which means 'to come down'.
4. In Radhakrishnan's translation, Kṛṣṇa says about himself: 'Whenever there is a decline of righteousness and rise of unrighteousness, O Bharata (Arjuna), then I send forth (create incarnate) Myself. For the protection of the good, for the destruction of the wicked and for the establishment of righteousness, I come into being from age to age' (Radhakrishnan, 1948, IV: 7–8).
5. *Mālikā* comes from the Sanskrit *mālā*, which means 'garland' or 'wreath'. The ending *-ikā* indicates a diminutive. *Mālikā* therefore means 'little garland'.
6. On the basis of Bhima Bhoi (1992), an English translation was made by Aniruddha Das. Composed during the first phase of the ORP in the 1970s, the manuscript is kept in Heidelberg's South Asia Institute (MSS 798). My quotations are mostly from this translation.
7. Unfortunately, the English translation, which is kept in the Orissa Archive in Heidelberg, is anonymous. It might have been translated by A. Das.
8. I found this interesting quotation in Heidelberg's Orissa Archive. Unfortunately it is not known to me from where Anncharlott Eschmann collected it. The copy was kept without further bibliographical details.
9. The recitation of the Gayatri *mantra* is probably the most important sign of reconnaissance in being a 'real' Hindu. It is used during *pūjā* performance and individual chanting. It goes like this: *Om tatsavitur vareṇyam, bhargo devasya dhīmahi, dhiyo yo naḥ pracodayāt* ('Oh Divine Beings of all three worlds, we meditate upon the glorious splendour of the vivifier divine. May He Himself illuminate our minds').
10. *Surabhi* means 'sweet smell'. It is also the name of a mythological cow. Here, she figures as the wife of Vāsuki.
11. Pṛithivī is the earth goddess.
12. Lakṣmī is the goddess of fortune.
13. Pox and smallpox are traditionally attributed to the goddess, Mātā.
14. *Anantayuga* literally means 'the age of no end'. But *ananta* is also an epithet of Viṣṇu. Could it therefore be a synonym for *satyayuga*? This would mean that there is eternity and no new beginning. The endless cycle stops, which would indicate a different cosmological concept.
15. According to the orthodox code of purity, *mlecchas* are impure people, such as 'untouchables' or foreigners.
16. *Anādi* means 'the one without beginning'. It is an epithet of Brahmā, the Lord of the void.

17. The burning of a *dhuni* (celestial fire) is a ritual practice of Mahimā Dharma ascetics.
18. An *akṣamālā* is a necklace of beads.
19. For further details referring to the question of children and progeny in hagiographic texts, see the paper by Beltz and Mishra in the present volume.
20. See the letter written by the Assistant Secretary to the Chief Commissioner of the Central Provinces (no. 3069-161), dated 17 August 1881. A copy is kept in the Orissa Archive in the South Asia Institute, Heidelberg.
21. Interview with Pabitra Sahu in Madhupur.
22. The only passage known to me, which refers to a German, is from *Padmakalpa*. In Chapter 27, it says: 'A German prince will be born in the dynasty of Viswabasu. He was the son of Indra in his previous birth. The son of Surya will also come with him. They will certainly earn name and fame, says Bhīma'. I would find it difficult, however, to relate this text to my presence.
23. In Oriya, *abda* corresponds to the Sanskrit word, *abda*, meaning 'year'.
24. *Meṣa* is a zodiac sign corresponding to Aries.
25. I owe this information to Lidia Guzy.
26. I should add that I also checked the Internet. The only reference I could get for *mālikā* concerns Orissa. It is Nancy C.M. Ross and Manmohan Mahapatra's report on oracles. See 'Pothi Oracles', www.tagmeme.com/index.html.
27. This text was translated by Amita Nathwani from Bengali into Hindi and published by Motilal Banarsidass, Delhi in 2002. It is interesting to note that its 'author', Dr Hajari, denied being the original poet and insisted that the text was revealed to him by Śiva.

References

Banerjee-Dube, Ishita (2001), 'Kali y sus contemporáneos', *Estudios de Asia y Africa*, vol. 36, pp. 11–33.

——— (2003), 'Reading Time: Texts and Pasts in Colonial Eastern India', *Studies in History*, vol. 19 (1), pp. 1–17.

Beltz, Johannes (2001), 'Healing Practices and Mahimā Dharma: A Short Note from Recent Fieldwork in Western Orissa', *Adivasi*, vols. 40 and 41, pp. 92–102.

——— (2003), 'Bhima Bhoi: The Making of a Modern Saint', in A. Copley (ed.), *Hindu Nationalism and Religious Reform Movements*, New Delhi: Oxford University Press, pp. 250–3.

——— (2004), 'Devotion, Poetry and Healing: Exploring Bhīma Bhoi's *Stuticintāmaṇi*', in Angelika Malinar, Johannes Beltz and Heiko Frese (eds.), *Text and Context in Orissa*, New Delhi: Manohar, pp. 143–70.

——— (2006), 'Contested Authorities, Disputed Centres, and Rejected Norms: Situating Mahimā Dharma in its Regional Diversity', in Georg Pfeffer (ed.), *Periphery and Centre : Studies in Orissan History, Religion and Authropology*, New Delhi: Manohar, pp. 79-104.

Bhima Bhoi (1992), *Bhaktakavi Bhīmabhoi Granthāvalī*, ed. Karunakar Sahu, Cuttack: Dharmagrantha Store.

——— (1971). *Bhīma Bhoi Māḷikā bā Padmakalpa*, ed. Vidhyadhar Sahu, Cuttack: Dharmagrantha Store (new edition 2000).

Biswanath Baba (1987), *Philosophy of Mahima Dharma*, translated from Oriya by Sarbeswar Das, Cuttack: Mahima Dharmalochana Samiti.

Chaini, Ratnakar (1998), *Makers of Indian Literature: Achyutananda Das*, New Delhi: Sahitya Akademi.

Dās, Acyutānanda (nd), *Agata Bhaviṣyata Mālikā*, Cuttack: Nityananda Pustakalaya.

Das, Aniruddha (nd), 'Bhima Bhoi's Nirvedasādhanā' translated into English (unpublished typed manuscript), Heidelberg: South Asia Institute, Orissa Archive, MSS 854.

Das, Chittaranjan (1951), 'Studies in Medieval Religion and Literature of Orissa', in *Vishva Bharati Annals*, vol. 3, pp. 107–94.

Dās, Shri Balaram (nd), *Jaśobanta Mālikā o Varṇaṭikā Avatāra Mālikā*. Cuttack: Nityananda Pustakalaya.

Dash, Kunja Behari (1991). *Folklore of Orissa*, Bhubaneswar: Orissa Sahitya Akademi.

Eschmann, Anncharlott (1975), 'Spread, Organization and Cult of Mahima Dharma', in Nilamani Senapati, ed., *Mahima Dharma*, Cuttack: Dharmagrantha Store, pp. 9–22.

——— (1978), 'Mahimā Dharma: An Autochthonous Hindu Reform Movement', in Anncharlott Eschmann, Herman Kulke and Gaya Charan Tripathi (eds.), *The Cult of Jagannath and the Regional Tradition of Orissa*, New Delhi: Manohar, pp. 375–410.

Goswami, Acyutananda (1977), *Bhabiṣyata Mālikā*, Cuttack: Hadibanda Jena.

Halbfass, Wilhelm (2000), *Karma und Wiedergeburt im indischen Denken*, Munich: Hugendubel Verlag (Diederichs Gelbe Reihe, 161).

Hiltebeitel, Alf (1999), 'Two Ways to Tell a Story: Ālhā in the Bhaviṣya Purāṇa', in Jackie Assayag (ed.), *The Resources of History, Tradition, Narration, Nation in South Asia*, Paris: Ecole Française d'Extréme Orient, pp. 95–111.

Mahapatra, Sitakant (1983), *Bhima Bhoi*, New Delhi: Sahitya Akademi.

Michaels, Axel (1998), *Der Hinduismus, Geschichte und Gegenwart*, Munich: C.H. Beck.

Mohapatra, Bishnu N., unpublished. '"Fish will Swim over the Twenty-two Steps of the Jagannath Temple". Time, Order, and Cosmology: Exploring the Career of an Apocalyptic Imagination', paper presented at the ORP Conference in Salzau, 10–13 May 2000.

Pal, Bhakta Sri Nakamudhia (1997), *Mahima Alekha Purāṇa*, Cuttack: Dharmagrantha Store.

Radhakrishnan, S. (ed.) (1948), *The Bhagavadgītā, with an Introductory Essay, Sanskrit Text, English Translation and Notes* (new edition), New Delhi: Blackie & Son.

Sahu, A.K. (ed.) (1999), *Ghora Kali Yugānta 1999–2010* (Oriya), Cuttack: Dharmagrantha Store.

von Stietencron, Heinrich (1986), 'Kalkulierter Religionsverfall: Das Kaliyuga in Indien', in Hartmut Zinser, ed., *Der Untergang von Religionen*, Berlin: Dietrich Reimer Verlag, pp. 135–50.

CHAPTER 5

A Note on the Mystic Poetry of Bhima Bhoi

SANJEEB KUMAR NAYAK

Nineteenth-century India witnessed an upsurge of religious reform movements in different corners. Some of the most prominent of these were the Brāhmo Samāj in Bengal, the Ārya Samāj in north India and the Prārthanā Sabhā in Maharashtra. These were the results of engagement on the part of Indian elites with colonial and missionary critiques of Hinduism that kindled in them a need to rethink and reinvigorate tradition. In the middle of the nineteenth century, Mahimā Dharma emerged in Orissa as a faith that gathered impetus from indigenous traditions, unaffected by western ideas of religion. Bhima Bhoi, one of the first disciples of Mahimā Svāmī, the expounder of Mahimā Dharma, was not only a devotee, a *siddha sādhak*, but also the foremost poet of Mahimā Dharma who enriched Oriya literature with his myriad devotional songs and lyrical compositions—*bhajanas*, *gītas* and *cautiśas*.[1] Meant primarily for the propagation of Mahimā Dharma, its philosophy and practices, these works are of immense literary value and poetic plenitude, characteristics that have led scholars to consider Bhima Bhoi to be 'the greatest gift of Mahimā Dharma to Oriya literature' (Das, 1952: 68). This short essay will look at some distinguishing features of the compositions of this literary genius.

Beginning the Beginning Again

Bhima Bhoi, a Kandha (tribal) from the remote territory of the *garhjats* (feudatory states) who grew up without formal education, gathered material from his own soil, from age-old Oriya culture and literature. He chose poetry as the medium through which he made his radical ideas known to ordinary men and women who inhabited the hills and forest of western Orissa. In his efforts to communicate with these people, he drew his metaphors from nature and tradition. Thus, making his poetic discourse in the language of common people, Bhima Bhoi created a style of a poetic language that is ordinary and common, yet highly suggestive and emotive. As a whole, in both content and manner, he 'revived' poetry from its beginning. By his phenomenal talent he actualized ancient traditions, both spiritual and poetical. He did not claim to be the founder of a new sect or cult, but was in fact a radical visionary who went back to the sources of the traditions and adapted their resources to his own time and condition. In this sense, he can be called a 'revolutionary classicist' who broke free from the rigid structures of orthodoxy and yet remained loyal to its original foundation.

Bhima Bhoi's poetical works, comprising *Stuticintāmaṇi*, *Brahma Nirupaṇa Gītā*, *Nirvedasādhanā*, *Śrutiniṣedha Gītā*, *Ādi-Anta Gītā*, *Bhajanamālā*, *Cautiśa Madhucakra*, *Padmakalpa*, *Brahma Calak Gītā*, *Manusabhā Maṇḍala*, and the unpublished *Mahimā Vinod* among others, elaborate the philosophy and practices of Mahimā Dharma along with records of his own spiritual growth and his quest for Brahma, whom he calls Alekha. Thus, in his poetry, 'feeling and thought, emotion and ratiocination, poetry and philosophy are inextricably blended' (Nayak, 2001: 118).

Bhima Bhoi, departing from the over-ornamented Sanskritized poetic technique of his predecessors[2] that was being employed to camouflage the sensuality of physical love, returned to the poetic simplicity of the *sant* (saint) tradition. Instead of using sophisticated figures of speech and Sanskritized diction, Bhima Bhoi used in his poetry colloquial words and idioms of the common man. His poetry depicted naked emotions, unpremeditated spontaneous feelings in a language simple and sincere, fluent and direct. He derived images from the ordinary day-to-day life of village folk and used them to describe extraordinary other-worldly subjects in a way that they look fresh and new, inordinately beautiful. Thus, Bhima Bhoi, the poet-prophet of Mahimā Dharma, set an unprecedented example in Oriya poetry. His works have a lucid classical simplicity and directness that are rich in expression but devoid of superfluous ornaments; a swift, vigorous, flexible and fluid verse resonating the epic cadence.

As stated earlier, Bhima Bhoi was not influenced by the currents of Westernization, whereas Radhanath Ray, Bhima Bhoi's contemporary, who is given the credit for beginning the era of modern poetry in Oriya literature, paved the way for modernity by deriving from Western literature. Bhima Bhoi refurbished the native tradition, making it relevant to his own time. According to Haraprasad Das, 'mystic poetry is the original identity of Oriya poetic-consciousness. Bhima Bhoi, renovating this native mystic poetic tradition, that was pushed aside by the Riti poets, began the modernist phase of Oriya poetry' (Das, 1995: 163). In doing so, Bhima Bhoi made Oriya poetry search for its original sources.

Śūnya Darśana and its Literary Delineation

Bhima Bhoi's poetry depicts the supreme being as *alekha* (indescribable), who is again *anākāra* (without form), *avyakta* (unmanifest), *anādi* (without beginning), *mahāśūnya* (great void), *śūnya puruṣa* (void personified)—epithets of Brahma that have appeared and reappeared in Oriya poetry long before him.

Right from Sarala Das's *Mahabharata* through a long chain of literary works including Balaram Das's *Brahmanda Bhugola*, *Virata Gītā*, Jagannath Das's *Tula Bhina*, the writings of Achyutananda, Dinakrushna and Arakshita Das and many other lesser writers, the supreme Reality has been delineated as one without form, without end or beginning, without shape and without qualities (Mahapatra, 1983: 24).

This tradition of *śūnya* as the supreme reality has its philosophical roots in Buddhism, the Sahajiā and the Nātha traditions. In the works of the Pancasakhās, the five medieval mystics, the Buddhist void came to embody both consciousness and energy. They conceived the Void not as complete nothingness, but as transcendental and immanent at the same time. Thus, for these mystics, the Void was embodied in a person. For the Vaiṣṇavas, again, *Alekha* is *Anākāra* Viṣṇu, whose creativity is *nirākāra.*

When Alekha the formless assumed form
As Nirakara he became known (Das, 1989: 11).

Over time, this *Alekha Anākāra* was transformed and came to be identified with Kṛṣṇa. Achyutananda described a formless Kṛṣṇa dwelling in eternal Golaka. Later, in his *Śūnya Saṁhitā*, he brought about a synthesis between the idea of an Absolute beyond attributes (*nirguṇa*) and that of a deity with form and attributes (*saguṇa*) symbolized by the Jagannātha cult, by identifying the Void with Jagannātha, the presiding deity of Orissa (Das, 1952: 68). This synthesis brought about by the Pancasakhās has been vehemently criticized by Mayadhar Mansingh, who writes: 'All these [Pancasakhā poets] brought into their writings intellectual indiscipline and incongruity. They could not avoid the impact of Jagannath and attached Shunya and Alekh to Jagannath' (Mansingh, 1996: 103).

The concept of Śūnya Brahma pervades in all of Bhima Bhoi's poetry: He is the one who is the uncaused cause, the one without beginning and end, from whom the void was born, from the void space and sky, from the sky the colours. Later, from the *nāma* came fire, ether and water. This was followed by the sun and the moon, the trinity of Brahma, Viṣṇu and Maheshvara, and all other moving and unmoving (static) objects, all of which arose from the nameless one (Das, 1977: 755–6). Bhima Bhoi defines this Brahma thus:

He is the formless Brahma who has no form, no colour, no body.
He is Brahma of the unfathomable sea, unheard is his glory (ibid.: 757).

The poet attempts to describe the indescribable Brahma. But language is not adequate for the purpose; hence, due to its inherent inadequacy, it becomes paradoxical:

He has no hands nor feet but hands and feet he has . . .
He has no nail but has lakhs of nails . . .
He has no anus but he has one . . .

He is the solid body with no pore absolutely. . . .
He has no teeth, nor tongue, but he has teeth and tongue
without tasting or eating he knows all taste . . .
He has no ear, but he has a pair of them
hearing all he remains silent as if he hears none. (ibid.: 246)

Such is the character of Brahma, who is neither this nor that, neither being nor non-being, nor anything in between. He is nothing yet He is all. It is the Nothing beyond nothing.

Bhima Bhoi uses the imagery of human features in order to describe Alekha Brahma lucidly, to make something nebulous comprehensible, yet to express His transcendental and immanent nature at the same time. The poet's imagination does not end there. The definition of the Alekha is always inadequate and therefore unsatisfying. How can the poet's imagination be satisfied?

Brahma slips when caressed.
So tender Brahma has become slippery
soft like cotton is the body of Brahma.
Brahma is playing like a child,
like a leech that never leaves,
out of unbearable terror.
The secret of Brahma has become subtle. (ibid.: 248)

The use of images like cotton and leech not only adds a colloquial flavour, but also makes the epithets for Brahma more suggestive. Brahma is like a leech, which is not only soft but also clings to the body. This unravels another characteristic of Brahma, namely, that once a person attains Brahma or He embraces a person, they are inseparable. Another point is also highly significant. The poet introduces the word *pua* (son), which is indicative of filial love. A Vaiṣṇava motif is thus introduced into the concept of Brahma. 'If you try to caress the Brahma, it slips away from the hand'—this reflects His elusiveness. The indeterminable Brahma is defined by negating known things and relationships, but this negation does not exclude what is negated; rather, it includes all in a large framework, which can be comprehended intuitively but not understood cognitively. Who is Brahma? He is neither the Guru, nor the disciple, nor the Brāhmaṇ nor the lowly *caṇḍāla*.[3] He has no caste or creed. At the same time, he is part of all souls, complements humans and rules the world.

He is neither a guru nor a disciple, neither a master nor a servant
He is neither a Brāhmaṇ nor a Caṇḍāla, nor is he great.
He has no caste or creed, nor has he any discrimination.
Both, becoming one in soul and mind He creates the universe. (ibid.: 689)

From this set of negation, the poet moves to a set of affirmation to define Alekha:

He becomes a disciple and also a preceptor.
He assumes the form of a grass and also the form of a mountain.
He becomes the master and a servant.
He shows himself to be ignorant and acquires all knowledge. (ibid.: 237)

This paradoxical stance of the poet suggests that he accepts the Lord's all-exclusive and all-inclusive nature: His nature as both transcendent and immanent at the same time. Through these lines, the poet suggests some basic ideas of Mahimā Dharma too. The Lord is above all castes and creeds, his creation is also supposed to be casteless. The Lord is both the disciple and the Guru, he is the same residing in all. Thus, Brahma is both being and becoming, the creator and the created, the 'all' and the 'none', the indescribable formless and all the forms:

He, the Brahma, becomes the void himself.
He manifests himself in forms, and is indescribable himself. (ibid.: 239)

Mahimā the Alekha creates the multiplicity of creation by his will out of his own Mahimā. He is both the consciousness and the creative energy:

He creates the whole universe by his own will
while being revealed as all possible objectivity. (ibid.: 478)

Brahma resides in *Nigama Bhubana*, an inaccessible region where there is no sense of time or sound:

Where Brahma resides is *Nigama Bhubana*.
There is neither light nor darkness, neither day nor night.
That is the temple of silence, no sound can penetrate.
There is no trace of *raja* or *birjya*, *bindu* or *nāda*. (ibid.: 222)[4]

Bhima Bhoi allegorically constructs the temple of his faith by re-organizing radically the images of traditional ritual and liturgy. The Lord Alekha resides in Alekha Mandira, guarded by Ananta in the west, Jagannātha in the south, Rāma in the north and Kṛṣṇa in the east. It is the *śūnya* temple built of the bricks and stones of *karmakāṇḍa*, plastered with the soil of *puṇya* (merit), washed with the lime of *yajña* (sacrifice). This (non-existent) temple is swept with the broomstick of dharma, shut with the doors of Rāma-Kṛṣṇa, decorated with the motifs of the twelve *avatāras* (incarnations). This *śūnya* temple is built upon the pillars of the four directions, roofed with the beams of gods and thatched with the straw of the revolving worlds (ibid.: 452). Thus, Bhima Bhoi metaphorically says that Brahma can be attained with the help of truth and virtue, wisdom and steadfastness. Rāma, Kṛṣṇa, Jagannātha and Ananta are not the ultimate Reality, but the personified representations of the Real.

Bhima Bhoi depicts the Hindu gods and goddesses as adornments of Alekha—cosmetics and clothes—and thereby dislodges them from their conventional positions to make them serve the higher principle:

Śaṇkara and Narasingha are the sari and the loin cloth.
Brāmaṇa and Rāmacandra have become the helms of the sari,
Kṛṣṇa and Balarāma are its two ends . . .
The ten incarnations have become the sari threads,
Sarasvatī has become the voice, Lakṣmī the grace, the vermilion. (ibid.: 274)

To describe the beauty of the Lord, Bhima Bhoi takes help of the traditional images referring to brightness:

The form is brighter than millions of flames.
The limbs dazzle like millions of suns.
The body more transparent than millions of moons,
The face more radiant than millions of illuminations. (ibid.: 269)

The imagery of light used here is manifold, such as fire, sun, moon and pure radiance, and they all signify the symbolic nature of light as a divine presence. To give another example, he compares the lotus-feet of the Lord with moonlight. This is not merely a lyrical analogy, but a profound philosophical paradox in which the formless, shapeless moonlight comes to function as a metaphor for the lotus-feet of the Lord. Like the soothing luminosity of the moonlight, which has no form of its own, but reveals the form of real objects, the Lord is a self-revealing reality of the ultimate abstraction that contains his concreteness. Brahma resides in the human body as well:

The abode of Brahma is at the opening on the top of the head
Alekha Puruṣa resides there at the top of the *brahmarandhra*[5]
and through *śiśurandhra*[6] he gets in and out. (ibid.: 222)

However esoteric the language of these lines might be, this conception invokes the tantric *piṇḍa-brahmāṇḍa* concept of Vajrāyana. It implies an affinity between the microcosm and the macrocosm. One can attain Brahma through body culture. Bhima Bhoi uses imagery of sexuality abundantly in *Ādi-Anta Gītā*.[7] We find Bhima Bhoi and Mahimā Dharma giving equal importance to body and mind, matter and consciousness. To explain the presence of the Brahma in human body, Bhima Bhoi uses two common metaphors:

There is Brahma in the body
as there is water in the coconut . . .
As the fish play while swimming in the pond
Brahma plays in the human body. (ibid.: 224)

It is evident that Bhima Bhoi has synthesized various elements of yoga and tantra in a heterodox manner. In the process, he has reinterpreted some of the basic ideas of both traditions in a new vein, integrating them. The significant point of his discourse is that the path of salvation is an open secret accessible to all. In this way, he disseminates the insights of the classical traditions within a popular ambience by using a folk idiom.

The Guru: Dynamics of Devotion

The age-old *guru-śiṣya* tradition in India is usually held to be the most holy and pivotally important in spiritual growth. The Guru is an agent, a guide on the road to spirituality. But Bhima Bhoi differs from this tradition in his conception of the Guru as the vehicle of spiritual metaphor. His Guru, Mahimā Svāmī, the expounder of Mahimā Dharma, is the Lord Alekha incarnate, who, leaving his *Śūnya Mandira* had descended upon the earth to save the universe from degeneration and destruction:

The creator himself has come to this earth . . .
The Guru, the Lord Brahma, is incarnate in this world. (ibid.: 825)

The Lord reveals himself to grant liberation. As the Lord of the lords, the only master of the universe, He has come to alleviate the suffering of his creatures, and to restore dharma on earth where sins and falsehood reign supreme:

To save all the fifty-six millions of creatures
the Buddha incarnated as Vaiṣṇava Gosain. (ibid.: 825)

The Lord has assumed human form as the Guru Mahimā Gosāin out of his unfathomable compassion to annihilate the suffering of the universe. Bhima Bhoi poetically narrates:

Appareled in ochre, the compassionate form
with attributes innumerable
wanders through rain and summer
the Lord himself suffers to sustain the universe. (ibid.: 670)

The Guru, the Lord is the embodiment of compassion. The poet portrays him in a unique image of endless renunciation and pathos who, in his mission to save the universe, travels through rain and summer without rest. The originality of Bhima Bhoi as a poet and a devotee lies in this image of god as a figure of endless compassion who suffers to annihilate the suffering of his creatures. The poetic sensibility of the devotee Bhima Bhoi makes it possible for him to articulate the indescribable reality of god. 'God had never appeared beforehand as human as he appeared in the poetry of Bhima Bhoi' (Das, 1995: 173). Although the line *puruṣa ratana jivanara dhana*' reflects Vaiṣṇavite influence in tone and imagery; yet, it goes beyond Vaiṣṇava philosophy. In Vaiṣṇava bhakti tradition, the guru is the master, and the *śiṣya* is the servant and sometimes a friend, a companion. But in Bhima Bhoi's poetry, this relationship receives its ultimate expression in the devotee's complete surrender at the feet of the Lord.

Here, the tone is on the whole devotional, but the imagery involves a paradox: the Lord is at the same time majestic and mendicant. He is suffering, yet blissful: out of his ever-blissful state, the Lord has taken human form as a *sannyāsī*. So He appears as both human and divine. In the last line, the paradox dissolves when the intention of the Lord is revealed. The majesty of the Lord lies in his compassion for his creation. His grandeur lies in his suffering for the cause of the universe. Before such a grand and great Lord, the devotee feels humble and insignificant, and in the words of Ishita Banerjee (1993, Chapter 2), asks for his *karuṇā*, mercy and compassion rather than his love and companionship. To the Lord who commands power and authority, the devotee can only submit his total faith and wait for his mercy. Still Bhima Bhoi expresses his impatience, worry and helplessness:

We are all waiting for you, mighty Lord, till the date you have given.
We are all going to be ruined if there is the slightest neglect on your part.
We are tumbling over the earth, oh revered Guru. (Das, 1977: 792)

It is important to mention here that the poet speaks on behalf of the common people, using verbs that indicate their reference to plural subjects. He also appropriately uses colloquial words and idioms to represent the voice of poor, subordinate people. The poet never prays for his personal liberation; he asks for the salvation of all.

The spirituality attained by Bhima Bhoi is not a state of peaceful equanimity and bliss, but is disturbed by the suffering of others. Therefore, his poetic mood is also an ever-changing one and his articulation takes many tones and forms. His devotion to Lord manifests itself in myriad dramatic ways. Sometimes he prays to the Lord like a slave, at times he explodes in anger; and at yet other times, in desperation, he orders Mahimā (the Lord) to fold His banner and go out of sight, for He has no right to persuade (people to accept his faith), if He cannot make the universe perfect (ibid.: 603). Thus, the poetic soul of the devotee Bhima Bhoi oscillates between persuasive prayer and angry explosion. The poet also prays to the Lord in total devotion, offering himself at his lotus-feet:

How long can I carry these bundles Lord?
Bundles on both the shoulders, left and right?
Take my body, my life, my Lord!
I offer myself at thy feet. (ibid.: 637)

Bhima Bhoi rages against Mahimā Svāmī in another poem:

Are you my master?
Aren't you ashamed of torturing your devotee?
Get lost in the nether world. (ibid.: 602)

A deep sense of unbearable agony persists all through Bhima Bhoi's *Bhajanamālā*, *Stuticintāmaṇi* and *Cautiśa Madhucakra*. This agony springs from and is controlled by devotion and the poet's ultimate faith in Lord Alekha. The mournfulness is not caused by the suffering and distress of the poet's personal life alone, but it is also the consequence of the sorrow of a devotee who empathises with mankind's suffering in a world that is ethically and spiritually decadent. The decadence is partially caused by 'time', through *yuga jantraṇā* (pain brought about by *kaliyuga*), and partially by man through casteism, idolatry and Brahmanical supremacy. Accordingly, the agony of the devotee finds outlets in different poetic moods and expressions. Out of this agony comes wisdom and compassion.

The poet's compassion results in a rebellious attitude that finds expression in two different modes: the first expressed as a revolt against high-caste men, particularly Brāhmaṇs who hold the authority of Vedas and mislead people into worshipping false gods; the second expressed as a revolt against god and a denunciation of his greatness as the Creator:

Why do you neglect me, for which sin, o Hari!
Yours is a cruel heart without pity,
devourer of your devotee. (ibid.: 638)[8]

This reminds us of an 'existentialist' reaction to the cruelty and injustice of destiny. The sensitive involvement in and identification with the suffering of others makes the poet consider his personal suffering as less important than that of the universe, and hence he becomes compassionate towards all living beings. The sorrows, personal and universal, blend to create an extraordinary depth and wisdom:

Let my soul be condemned to hell
but let the universe be redeemed. (ibid.: 676)

The poet has internalized the endless suffering of all living beings, 'For I am flesh and blood, Lord, I cannot bear the miseries of mankind' (ibid.: 676). The poet's unfathomable compassion for the universe and his intense faith upon the Lord makes him a rebel to the extent of religious transgression:

Sitting on the bank of Mahānadi I have taken a vow touching water.
Transgressing dharma I will drink wine and abduct Brāhmaṇ women.
(ibid.: 675)

The poet's immense faith in his Lord gives him the courage to voice his frustrations:

I could overturn the earth in a day in a moment
But what can I do but clench my teeth without the Guru's warrant. (ibid. 675)

The poet is aware of his own power and yet accepts his limitation as a human being. He recognizes the absolute authority of the Lord, without whose command even a leaf cannot shake.

Bhima Bhoi was a genius. He was not only a devotee but also a poet. Or, to put it more succinctly, he was more a poet than a devotee or a spiritualist. The following lines from *Stuticintāmaṇi* bear testimony to this:

Consider my prayer, otherwise I will leave the body, this is my judgment.
You will carry the sin of killing the poet of the three worlds. (ibid.: 672)

This shows that Bhima Bhoi thought of himself primarily as a poet who used his poetic talent to express his spirituality. His poetry is thus a medium of self-expression, 'the intimate revelation of his changing moods of anger and surrender, humility and tranquillity, confrontation and conciliation, forgiveness and submissiveness, passion and pathos, self-pity and self-abnegation' (Nayak, 2001: 123). Here, then, is a highly sensitive poet for whom religion was less important than the survival of the world: 'Let theology be condemned, but let the world survive' (Das, 1977: 836). These lines reveal how the poet gave primacy to the world here and now, over and above the sanctity of doctrine or dogma and affirm the precedence of experience over idea in Bhima Bhoi's existentialist schema.

Conclusion

The poetic style and language of Bhima Bhoi is simple, however complex his feelings, thoughts and philosophy might be. His love and compassion for the low and the high, literate and non-literate, give his poetry both personal and universal appeal. It bridges the gulf between the high and serious esoteric literature and philosophy, and religious beliefs and literary feelings of the common people. As a mystic poet, he was remarkably effective in capturing the 'dazzling darkness' which lies beyond language and sensory perception. In fact, his poetry can be called an incantation, which invokes the soul of silence in human language—the silence of the absolute meaning beyond the relative contingency of verbal events. To use the words of Sri Aurobindo (1994: 9) in this context, Bhima Bhoi's poetry is of the 'mantric' spirit, which 'rises at once from the heart of the seer and from the distant home of the truth'.

Notes

1. A *cautiśā* is a poem of 34 couplets in alphabetical order.
2. The 'medieval' period in Oriya literary history was dominated by the works of Upendra Bhanja.
3. Sanskrit term for outcaste.
4. *Raja*, *birjya*, *bindu* and *nādā* are different names of semen at different levels of erotic ecstasy.
5. According to a communication with Sadananda Das, *brahmarandhra* denotes the opening at the top of the head of newborn babies. The top of the head is very soft.
6. According to a communication with Bettina Bäumer, *śiśurandhra* may denote the *nābhi-cakra*, the navel, through which the child is connected to the mother at the time of birth. After birth, the navel cord is cut-off.
7. See the paper of Bettina Bäumer in this volume.

8. The Oriya text reads: *Taki achhu tia parijante, tana prabhunku chahin samaste, tike hela kale nasilu gosain, tali padu achhu mahigate he shriguru.*

References

Sri Aurobindo (1994), *The Future Poetry: Letters on Poetry, Literature and Art*, Pondichery: Sri Aurobindo Ashram Publication Department.

Banerjee-Dube, Ishita (1993), 'Religion and Society in Eastern India: Mahima Dharma in the Nineteenth and Twentieth Centuries', Ph.D. thesis, University of Calcutta.

Das, Bir Kishore (ed.) (1977), *Bhīma Bhoi Granthābalī*, Cuttack: J. Mahapaatra & Co.

Das, Chaitanya (1989), *Viṣnugarbha Purāna*, Cuttack: Dharmagrantha Store.

Das, Chittaranjan (1952), *Odisare Mahimā Dharma*, Calcutta: Vishwabharati.

Das, Hara Prasad (1995), *Adhunikatara Paramparā*, Cuttack: Bharat Bharati.

Mahapatra, Sitakanta (1983), *Bhima Bhoi: His Life and Works*, New Delhi: Sahitya Akademi.

Mansingh, Mayadhar (1996), *Odia Sahityara Itihāsa*, Cuttack: Grantha Mandir.

Nayak, Pabitra Mohan (2001), *The Voice of Silence*, Bhubaneswar: Odissa Sahitya Akademi.

CHAPTER 6

The Guru in Bhima Bhoi's Stuticintāmaṇi

SADANANDA DAS

Let me begin with a few verses of Bhima Bhoi on guru as a prayer to the preceptor.

Satya dharma vinu kichi na jāṇai pāpa puṇya bhalamanda.
vasi divā niśi ghoṣi aharniśi śrīguru caraṇābinda.
guru pāda vinu na diśai mote baḍa hoi yete dravya.
muhiṁvicāruchi mohara manare guru pādapadma sarva.
E marttyadhāmare ajñāna paṇare jīva mohara na yiba.
guru jñānadātā jagatara pitā jñānapatha dekhāiba.

I am repeating the name of my master (guru) sitting all the day and night. Thus, I know nothing else, neither sin nor merit, neither good nor bad except the true religion.

Nothing seems to me to be greater than the feet of my master. I myself consider that the lotus feet of my master are everything for me.

Let me not die in this world out of ignorance. Let my guru, the bestower of knowledge and the father of the worlds show me the path of wisdom.[1]

Introduction

The term *guru* is very significant in Indian culture from the very beginning, i.e. from the Vedic period. It has an old and a long tradition in different spiritual and religious schools in India. Starting from the Vedas and Upaniṣads throughout Tantra, Āgama, and Bhakti period up to the present day, the role of a guru has been very important.[2] The term has different meanings such as a teacher in general, a religious teacher, a spiritual preceptor in particular, a master of any science, a respectable person, a father, a mother, and forefathers. It also means venerable, respectable, important and great. As an adjective it means heavy or weighty. Technically a guru is one who performs purificatory ceremonies over a boy and instructs him in the Vedas.[3] 'Orthodox' Brahmanical texts of major importance such as the *Manusmṛti* define guru in the following words:

> That vipra who performs in accordance with the rules (of the Veda) the rites, like garbhādhāna (conception-rite) and others, and gives food (to the child), is called the guru.[4]

The etymology of the word *guru* is *gṛṇāti, upadiśati iti guruḥ* one who teaches or imparts knowledge is guru. It has another meaning which means the Lord, the Supreme Spirit. All these meanings are not very different from each other, except when it is used as an adjective, and all these senses are found in Bhima Bhoi's *Stuticintāmaṇi.*

Stuticintāmaṇi, 'The jewel of spiritual hymns' is one of the major works of the saint poet Bhima Bhoi. It contains a hundred *bolis*, each *boli* having 20 stanzas. The text deals with a variety of subject matters among which the description of Śūnya Brahma, the eulogy of *Mahimā*, the narration of different *yugas*, *anāma* cosmology, description about the characteristics of a guru and *śiṣya* and some autobiographical as well as personal or devotional verses are of key importance. This paper focuses on the idea of guru and his importance in relation to his *śiṣya* as found in *Stuticintāmaṇi* with references from other works of Bhima Bhoi like *Bhajanamālā*. *Stuticintāmaṇi* deals with the devotional aspect of the saint-poet Bhima Bhoi and explains his ideas about the guru and his relationship with his guru in great details. He is beyond description (*alekha*), beyond names (*anāma*), beyond forms (*arūpa*), beginningless (*anādi*), yet having human form, and has rescued Bhima Bhoi.[5] From the description of the poet one gets an idea that Bhima Bhoi had a very close and personal relationship with his master. He sings the glory (*mahimā*) of his great guru and narrates his personal matters and his life experiences to him. He is so much in close contact with his guru that he cannot live even for a moment without him. Suffering because of the absence of his guru, Bhima sings thus:

Śrīguru payare koṭi namaskāra mūrchi na pārai daṇḍe.
pākharu antara hele satyabrahma vajra paḍuthāi muṇḍe.

Without missing him even for a moment, I offer my salutations at his feet. If he is (*satyabrahma*) away from me I feel as if a thunderbolt has fallen on my head.[6]

Bhima's Meeting with his Guru

Bhima Bhoi remembers his childhood days very clearly and describes his first meeting with his guru. He mentions that when he was two years old he got his wisdom.[7] In the month of *Jyeṣṭha* (May-June) when he completed four years of age, he saw a *yogī* wandering in the villages. He was wearing a *kaṣā kaupīna* (a dark-red coloured ragged garment worn by ascetics) and looking dirty. Bhima Bhoi recalls clearly that he had seen the auspicious signs of a *śaṅkha* (conch) and *cakra* (disc) on both his arms. He was moving in the villages with an earthen pot in his hands and asking the village women for food. Child Bhima was standing close to him knowing very little about him. The guru was asking, 'O my child, give me a little water'. Bhima remembers that moment when people gathering around the *yogī* only looked at each other and nobody offered him food or water. The Svāmī uttering the word *dharma*, left the place. Memories of that day were too painful for child Bhima. It was a mixture of both sorrow and joy for him. He says that when he recalls the incident, his body shivers and his heart gets excited. He further says that thoughts of that day burn me with sorrow: 'My body and soul cry losing consciousness'.[8] Another instance of meeting with his master is narrated in *Bhajanamālā*:

Vijaye śriguru avanā mandiru śūnye yā vānā prakāśa
jñāna netre dekhi uṭhili camaki rūpa bijuḷira trāsa se
puṇya kārttika māsa, śukḷapakṣa daśamī divasa
tahiṁ bheṭa hele guru śiṣya, daṇḍa praḷambita gurupāśa
kṛpā bhakta bāndhava viśvāsa ye.

The great master whose glory shines in the void, revealed himself from the indescribable temple (*avanā mandira*). I saw him with my eyes of wisdom and was surprised to see the frightening form like lightening. It was the tenth day of the bright fortnight, in the month of holy Kārttika (November/December). There met the *guru* and disciple. He (the disciple) fell prostrate before the *guru* who was full of mercy, trustworthy and dear to his devout.[9]

Elsewhere it is vividly mentioned that in the middle of the night the great master Mahimā Svāmī along with Siddha Govinda Bābā came to the place of Bhima Bhoi. Bhima Bhoi remembers that moment and writes:

Hoichi daśa ghaḍi rātri vijaye aṇākāra jyoti
praveśa śayana mandire timiri phiṭilā tejare
chiḍā hoile divya jyoti jājulyamaya rūpakānti
śravaṇe śubhilā ḍākile anādi prabhu ājñā dele
boile uṭhasire bāpa dekha anādi brahmarūpa
ceti uṭhili tatakṣaṇa pāruśe vije śūnya brahma
cakṣu maḷiṇa deli cāhiṁ samāna guru śiṣya dui
kali muṁ daṇḍa ye praṇāma labhili puṇya muktakāma.
kalyāṇa vaṃchile turita mathāre māridele hasta.

It was about ten *ghaḍis*[10] of the night when that formless light entered my sleeping room. The darkness was conquered with the divine light. The divine light with a lustrous body stood up and addressed me. I heard the command of the beginningless Lord in my ears, 'Oh my dear son, wake up and behold the beginning-less form of Brahman'. I woke up all of a sudden and beheld the śūnyabrahma by my side. I refreshed myself and saw both the master and the disciple. Desiring liberation I paid my salutation to him and fell at his feet. He put his hands on my head and blessed me.[11]

Bhima Bhoi waits for a few more years to be graced. When he attained youth, he was blessed by the Lord. By that time his body and mind had undergone so much suffering that they had become purified and capable of receiving initiation. The great guru Mahimā Svāmī came to him and initiated him in the true glorious religion or *satya mahimā dharma*. In other terms it is called *gurudharma*.[12] Bhima further says that seeing the three worlds engaged in untruth the Lord revealed this *gurudharma*. He gave the *mantra* of six letters (*ṣaḍākṣaramantra*) such as *alekha-mahimā* to the world.

Bhima having become initiated in this *satyadharma* or *guru-dharma* did not feel proud of it, rather he felt more humble and obedient. Thus he speaks that I feel humble and consider myself as small as a fly or an insect in the teaching of the *nirveda* initiation of my master. Realizing his own limit he is afraid of seeing the glory of the Lord.

Nirveda dīkṣāre śrīguru śikṣāre aṭai kīṭapa māchi,
nija rūpa cāhiṁ kāhiṁ muṁ bhajanti vānā dekhi maruachi.

I am like a fly or an insect in the teaching of this initiation of dispassion of my master. Seeing my own limit how can I worship him? I am afraid of seeing the glory of my Lord.[13]

Further he approaches the Lord with folded hands and asks for his blessings. The Guru is the Lord of all the three worlds. He is the sole saviour of mankind. He is the father, and mother. He is all-powerful, all-mighty. He is the creator of the micro-cosmos and the macro-cosmos (*piṇḍa-brahmāṇḍa*). He is the creator and the protector of all this.

Guru baḷabanta guru sāmaratha guru sinā pitā mātā,
e piṇḍa brahmāṇḍa āya vyaya yete aṭa haratā karatā.
Jagata yākare guru pitā mātā sakaḷa samāna cāhiṁ ,
dārā suta vitta bandhu varga boli manare ghenuchi muhiṁ.
pitā mātā rūpe hoi acha tumbhe ākāśamaṇḍaḷu āsi,
guru pitā mātā koḷare e pāda hoichi bahuta doṣī.

The Guru is all mighty. He is capable of (doing everything and anything). He is father and mother. He is the sole saviour of the micro- and macro-cosmos and other activities. In the whole world, the guru is my father and mother. He looks after everybody equally. He is my wife, son, wealth, and relatives, thus I think in my mind. Manifesting from the Void you have become like my father and mother. This soul has become a sinner in the lap of my master, who is father and mother to me.[14]

Being the creator and protector of all the creatures he is compassionate. He is the sovereign Lord of the universe, which consists of nine earths. He is all-pervasive. He protects his devotees and saves the world, therefore he is called *Viśvambhara*. He is the only protector of weak people and the saviour of the poor. He is the incarnation of *dharma* and *karma*. He is the father and mother of all the animate and inanimate beings. He pervades everywhere within and outside. He protects the noble and the wicked equally. He is the giver of food to all.[15] In the following verses the identification of guru and Brahman is clearly stated by Bhima Bhoi.

Alekha prabhu se mahimā sāgara piṇḍa brahmāṇḍara guru,
cāri yugamadhye cāri khāni jīva jāta hvanti se brahmaru.

The indescribable Lord is the ocean of Glory. He is the master of micro- and macro-cosmos. All the four varieties of creatures are born out of that Brahma in four ages.[16]

In the *Bhajanamālā* the identification of the guru (Mahimā Svāmī) with Brahman is explicitly described by Bhima Bhoi. He has experienced himself the presence of the absolute Brahman which he expresses in these words:

Eka brahma rūpa goṭi cāhiṁcakṣu yiba phuṭi
yāhā muṁ dekhichi kisa kahibi tuṇḍe.

The sight of the one and absolute Brahman blinds one's eyes. How can I express in words what I have seen![17]

Further he explains that the true Bṛahman is of one form and the father of all living beings (*sakaḷa jīvaṅka bāpa*). Only his devotees know the essence of Brahman and adorn his blessed feet. Merging with undecaying Brahman, he appears in one form. None is comparable to him in the three worlds. Here there is a complete identification of the guru and Brahman. Everybody sees him through their eyes that he wears the bark of a tree and roams like a guest on the path of dharma. Bhima Bhoi says that no one has understood this. *Bhajanamālā* 45 and 46 describe the identification of Mahimā Svāmī and Brahman again. The peculiarity of these two *bhajanas* is that here the Divine is conceived as a child and the poet here expresses the *vātsalyabhāva* (mood of affection) in a devotional way. There are many expressions which express more than are meaning, a feature common to *bhakti* literature. Thus Bhima describes:

Vṛddha vayasare atithiveśare yāuthile ehi pathare
kehu dekhichaki veni netrare.

Has anyone seen him with his own eyes?
In the guise of a guest he was going on this path
in his old age.

Rūpa varṇa nāhiṁ jhaḷi diśanti
pāda pāṇi nāhiṁ cālu achanti
vastra nāhiṁ vṛkṣa vakaḷa pindhanti
āḍabandha nāhiṁ kaṭire

He has neither form nor colour, yet he glows,
neither feet nor hands, yet he walks.
He has no clothing but wears around his waist the bark of a tree.

Mote dharatī ākāśa kahile
putra yogīndra heleṇi boile
brahmāṇḍa uddhāra karibe kumara
ghora kaḷikāḷa yugare.

The earth and the sky told me
the son has become a supreme *yogī*.
In this age of Kali the son will liberate the world.[18]

Here the son who is addressed as a *yogīputra* is none other than Mahimā Svāmī who has come down to the earth to liberate the world.

The Relationship of Guru and *Śiṣya*

The relationship of guru and *śiṣya*, the master and disciple is an age-old tradition.[19] There is a mutual relationship between the master and disciple. One compliments the other. Both guru and *śiṣya* are interdependent. In the context of tantric initiation the role of both guru and *śiṣya* are very important. While explaining the importance of a guru in tantric ritual Abhinavagupta in his commentary *Gītārtha Saṅgraha* to the *Bhagavadgītā* (IV.29–30) speaks:

Through the process of uniting the self of a student with his own self, a teacher, by causing the disciple's exhaling breath (*apāna*) to enter into his inhaling breath (*prāṇa*), generates the experience of liberation (*apavarga*) in the self of a disciple and in his own self. In this way he offers *apāna* into *prāṇa* in the fire of *svādhyāya* which enables both to abide in the state of bliss.[20]

Bhima Bhoi describes the relation of guru-*śiṣya* in detail.[21] The guru and *śiṣya* are one and inseparable like *jīva* and *parama* (human soul and the supreme) in the body.[22] Their relation is very close and inseparable. In the words of Bhima:

Vāmphīre yesane jala pūrithāi gāra kāṭile ki chiḍi.
yugayugāntare tini trailokyare guruśiṣya sehipari.

As one cannot separate the water of a pond by drawing a line, in the same way the relation of guru-*śiṣya* is inseparable in all the ages in the three worlds.[23]

There is a unity between them. Nobody can make a distinction in their relationship. If anyone differentiates them he will be destroyed. As Bhima Bhoi puts in his own words:

Kehu aṭe guru kehu aṭe śiṣya tahiṁ na thāi vāraṇa.
bhakta bhagavāna eka aṅga jāṇa ekānta ṭhābe bhojana.
E beni prakāra ye kare vicāra se prāṇī huanti nāśa.
bhaṇe bhīma bhoi sātaśa padare abhaya pañjare vāsa.

One should not make any distinction between guru and *śiṣya*. Both the *bhakta* and the Lord is one limb and they partake meals together. One who sees difference between them will perish. Thus speaks Bhima Bhoi in seven hundred *padas* dwelling in the abode of fearlessness.[24]

In fact, the body of the disciple is like that of the Lord. The Lord appears in the human form as the body of a devotee. They worship each other. The disciple worships the feet of the master and the master takes care of him.[25] This interdependence between them is very significant. This is not just an outward relationship in an academic sphere, but much more than that. However it may be difficult to understand this relationship in the modern days. This relationship is not possible among others. One should not look at them as two. They are one.

Ementa ye gururśiṣyaṅka carita ānare sambhava nohi.
Guruśiṣya duheṁ ekatva aṭanti antara maṇiba nāhiṁ. . .

Such is the characteristic of a guru and disciple, this is not possible with others. Both guru and disciple are one. One should not think (*maṇiba*) of them as two.[26]

They take care of each other (*parasparaṃ bhāvayantaḥ śreyaḥ paramavāpsythaḥ, Bhagavadgītā*). It is not a one-sided relationship. There is communication from both sides. In Bhima's words:

Śrīguruṅka aṅga vyathā karuthile bhaktaku lāgai cintā.
Bhakata duḥkha phāndare paśithile śrīguruṅku lāge vyathā.

If the limb of the revered master feels pain the disciple becomes worried. If the disciple is in difficult situation, the master too feels pain.[27]

Not only this, both need each other's help. Without one the other is incomplete. Both support each other. In Bhima Bhoi's language:

Śrīguru loḍai dayā karibāku sevaka loḍai dayā.
Veni jana tahiṁeka prāṇa hoi na thāi antare māyā.

The master wants to show his mercy to the disciple and the disciple needs it. In this way both are united and there is no place for illusion.[28]

The guru is regarded as a divine being in different traditions throughout the whole of Indian culture. As it is said by Padoux: 'In the Śaiva *kaula* traditions, the *gurupaṅkti* is sometimes described as consisting of a threefold succession or 'flow' (*ogha*) of masters, the first group being 'divine' (*divya*), the second 'accomplished' (*siddha*) and the last 'human' (*mānava*). If not historically then at least mythically, this flow links all the succeeding gurus to the supreme godhead by whom the tradition is supposed to have been originally revealed. In this threefold succession, the gurus are progressively less perfect as they pass from a divine to a mere human condition. However, even human gurus are incarnations of the godhead and are to be worshipped as such by the disciples'.[29] In *Stuticintāmaṇi*, Bhima Bhoi regards Mahimā Svāmī as the incarnation of the Absolute Brahman. This is evident from the adjectives he uses in the text such as: *nirguṇa-puruṣa, nirveda-puruṣa, apāpa-puruṣa, śūnyabrahma prabhu, antaryāmī*, *alekha-puruṣa*, *śūnyabrahma* and so on. Sometimes he identifies the guru with Brahman.

Sādhu sujñanara gurusevā kara brahmare hua bhagati.
Aśeṣa janmara kaluṣa nāśibe avaśya debe mukati.

O sages and wise men, serve the guru and be devoted to Brahman. He will destroy sins from many births and grant you liberation surely.[30]

Elsewhere he says that the Brahma, who is beyond description, who is beginningless, takes the form a guru to teach his disciples.[31]

Service to the Master (*Gurusevā*)

Thus knowing the importance of the guru one has to serve him. One has to take recourse at the feet of one's guru. He is the bridge to cross over this ocean of world. He is the power who protects the disciple from all the difficulties, sins of this life as well as the previous lives. Therefore *gurusevā* is very much essential, especially in this *kaliyuga*. As Bhima Bhoi writes:

Cāriyuga madhye gurupādagoṭi aṭai ṭi dharma nāva.
Yahiṁ jātahele tahiṁ hata hele bhāsuchanti bhavārṇava.

All the beings are created here and they also die here. They are floating in the ocean of world (*bhavasāgara*). In all the four ages the feet of my master are indeed a boat of merit (*dharma*) (which takes us to the further shore of immortality).[32]

Therefore one should serve one's master and take recourse in the Brahma, because he destroys the sins of many lives and certainly gives liberation (77, 19). This very idea has been discussed long before in *Śivasūtras,*[33] a text of Kashmir Śaivism on the *yoga* of Supreme Identity. Thus the text (II, 6) says: *gururupāyah*, the guru himself is the means to liberation. Bhima Bhoi, the saint poet, is very much confident in this process. Therefore emphasizes on *gurusevā*, which is a means for liberation, and says:

Gurudeva binu mokṣa nohe tanu anyare bharasā nāhiṁ
prabhupāda dhyāyi bhaṇe Bhīma Bhoi hetu ghare nāma thoi.

Without the master there is no liberation of this body. I have no faith in others for this. Thus says Bhima Bhoi taking the Name consciously and meditating on the feet of the Lord.[34]

Bhima Bhoi is very much concerned about the liberation of human beings. Therefore he sings the most heart touching verse, any poet has ever sung.

Prāṇīṅka ārata duḥkha apramita dekhu dekhu kebā sahu.
Mo jīvana pache narke paḍithāu jagata uddhāra heu.

How can one tolerate seeing the limitless agony and sorrow of the beings? Let my life go to hell and the world be saved.[35]

One who has attained a highest state or who has experienced god's grace can only sing in such a tone. Bhima Bhoi was one of these persons who had experienced god's grace in his life. In other words we may say that a guru only can sing such a song for the sake of his fellow disciples. Bhima Bhoi by this time had already become a guru to his followers. This is known from his *Stuticintāmaṇi* (63, 1–4), where he writes about the criticism of people towards his teaching and preaching of Mahimā Dharma. Thus he says,

Others criticize me saying that being a householder I have become a preceptor (*guru bolāuchi gṛha kariachi boluchanti rājā prajā*). The Brahmans, the learned people, all say that I have become a guru, I know nothing and am doing wrong (*guru pane vasi kichi na jāṇilā anyāya karuchi ehā*). Other people say that I, being a Kandha (a tribal), receive the worship of Brāhmaṇs and this is not possible without having the lustre of Lord Viṣṇu. Such is the comment of the wicked people towards me.

From this it is very clearly understood that by this time Bhima Bhoi was raised to the status of a guru. This shows that Bhima Bhoi had some spiritual power for which he was worshipped by other people. From this statement it is clear that Bhima Bhoi loved fellow human beings so much that he could not desist from throwing himself to hell for the sake of the world. Further he sings:

Prāṇaru adhika kariṇa tāhāku kahuthāi sadabuddhi.
Gurusevā kale niśce antakāḷe tariyiba vārānidhi.

I love them more than my soul and hence I give them true wisdom. If they do serve the master, at the end of their life they will certainly cross over this ocean of *saṃsāra*.[36]

He further reminds householders that: 'Do your respective duty. Remember your religious obligations. Have faith in the feet of the guru. He will rescue you truly'.[37] Bhima Bhoi gives importance to *gurudharma* or *satya mahimā dharma* and says that whatever your profession may be, do your duty. But if you take recourse to Mahimā Dharma and have mercy on the beings, if you take shelter in *gurudharma*, you will be liberated.[38] If the master is kind towards you, you will be definitely liberated; there is no doubt about it. If you have devotion at the feet of your guru, you will be absorbed in Brahman.[39]

Conclusion

From the above observation what we have to take into account in Mahimā Dharma of the present day is that: the place of Bhima Bhoi in Mahimā Dharma after Mahimā Svāmī was very important. His writings were very significant which served as first-hand literature in Mahimā Dharma. Even today they have a special place in the literature and among the devotees of Mahimā Dharma. After Mahimā Svāmī, Bhima Bhoi continued the *guru* tradition and the teachings of Mahimā Svāmī through his writings and *bhajanas*. Though under the guidance of Viswanath Baba certain ascetics from Jorandā neglected Bhima Bhoi by calling him a householder, a Kandha, and so on, but still he is regarded as a guru by his followers at Khaliapali *āśrama*.

There is no *guru-paramparā* (tradition of gurus) in Mahimā Dharma as in other schools of Hinduism. But the *guru-śiṣya* relationship and the faith in a human guru is very significant and still very much alive in present-day Mahimā Dharma. Keeping this in mind the householders, the devotees, the *tyāgīs*, *vairāgīs* and younger *sādhus* take initiation from the oldest (*bābās*) *sannyāsīs* and regard them as their guru.

Notes

1. *Stuticintāmaṇi* 58, 6–7, 56, 19.
2. See Bäumer 1990 and Padoux 2001.
3. See Apte, 1957, 409.
4. *Manusmṛti* II.142; based on the translation of Bühler 1975; see also *Amarakośa,* (II.7.7).
5. *Stuticintāmaṇi* 39, 13.
6. Ibid., 22, 17.
7. Ibid., 21, 3.
8. Ibid., 21, 7–13.
9. *Bhajanamālā* 257.1.
10. One *ghaḍi* is about 45 minutes.
11. *Nirvedasādhanā*, Chapter 1, 2.
12. See *Stuticintāmaṇi* 91, 8 and 97, 7.
13. Ibid., 29, 11.
14. Ibid., 39, 16; 33, 18; 74, 10.
15. Ibid., 6, 11–13.
16. Ibid., 43, 3.
17. *Bhajanamālā* 10, 1, translation by B. Bäumer and J. Beltz.
18. *Bhajanamālā* 45, 3–5, ibid.
19. See n. 1.
20. Marjanovic 2002, 124.
21. *Stuticintāmaṇi*, see *bolis* 35–7.
22. Ibid., 37, 1.
23. Ibid., 37, 9.
24. Ibid., 35, 19–20.
25. Ibid., 36, 11.
26. Ibid., 37, 18.
27. Ibid., 37, 19.
28. Ibid., 37, 7.
29. Padoux 2001.
30. *Stuticintāmaṇi* 77, 19; see also *Stuticintāmaṇi* 22, 17 and 43, 3.
31. *Gururūpa hoi batāu achanti alekha anādi brahma* (89, 19); see also 97, 3.
32. *Stuticintāmaṇi* 43, 19.
33. See Hughes, 2002.
34. *Stuticintāmaṇi* 17, 20.
35. Ibid., 27, 7.
36. Ibid., 34, 19.
37. Ibid., 90, 6.
38. Ibid., 91, 6–7.
39. See other verses for further references such as 45, 8–10 and *boli* 57 for more details.

References

Apte, V.S. (1957), *The Practical Sanskrit–English Dictionary*, New Delhi: Motilal Banarsidass.

Bäumer, Bettina (1990), 'The Guru in the Hindu Tradition', in *Studies in Formative Spirituality*, JSF, vol. 11, 3, pp. 341–53.

Bühler, G. (ed.) (1975), *The Laws of Manu*, New Delhi: Motilal Banarsidass (Sacred Books of the East Series, 25).

Dadhimatha, Sivadattam, B. Panshikar, and L. Shastri (eds.) (1985), *Amarakośa of Amarasimha*, Delhi: Chaukhamba Sanskrit Pratisthan.

Banerjee-Dube, Ishita (1993), 'Of Poets and Texts: Bhima Bhoi and Mahimā Dharma', in 'Religion and Society in Orissa: Mahima Dharma in the Nineteenth and Twentieth Centuries', Ph.D. thesis, University of Calcutta.

Hughes, John (ed.) (2002), *Shiva Sutras*, '*The Supreme Awakening*', with the commentary of Kshemaraja, revealed by Swami Lakshmanjoo, USA: Universal Shaiva Fellowship.

Marjanovic, Boris (ed.) (2002), *Abhinavagupta's Commentary on the Bhagavad-Gita: Gītārtha Saṃgraha*, Varanasi: Indica Books.

Padoux, André (2001), 'The Tantric Guru', in David G. White (ed.), *Tantra in Practice*, New Delhi: Motilal Banarsidass, pp. 41–51.

Sahu, Karunakara (ed.) (1992), *Bhaktakavi Bhīma Bhoi Granthāvalī*, Cuttack: Dharmagrantha Store.

Shastri, J.L. (ed.) (1983), *Manusmṛti, with the Sanskrit Commentary Manvartha Muktāvalī of Kullūka Bhaṭṭa,* New Delhi: Motilal Banarsidass.

Singh, Jaideva, (ed.) (1979), *Śiva Sūtras: The Yoga of Supreme Identity*, New Delhi: Motilal Banarsidass.

CHAPTER 7

Ascetic, Layman, or Rebellious Guru? Bhima Bhoi and his Female Consorts

JOHANNES BELTZ
KEDAR MISHRA

Introduction

The rise of Mahimā Dharma in the mid-nineteenth century spread a new wave in the social and religious life of Orissa. It is said that by the end of the nineteenth century, one-sixth of the population of the Orissa-Chhattisgarh *garjhat* division, especially farmers and low castes, got initiated to this new religion. From Jepore to Sambalpur, a major portion of Orissa was populated by the devotees of Lord Mahimā. Mahimā Dharma attracted the downtrodden segments of the population. It conferred on subordinate people—women and untouchables—a new sense of dignity that enabled them to question the discrimination inherent in Brahmanical Hinduism. Bhima Bhoi affirms in his *Stuticintamaṇi* that 'men and women . . . with no discrimination of high and low take refuge in the Name' (*Stuticintāmaṇi*, 92). This was an exalted saying appealing to women and men: 'When the Kuṃbhipatias came, they made men and women mad.'[1] In other words, those who were excluded from rituals and worship, to whom the entry to temples was previously denied, got free access to Mahimā Dharma. Bhima Bhoi was the hero propagating the glory of Mahimā Svāmī among the villagers to such an extent that many believed that Bhima Bhoi was the expounder of Mahimā Dharma.[2]

Indeed, several women received initiation directly from Mahimā

Svāmī and it is said that Malbiharpur, which was one of the principal seats of Mahimā Dharma, had even a *maṭha* (monastery) for women. In an interview conducted in 2001, we were told that a Karana girl came to the Malabiharpur *āśrama* (sanctuary) for the *darśana* (sight) of Mahimā Svāmī and was later ostracised by her family. It is further stated that this girl took refuge at the feet of the Guru. Apparently the Lord himself commanded her to stay in this *āśrama*. Her son Brindaban Das became an enlightened *sannyāsī*. The *maṭha* for women exists till today.[3] Reports in the newspaper *Mukura* also indicate that Mahimā Svāmī had women disciples among his companions: 'The *sannyāsīs* who wear loin cloth are found having their wives with them but they do not stay in their houses.' The *Journal of the Asiatic Society of Bengal* confirms in 1882 that there were *bābās* (*sannyāsīs*) and *mātās* (*sannyāsins*) in both the ascetic groups of *kumbhipatias* and *kanapatias*.

The apparent free access of women to both the lay (*gṛhastha*) and monastic (*sannyāsa*) orders of Mahimā Dharma led to its social maligning by the rest of Oriya society. It was common for many writers of that time to ridicule the *kumbhipatias*' cohabitation with their wives and their eating of dry salty fish (*Mukura*, 1907–8). The spread of Mahimā Dharma seems to have enraged the elites, that is high castes and conservative Hindus. Mahimā Dharma was resented as anti-Brāhmaṇ, heathen and anti-royal (*Utkala Sahitya*, 1883: 66–7). Consequently, writings extremely critical of Mahimā Dharma, Mahimā Svāmī and Bhima Bhoi appeared in several magazines and newspapers of the time, with certain writers going to the extent of demanding the prosecution of Mahimā Svāmī for causing social indiscipline (*Utkal Deepika*, 1871). The British government considered these demands and directed the district magistrates to keep vigilance on Mahimā Dharmīs (idem).

Let us now turn to the official report of the Superintendent of Police, Puri, regarding the famous attack on Jagannātha Temple on 1 March 1881. It states that among the attackers were three women, and eleven women from another group of attackers were arrested near Sakshigopal.[4] There were also women who had entered the premises of the temple of Lord Jagannātha holding babies in their arms to burn down the wooden idol of Jagannātha (*Utkal Deepika*, 1881). This incident, in our opinion, added a new chapter to the history of Orissa. Did Mahimā Dharma allow women to play a vital role as rebels in the attack on the symbol of orthodox religion in Orissa, Lord Jagannātha's idol? In traditional Oriya society, the role of woman was confined only to the house. Though there had been female ascetics in the Oriya Vaiṣṇava tradition, the social positions assumed by them is unknown. Is it far-fetched to assume that the liberal call of Mahimā Dharma made a lot of women leave their homes and inspired them to become the disciples of Mahimā Svāmī and Bhima Bhoi?

Bhima Bhoi in the Company of Women

We know little about Bhima Bhoi, the great poet of Mahimā Dharma, as a person. 'Authentic' historical sources are almost non-existent and Bhima Bhoi did not reveal much in his poetry. The few instances where he talked about himself are open to diverse interpretations (Banerjee-Dube, 1993 and 2001; Eschmann, 1978; Mahapatra, 1983; Mishra, 1998; Nath, 1990; Nepak, 1997), as are the large number of stories and legends surrounding Bhima Bhoi, which were transmitted orally and saved in administrative reports. Themes like Bhima Bhoi's origin or his blindness have been a matter of scholarly and polemical discussion, and there has been no easy solution to these debates. In this paper, we would like to address another, but no less important controversy: Bhima Bhoi's relation to women.

This is a crucial, if not controversial, issue which helps to put Bhima Bhoi's works as well as his hagiography in proper perspective. It is widely accepted that Bhima Bhoi lived with four women, two 'worldly' and two 'spiritual' consorts. To understand what this means, we need to go beyond his posthumous deification and look into the many instances where Bhima Bhoi deals and interacts with women. This thematic choice might seem to be a little unorthodox, since most books on Bhima Bhoi mention only the fact that he had female consorts without indicating its background and implications. However, most of the stories relating to his life touch upon the question of whether Bhima Bhoi had a sexual life. Mahimā Dharma is open to both ascetics and householders. Was Bhima Bhoi a *sannyāsī*? It does not seem so. But he was definitely not an ordinary householder who married and had children. He stayed in an *āśrama* and had the status of a religious leader. Let us turn to the oral tradition and quote some stories which highlight the controversy.

It is said that Bhima Bhoi moved to Gurunda, a place situated near the small town of Binka in today's Sonepur district. It was there that a certain Vaiṣṇava, Mohan Das, accepted Bhima Bhoi as his guru and offered his daughter Sumedha at the feet of Bhima Bhoi as a sign of his devotion.[5] Following this example, Mohan Das's brother-in-law Narayan Das also gave his daughter, Rohini to Bhima Bhoi. Rohini, therefore, also comes from a Vaiṣṇava background.[6] The third woman associated with Bhima Bhoi, Annapurna, was not offered but joined the *āśrama* herself. Some people say that she was originally the maidservant of Lord Mahimā and that she joined Bhima Bhoi's sanctuary after his death. According to another story, she followed the order of Mahimā Gosāin who asked her to leave Dhenkanal in order to get *darśana* of Bhima Bhoi. Once she had reached Bhrusrapali, she decided to stay with him. Her decision was based on her sole desire to offer her service at Bhima Bhoi's feet (*padasevā*).[7] It was in the *āśrama* of Khaliapali that the fourth woman appeared on scene: Iswar Das of Rampela village handed over his daughter Sarasvati to Bhima Bhoi.[8]

So far we have mentioned three women who were offered to Bhima Bhoi, and another, Annapurna, who joined of her own volition. This raises the thorny issue of the nature of relationship between Bhima Bhoi and these women. Did he adopt an ascetic lifestyle in his *āśrama*? Hagiographies generally tend to depict saints as ascetics who led a chaste life (Bouez, 1992; Gross, 1992). But with regard to Bhima Bhoi, it is widely accepted that he was a householder, and a householder can have wives. Some followers of the faith, however, suggest that he was never married and that his relations with women were only 'spiritual'. It is said that Annapurna, Rohini and Sarasvati lived a life of austerity and moral purity. As a final statement on the tricky question, Mahimā Dharmīs argue that Bhima Bhoi was neither male nor female and that these women were in fact goddesses. But the repeated depiction of Bhima Bhoi's celibacy gives a one-sided picture. Before we approach this question again, let us quote Bhima Bhoi from his *Brahma Nirupana Gītā* where he says: 'The door of the Guru equally welcomes all; Man and Woman, high and low, big or small.'

Bhima Bhoi, the first and foremost writer of Mahimā Dharma, declared that one who discriminates between male and female gets damned in hell. Both men and women are born out of one and the same Brahma. Although he did stress the Hindu idea of a wife's devotion to her husband and her feminine qualities, yet he never made any distinction of superiority and inferiority among men and women.[9] One could conclude that Bhima Bhoi urged women to break out of the limits of domestic life and sensual pleasure and to take up spiritual and religious activities. Did he advise women to walk on the path of Brahma? Would it be an exaggeration to conclude that he strongly sympathized with the sufferings of exploited women?

Annapurna

It is often told by devotees that Annapurna had been attracted to Mahimā Dharma since her childhood. Some identify her as the youngest daughter of Bhagabana Dash of the village Maddhi of Dhenkanal district. Bhima Dash, Nirakara Dash and Arjun Dash were her brothers and also devotees of Mahimā Dharma. But many questions remain. One has to note here that in the village of Khaliapali, people regard Annapurna as the divine sister (*guru bhaginī*) of Bhima Bhoi, because they were both the direct disciples of Mahimā Svāmī. Was Annapurna really Mahimā Svāmī's fond disciple? The two loving disciples of Mahimā Svāmī are buried at one place, and their *pādukās* (wooden sandals), are still worshipped.[10]

If one believes Daya Sagar Das, Annapurna was the daughter of a farmer from Badhigan; she came from an aristocratic family and her brothers wore sandals made of silver. Others think that she came from a Brāhmaṇ family. Her aristocratic and upper-caste background makes her liaison with an illiterate tribal even more scandalous. Baishya Charan Thakur, from the village Haldipali near Sonepur recounted:

> Annapurna was Bhima Bhoi's disciple and follower. This was considered as a sin in the society. A saint could not have the company of a Brāhmaṇ girl, not even as a disciple. So, Bhima Bhoi had had to bear a lot of reproof in Khaliapali.[11]

This is confirmed by many narratives. After Annapurna left her village, the family accused Bhima Bhoi of abducting her. The brother of Annapurna, misunderstanding the spiritual relationship, attacked Bhima Bhoi at Gulunda village. Let us quote a passage from another interview:

> Annapurna, a Brāhmaṇ girl, devoted her life to Bhima Bhoi and came with him to Khaliapali. Annapurna's relatives were not happy with that. They spread the rumor that Bhima Bhoi had absconded with a Brāhmaṇ girl. Furious as they were, they went to see Bhima Bhoi. They disrobed him. But what did they discover? They saw that he had no penis. After that they understood that his relationship with Annapurna was only spiritual.

These accounts point to the controversy indicated above. Bhima Bhoi is suspected of having abducted women for his sensual pleasure. This accusation is negated with the indication that Bhima Bhoi had no genitals. In other words, there was no possibility of an illicit relationship between the two. One can easily conclude that the presence of women in the *āśrama* was opposed by certain people. From a rather different perspective, but nevertheless arguing in the same direction, the following statement is interesting—Maheswar Das Baba, 70 years old, originating from the village Banjani told us:

> Annapurna was the wife of Bhima Bhoi. But Bhima Bhoi did not want to get married. His marriage with her was against his own will. Annapurna was in love with Bhima Bhoi. But she was punished for that. Her family vanished. Nobody should stay with Bhima Bhoi to testify his credibility as a saint and poet.

Here, Annapurna appears in a slightly negative perspective. It is she who forces Bhima Bhoi to marry and renounce his celibacy. It is said that their wedding was performed on the full moon day of the *Māgha* month. In other words, they were a couple. But irrespective of her mysterious origin and her contested relations to Bhima, all accounts state that Annapurna began playing a decisive role in the daily activities of the *āśrama* soon after she began residing there. It is stated again and again that she was very kind and gave *sadopadeśa* (good advice) to the *bhaktas*. The *bhaktas* also offered *pūjā* to her. The story also goes that both of them were worshipped on an altar with 108 *kalaśas* and a sacred flame at the Khaliapali *āśrama* (Nayak 2001: 105). Annapurna is also credited with many supernatural powers. She could bless childless couples with children and cure diseased persons. One should also note that after the death of Bhima Bhoi, the management of the *āśrama* came into her hands.

Let us quote an interesting passage from a letter written by the Assistant Secretary to the Chief Commissioner of the Central Provinces, dated 17 August 1881. In the sixth paragraph of the letter, of which a copy is kept at the Orissa Archive in Heidelberg's South Asia Institute, the author writes about Bhima Bhoi:

> He has erected an altar over which he and his wife sit in the morning. His followers worship them and move round the altar until the time for their morning meal arrives.

Here, it is confirmed that Bhima Bhoi was worshipped along with his wife. But what was the relationship between Bhima Bhoi and her? A common understanding among the *bhaktas* of Khaliapali is that their relationship was purely spiritual. It is said that Bhima Bhoi had accepted Annapurna as his 'guru sister'. She is also called *ādimātā* (lit. the first goddess). Others identify her with the Hindu goddess of grain, Annapūrṇā, and call her Ādi Annapūrṇā. After all, there is little doubt that she is the most important of Bhima Bhoi's disciples, be it women or men. She was his principal spiritual consort. Annapurna and Bhima Bhoi together accepted the adoration and services of the devotees. Her *pādukā* (shoes) are still kept with those of Bhima Bhoi's and worshipped in a specific shrine every evening before sunset. She was the head of Khaliapali *āśrama*. Giving due respect to her divine power, devotees of Mahimā Dharma got initiated and received *mahimā bāna* from her. Great also was her contribution to the construction of the Samādhi-Mandira (memorial) of Bhima Bhoi at Khaliapali.

As a souvenir, on the death of Annapurna, Bhima Bhoi's scribe Hari Panda wrote a long poem entitled *Mātru Biccheda* (Departure of the Mother) in which he praised the role of Annapurna in detail. On the divine glory of Mother Annapurna, he had this to say:

> In kindness, you are Alekha. Yet you never see my sorrow for a moment. Who will then narrate your charity and kindness? The world is beautified by you. You, the couple, brought down to earth the fountain of religiousness. Brahma, you are the Goddesses. Do pour nectar upon me. If not, definitely I will die.

In this unpublished poem of Hari Panda which is kept in the custody of the Bhima Bhoi Samadhi Pitha Trust at Khaliapali, Annapurna is described as the epitome of spirituality. Hari Panda used adjectives such as *brahma svarūpā* (the true image of the Divine), *mahāmayī* (greatness embodied) to characterize Annapurna, Bhima Bhoi's divine consort and the embodiment of divine energy. After the demise of Annapurna, the devotees of Mahimā Dharma felt orphaned. Hari Panda wrote:

> The throat chokes and
> lamentations grow from the heart
> and the body burns in the fire of anguish.
> We have got such parents and the preceptor
> as the result of good actions of innumerable births.
> Though laughing uproarious, she speaks sweetly
> and never separates us for a moment.
> Now our hearts are cut into pieces
> as she, the glory of the earth, departs.
> The temple which was looking beautiful with her presence
> is now dark like dense forest.
> We are burning from within.
> We, her children, are crying and rolling on the ground.
> The heat of sorrow in the limbs grow intense
> as we no more see your feet

beautiful like lightning.
Houses look ugly and our hearts dark,
Who will tell us about Brahma, the one-lettered and
the significance of the letters that constitute 'Om',
Who will then soothe us with delight?
The goddess beginning-less manifests all around
you departed.
Though you became invisible,
we are servants at your feet.
Let you not separate us for four ages.

In *Mātru Biccheda*, Annapurna is portrayed as the leader of Mahimā Dharma, but researchers and historians of Mahimā Dharma have seldom focused on her life and ideals. Occasionally, her name finds mention as the wife or spiritual consort of Bhima Bhoi; it is often said that they were one and the same—one is Śiva (Happiness) and the other is Śakti (Energy). Hence, it is impossible to write on Bhima Bhoi's life without the mention of Annapurna.

Our purpose here is not to write a new biography of Bhima Bhoi. Still, we wonder why there is not a single word about Annapurna in the history of Mahimā Dharma, in spite of the fact that she was a woman gifted with spiritual power.

Keeping the Heritage Alive

The tradition of initiating women to Mahimā Dharma prevailed at Bhima Bhoi's *āśrama* in Khaliapali. After the death of Bhima Bhoi, Annapurna, and following her death, Labanyabati, and finally the granddaughter of Hari Panda and Basu Panda, Śriyā Mātā, conducted the affairs of the *āśrama* as its chief (Mishra, 1998). Moreover, Annapurna and Labanyabati had inherited the extraordinary healing powers of Bhima Bhoi.[12]

Labanyabati, Bhima Bhoi's and Annapurna's daughter, led the *āśrama* at Khaliapali for some time after her mother's death. She was an extraordinary woman like her mother. Many legends circulate among the Mahimā Dharmīs about Labanyabati. She was a highly talented and knowledgeable woman. She knew a lot of medical sciences and wrote a book on Ayurveda titled *Latā*

Mañjarī, in which she gave elaborate descriptions in Sanskrit of various medicinal plants. But history is silent about her achievements.

With Labanyabati, once again, we see the same trend of depicting saints as asexual beings. The hagiographic records of the life of Labanyabati reveal her as an *ājanmabrahmacāriṇī*, a celibate all her life. Further, it is believed that her body had the holy marks of the conch, the wheel, the *gadā* (club) and the lotus, the holy marks of Viṣṇu. Thus, she clearly represented the ascetic ideal. Samantary (1976: 23–4) adds that she never spoke much. When she did, she uttered the name of Mahimā Alekha, sang the *bhajanas* of Bhima Bhoi and explained their significance to devotees. She was very affectionate, and attracted devotees to the *āśrama*. According to the tradition, she refused to talk about marriage. If somebody came to ask her for marriage, she would tell him: *gurunkāra ājñā nāhin* (there is no permission from the guru). She completed 54 years and was known in the area as *nārī* (respected woman). Let us look at a story, collected in Khaliapali and current among the followers:

> Once a prince . . . saw Labanyabati. She was very beautiful. He got interested in her. He wanted to marry her. He sent a message to Bhima Bhoi to ask him for his daughter. And Bhima passed on the message to Labanyabati. She replied: 'Let the prince come personally.' As she had said it, the prince came. He was riding on an elephant. When he arrived he stood in front of her. She asked him: 'Can you marry me? Can you bear my holiness?' And then she lifted her clothes and made him see her vagina. But what the prince saw was a burning fire. Siva and Labanyabati were playing in it. Seeing this, the prince prostrated in front of her. He touched her feet and asked for her forgiveness. He went away afraid of what he had done. After some time, the prince died. And Labanyabati said that she wished his death. He had to die because in the *kaliyuga* he had wished to marry his own mother.

The motif is interesting, referring to the *kaliyuga* and sexual transgression.[13] Labanyabati is identified as a manifestation of the *devī*, the great goddess. As the companion/wife of Śiva, she is divine, the mother with whom an ordinary human being cannot have sexual intercourse. Surprisingly, we collected several variations of the same story in our interviews. One goes like this:

Bhima Bhoi's daughter was Labanyabati. Once the king's barber went to visit Khaliapali and he saw Labanyabati. Being impressed by her beauty he thought that the girl should be offered to the king. He thought: 'If I tell this to the king, he will surely reward me'. When the king heard the story of the beautiful daughter of Bhima Bhoi, he took his guard and went to Khaliapali to catch her. . . . They came, asked for his daughter and forced him to bring her to them. Labanyabati came. She took a branch with dry leaves and touched her vagina with it. Immediately the branch turned to ashes. Seeing this miracle, the king bowed down to Bhima Bhoi and renounced his idea of taking away Labanyabati with him.

It is also stated that the devotees of Bhima Bhoi worship his daughter Labanyabati as *ādiśakti* (primal energy). These stories reinforce the belief of Labanyabati's holiness. In fact, after Bhima Bhoi's death, women such as Annapurna and Labanyabati were treated as demi-goddesses because they could perform miracles and heal people.

There is another woman to be talked about: Śriyā Mātā. Although she was not a child of Bhima Bhoi, her story fits very well into the framework of holy companionship depicted above. According to the narrative of Śriyā Mātā collected by Anncharlott Eschmann, she was offered by her parents to Mahimā Svāmī. Her mother was Padmavati and her father Laranidara Panda who was the son of a certain Madhu, the brother of Hari Panda and Basu Panda. According to the story, her mother died when she was one year old. Hari Panda reached her village when Padmavati was in her deathbed, and showering upon her the seven nectars, delivered her to Lord Mahimā. Annapurna, who had no child, nourished Śriyā Mātā with her own milk. When she was 28 years old, she started managing the temple and stayed there till her death. Many people still remember her. The late Anncharlott Eschmann (1978: 403) described her as a 'scintillating' woman 'with temperament'.

The Controversy about Bhima Bhoi's Procreation

The problem of Bhima Bhoi's sexuality seems resolved if one accepts the spiritual character of the relationship between Bhima Bhoi and his consorts. But trouble arose in Bhima Bhoi's life when the first children were born in Khaliapali. It is said that Kapileśvara was born of Sumedha. But devotees insist that his mother did not have any sexual intercourse with Bhima Bhoi. Labanyabati, the younger sister of Kapileśvara is also said to be the daughter of Rohini. But who is her father? Generally, there is no mention of a biological father. Very few admit that Labanyabati and Kapileśvara are the children of Bhima Bhoi. It is said that Sumedha's mother came once from Ragapali to Khaliapali to pray to Bhima Bhoi and have *darśana*. She prayed that her daughter should always be happy, and also that she should have a child. Bhima Bhoi smiled and promised to fulfil her desire. He smeared some *mantrapūta bibhūti* (holy ashes) on Sumedha's forehead. And, of course, the result came immediately. After three days, she gave birth to Kapileśvara.

The same story exists about Labanyabati. It is believed that when Rohini was offered to Bhima Bhoi, her mother requested him that her daughter be blessed with a child. Bhima Bhoi put *bibhūti* on her forehead and after some days Labanyabati was born. It is interesting that the same stories exist about the birth of Labanyabati and Kapileśvara. In both instances, it was the mother who came to see Bhima Bhoi and asked him to give a child to her daughter. The request was that the daughter should not be barren; nevertheless, she should beget children while remaining a virgin. Sometimes the two stories are linked. Johannes was told that

> Narayan Das and Mohan Das, fathers of Sumedha and Rohini, came to Bhima Bhoi and complained that they had gained nothing by delivering their daughters to him. Then Bhima Bhoi pasted vermilion on the forehead of Sumedha and Rohini. We have heard that as a result, Kapileśvara, a son and Labanyabati, a daughter were born of them.

We have an early indication of the problem in colonial administrative and police reports, drawn up after the attack on the Jagannātha temple to enquire into the Alekha religion of Orissa. Let us quote an interesting passage from a letter written by the Assistant Secretary to the Chief Commissioner of the Central Provinces. In the sixth paragraph of this text, the author writes this about Bhima Bhoi:

Formerly Bhima Kondh of Snepore (Sonepur) was the leader of the sect. Bhima was born blind, but he appears to have been endowed with natural talents of a superior order. Though unable to read and write, he had some Uriya religious books, such as *Mahabharat* and *Srimat Bhagbat*, read to him, and the education he thus received enabled him to compose two or three volumes of verses in praise of the Almighty, which, it is asserted, would do credit to any Uriya scholar of the present day. He exercised great influence over his followers. The relations existing between him and a female companion, however, excited suspicion among his adherents, who however, did not venture to question the purity of his conduct until the woman became pregnant. Bhima endeavoured to deceive his followers by telling them that the woman would give birth to Arjun, who would root out all unbelievers. The(y) believed this story, and waited until the child was born, when to their great surprise, they found that the woman gave birth to a girl. Bhima accounted for this by saying that it had recently been revealed to him that the woman would give birth to a female, who would destroy all the unbelievers by means of her charms. The child, however, died a few days later, and Bhima then tried to mislead his followers still further by saying that the fairy had quitted (sic) this world because she had found it filled with vices of mankind. He was now deserted by most of his followers, who formed a separate faction but he is still highly adored and honored (. . .). (Report no. 3069–161, dated 17 August 1881)

Interesting here is the rather negative characterization of Bhima Bhoi: that he misguided and cheated his followers. The same radical criticism is expressed by the authors of the *Census of India*, 1911, who repeated the same story in the fourth chapter. In the same year, B.C. Mazumdar wrote his famous article entitled 'Alekhism' as a part of his book *Sonpur in the Sambalpur Tract* (1911). In this article, we find the same statement that Bhima Bhoi begot children and that this fact created much dissent among his followers. However, his judgement is less harsh. Let us quote the passage:

Bhima Bhoi as a matter of fact did beget two children—one a son and another a daughter—on two women, who became nuns and lived at Khaliapali in Bhima Bhoi's *math*. Both these women are still living at Khaliapali with the children begotten upon them. It was nineteen years ago that first a daughter and then after two months a son were born having Bhima Bhoi for their father. The disciples were no doubt very much shocked at it, but Bhima Bhoi explained it to them that he brought one male and one female child into existence with a view to give to the world one ideal woman and one ideal man. How these two ideal beings are behaving now could not be ascertained by me. (Mazumdar, 1911: 134)

Apart from the dates of birth of the children, which differ, all texts mention the same problem. Bhima Bhoi had sired children when he was supposed to be a celibate. Let us cite B.C. Mazumdar from his paper:

Bhima Bhoi having, in the opinion of some Kumbhipatias, transgressed the rules regarding procreation, the Kumbhipatias of Dhenkanal and the disciples of Bhagavan Das and Kripasindhu Das regard the Sonput (Sonepur) section as heretics. But the Sonpur section of the Kumbhipatias still continues to be strong having the greatest number of followers. (ibid: 134)

According to all texts, Bhima Bhoi was almost compelled to justify the birth of these children. He did this always in the same manner: by promoting the idea that the children were quasi-divine, ideal beings who were the saviours of humankind, or embodiments of the perfect man and the perfect woman. These texts make it clear that his followers, or at least a section of them, disapproved of his behaviour. As a matter of fact, the birth of the children caused scandal at the *āśrama*. As mentioned above, two reactions can be analysed. Some devotees rejected Bhima Bhoi categorically and left him. Others justified his children by deifying him as well as his progeny. The following story collected in Khaliapali illustrates the second tendency clearly:

Once the villagers came to humiliate Bhima Bhoi because of his children. They scolded him to be a *bhaṇḍa* (cheater), an aberrant, a heretic. When they unclothed him, they noticed that he had no penis. They concluded that he was the incarnation of Rādhā.

This seems like a repetition of the story about Annapurna and Bhima Bhoi. As a holy man, Bhima Bhoi had no genitals. He could not, therefore, have illicit relations with women, nor sire children. This recurrent topic is mixed with another myth according to which Bhima Bhoi is the eternal Rādhā.

Plate 1: A. Eschmann with Biswanath Baba in Jorandā, Copyright South Asia Institute, Heidelberg.

Plate 2: A. Eschmann with Mahimā Dharmīs, Copyright South Asia Institute, Heidelberg.

Plate 3: Bhima Bhoi's Samadhipitha in Khaliapali,
photograph A. Eschmann, 1971.

Plate 4: Jorandā, Photograph J. Beltz, 2001.

Plate 5: Jorandā, Photograph J. Beltz, 2001.

Plate 6: Bhima Bhoi's Samadhipitha in Khaliapali, Photograph J. Beltz, 2001.

Plate 7: Śriyā Mā from Khaliapali, Photograph A. Eschmann, 1971.

Plate 8: Bishwanath Baba, photograph A. Eschmann.

This is a new aspect. This identification probably goes back to the Pancasakhā tradition.[14] According to this idea, Bhima Bhoi's appearance was predicted by Achyutananda Das, the famous Oriya poet of the fifteenth century. In his *Kalpa Saṃhitā*, he is quoted to have said that Rādhā would take birth again in the world, in the *kali* age, and would be called Bhima Bhoi. It is also said that he would be reborn in a Kandha family and that he would have poetic talent. Apart from that, the identification with Rādhā is a common feature of the *bhakti* movement. Rādhā is seen as the female counterpart of Kṛṣṇa; she is deeply in love with him. In our case, Kṛṣṇa is identified as Lord Mahimā Svāmī himself.

It is difficult to prove how far Bhima Bhoi really identified himself with Rādhā. This may be a later interpretation. But interestingly, Bhima Bhoi is reported to have been seen wearing women's clothes on certain occasions. We have been told that Bhima Bhoi sometimes made himself up like a woman; this is again a phenomenon which is not uncommon among *bhakti* poets.

Indeed, a certain ambiguity of gender exists. Bhima Bhoi is imagined as neither male nor female, being in fact both or none. Should one follow Lisa Lassel Hallstrom (1999) in her monograph about Anandamayi Ma who expressed that same ambiguity about her sexuality? Hallstrom has rightly pointed out that there is ambiguity within the Hindu tradition about the gender of self-realized beings, as well about the gender of God. In fact, analysing Bhima Bhoi and his relation to woman seems to show how the frontiers between male and female are crossed and re-crossed many times.

The dominant perception of Bhima Bhoi upholds his celibacy and disregards the women in his life. The ongoing deification of Bhima Bhoi as well as of his companions is the second interesting phenomenon, which needs our attention. The narratives about Bhima Bhoi and his female companions express competing concepts of holiness. Different ideas about him circulate among people who tell his story. He is simultaneously described as an ascetic, saint and social reformer, and sometimes as God. References are made to the Śaiva and the Vaiṣṇava traditions. Some narratives include topics which apparently oppose each other:

Nirguṇa bhakti and *saguṇa bhakti* seem to go hand in hand in them. Generally, the ideal of a *santa* is compatible with *nirguṇa bhakti*, whereas a *bhakta* is a typical term for the *saguṇa bhakti* tradition. But the notions often overlap and intermingle in the narratives.

Challenging Jorandā

As we have seen earlier, the presence of women at Khaliapali was right from the beginning a matter of discord. Later, monks at the new self-proclaimed monastic 'centre' of the Mahimā Dharma movement at Jorandā spoke vehemently against this. According to their spokesmen, asceticism is generally attributed to men, and not to women, female sexuality being perceived as dangerous. This is a general observation, which can be applied to other examples. Ascetic orders in India are indeed dominated by men. Kapileśwar Das Baba from Jorandā tells us more about this controversy:

> Women are not allowed to take *sannyāsa*. They are weak persons. Women are only allowed to stay at home. They cannot become wandering ascetics. Yes, it is said that there were eight *mātās* with Mahimā Svāmī. But there is a difference because they were goddesses. If women join the *sannyāsin* order, there are possibilities of moral degradation.

It seems very clear that for the monks from Jorandā, the propensity to procreate is the root of all evil. According to the ascetic ideal, a holy man has no sexual feelings; he dominates his body and gains full control over sexual desires. This is not a new development. Early on, S.P. Sharma (1942: 37) observed that the *kumbhipatias* were expected to contemplate on the organs of generation every morning without getting excited. According to him, they obtained complete detachment from sexual feelings. This idea still dominates. The female disciples of Lord Mahimā who were staying with him were not ordinary women. They were all goddesses, sent by the gods to serve and worship Lord Mahimā. If one follows this logic, only goddesses can be ascetics, but not ordinary women. This idea seems 'anti-women' and does not fit into the picture of an egalitarian community proclaimed by Bhima

Bhoi who always emphasized that woman and man are equal. In fact, he never looked down upon women. Like no other fact, Bhima Bhoi's attitude towards women manifests clearly the differences between him and the Jorandā faction of the Mahimā Dharmīs. One should note that this conflict is not only a matter of discussion.

Let us reiterate here that after Annapurna joined Bhima Bhoi's *āśrama*, the *balkaladhārī sannyāsīs*[15] from Jorandā came to Gurunda, quarrelled with Bhima Bhoi and burned down the *āśrama* house. Therefore, this is not simply an expression of disagreement, but an act of heresy. In fact, the *balkaladhārīs* contest Bhima Bhoi's role as a leader. According to them, he is clearly inferior to Mahimā Gosāin and the monastic order at Jorandā. But nowadays the opposition is expressed less violently and another strategy has been adopted. According to the *bābās* from Jorandā, Bhima Bhoi is certainly an important disciple of the guru, but he should not—under any circumstance—be compared with Mahimā Svāmī. We were told that Bhima Bhoi was a simple devotee. He was not *sannyāsī*, but a worldly poet and a *gṛhastha*. What matters is that he married and procreated, and thereby his religious authority has been undermined. Khaliapali is considered to be Bhima Bhoi's *āśrama* and looked down upon. It is compared unfavourably with the veneration for Jorandā among followers, which is regarded as Mahimā Svāmī's holy place. Another interesting point mentioned in this interview is that Bhima Bhoi never came to Jorandā and the story that he touched the grounds at the sacred centre is dismissed by Jorandā monks. People from Khaliapali told us that Bhima Bhoi did go to Jorandā after the death of Mahimā Gosāin but was horrified by the form of worship conducted there. He left Jorandā swearing that he would never return and founded his own *āśrama* in Khaliapali where he accepted women as disciples. The *bābās* at Jorandā reject such an event and claim that the guru himself, Mahimā Svāmī, forbade Bhima to come ever to this sacred place. The reason he gave Bhima Bhoi was that this was the holy *āśrama* of the guru, which had no place for a heretic like him.

The controversy is well documented by the news items published in *Utkal Deepika* criticizing the presence of women at the Khaliapali *āśrama* (*Utkal Deepika*, 1881). Again, we have to review these accusations. Could we read between the lines to argue that Bhima Bhoi's *āśrama* emerged as an important centre that rivalled Jorandā? Was there a danger of his group becoming more prominent than the monastic order? The stories collected at Khaliapali clearly attribute a superior role to Bhima Bhoi. Let us illustrate this with an example. In one story it is told that Bhima Bhoi was once sitting with his four scribes when four *sādhus* from Jorandā came to see him:

> The *sadhus* were so proud of themselves and arrogant that they disregarded and underestimated Bhima Bhoi. They thought, 'How can a tribal and a blind fellow preach such a great religion'? This was their idea of him. But Bhima Bhoi was *antaryami*;[16] he knew the inner thoughts of other people. He could already foresee their arrival and he ordered Basu Panda to get ready to welcome four *bhaktas*. Then the *sadhus* arrived at Khaliapali. The first *sadhu* saw Bhima Bhoi as Viṣṇu with his conch, wheel, club and lotus. He touched Bhima's feet. The second saw Bhima Bhoi as an old man, not as Viṣṇu and accused the first of seeing things. The third *sadhu* again saw Bhima Bhoi in form of the most beautiful Rādhā. He asked her: 'Ma, why did you leave Baikuntha?' And the fourth *sadhu* saw a child in Bhima Bhoi. Thus, these four *sadhus* each saw Bhima in a different form, and only after some time did they see the real Bhima Bhoi. The sadhus concluded that Bhima Bhoi and Mahimā Svāmī were equal. They asked Bhima Bhoi to excuse their arrogance and their pride.

As we have already seen before, Bhima Bhoi is often seen as an incarnation of God, and here he is linked to Viṣṇu. The relationship between Mahimā Dharma and Vaiṣṇava *bhakti* cannot be overestimated. When one adds to this other stories about his healing capacities and his fame, one can easily attribute either a superior role, or the role of the successor of Mahimā Svāmī, to Bhima Bhoi. Interestingly, there are some voices which accord more importance to Bhima Bhoi then we might expect. S.P. Sharma (1942: 35) wrote that Bhima Bhoi was the next leader after the founder died: 'On the death of Mukunda Das (Mahimā Svāmī), he became one of the important leaders of the sect. . . .' He states that Bhima Bhoi was initiated into Mahimā Dharma at Jorandā and that he appears to be the legitimate successor of his guru. Das also believes that it was

Bhima Bhoi who was responsible for the sect's dissemination outside Dhenkanal. It becomes clear that Bhima Bhoi had a significant role in popularizing the tenets of the Dharma as well, a fact downplayed by the Jorandā monks. The conflict, however, hinges not only on who or which centre is superior: we suggest that the tension between Bhima Bhoi and Jorandā results from the fact that Bhima Bhoi made his own rules and protested against established norms of the sect. He accepted women from different caste backgrounds as disciples and initiated them into the new *dharma*. This was an act of revolt because it was not a usual practice for a religious leader.

Let us turn to another text that records Bhima Bhoi's conscious refusal to accept asceticism. Nagendra Nath Vasu (1911) reports that Lord Mahimā Svāmī had asked Bhima Bhoi to wear nothing but a *kaupīna*, a red garment made of the bark of a tree and to adopt an ascetic lifestyle. Bhima Bhoi followed his order and wandered half-naked in the villages begging for alms. One day, Bhima Bhoi was ridiculed and beaten off a village. Vasu relates how Bhima Bhoi became enraged, cast off his *kaupīna* and belt, and proceeded towards Kapilāś to meet with his Lord. The latter took him to Jorandā in order to give him *siddhi* (sainthood). After that he freed him from wandering and Bhima Bhoi married in accordance with the wishes of his preceptor and attended to the household duties of a man. In other words, Bhima Bhoi was an ascetic and adopted the life of a householder after he had attained *siddhi*. However, one has to be very careful in reading this information, because Vasu's information is often contradictory and misguided.[17]

Based on the discussion, we may, therefore, conclude that Bhima Bhoi revolted against the discrimination of women, and the relationship between Annapurna and Bhima Bhoi can be interpreted as a protest against social sanctions. Even today an important number of *sannyāsins* reside close, but not inside the *āśrama*, and keep his legacy alive. Though they have to sleep outside the holy compound, they are present during the day. Bhima Bhoi's life may be contrasted with the ascetic life of the *bābās* at Jorandā, and his *āśrama* may be seen as a counterpart to the Jorandā *āśrama*. Bhima

Bhoi has democratized the Dharma by accepting women as disciples and by allowing lay persons to play a crucial role in its functioning. In this sense, he is indeed a religious reformer.

Biswanath Baba

Biswanath Baba was one of the most prominent *balkaladhārī* leaders of Mahimā Dharma in recent history. He was a reformer who reintegrated this heterodox *dharma* into the Hindu mainstream. What merits our attention is his *Mahimā Dharmara Itihāsa*, in which he narrates the history of the Dharma without giving any information about Mahimā Svāmī's women disciples.[18] It is difficult to accept the claim made by Biswanath Baba's followers that this book is an authentic and objective account. It is above all a religious narrative of its own. But one understands the silence with regard to Mahimā Svāmī's women disciples better if one keeps in mind that only three pages out of 300 in the book have been devoted to Bhima Bhoi, not only the guru's first disciple but also the foremost writer of Mahimā Dharma. Biswanath Baba's indifference towards Bhima Bhoi is clearly indicated. The exact reasons of the difference between Bhima Bhoi and the *balkaladhārī*s of Jorandā have not been investigated till today. It seems that the leadership of Mahimā Dharma had been shifted to the great poet Bhima Bhoi after the demise of Mahimā Svāmī. The wholehearted faith of the Mahimā Dharmīs in Bhima Bhoi, who considered wealth and servants, opulence of worldly life as the blessings of the guru (*Stuticintāmaṇi*, 67.16), might have created jealousy among the monks who had left their worldly life. For the monks of Jorandā like Krupasindhu Dash and Bhagawan Dash, Bhima Bhoi was a heretic, despite the number of Bhima Bhoi's devotees being quite high.

There are numerous examples of Bhima Bhoi justifying the rights of women to take up the spiritual path and to become involved in spiritual activities. But the disciples of Biswanath Baba claim that 'women and creeper never survive without support'. Biswanath Baba repeatedly stressed that Mahimā Dharma is nothing but *sanātana* (pristine) Hindu *dharma* and that there is no scope for women in it. Bhima Bhoi's slogan was that 'there is no division of big and small in man and woman'; but Biswanath Baba has defined the *viśuddha advaitavāda* as the root concept of Mahimā Dharma.

There are certain differences between the two preachers. Bhima Bhoi was not an intellectual, but he was a passionate devotee and a poet of universal consciousness. His anger with the kings and Brāhmaṇs is not an expression of his jealousy and rivalry, but rather of his rebelliousness. On the other hand, Biswanath Baba was an intellectual and a *sannyāsī* of the eternal (*sanātana*) Hindu *dharma*, which could be labelled here in comparison as 'orthodox' and 'conservative'. Biswanath Baba made categorical statements about the prohibition of female monks in Mahimā Dharma: 'Earlier, some women were wandering as *sannyāsīs* by the command of the guru, leaving their homes. So Lord Abadhuta commanded the *sannyāsīs*, Lord Alekha Śūnya ordered, from this day no woman will be a *sannyāsinī* leaving home.' (Biswanath Baba, 1991 [1935]: 232–3). Was the command of Mahimā Svāmī or was it Biswanath Baba's own statement?

The new group of Biswanath Baba introduced several restrictions (1971: 338–9). Baba is said to have wholeheartedly supported Shankaracharya's opinion that 'women are the gateway to hell' (Biswanath Baba, 1971: 490–2). Bhima Bhoi's *Ādi-Anta Gītā* was rejected as useless for devotees.[19] At present, *balkaladhārī* and *kaupīnadhārī*[20] groups at Jorandā consider each other as rivals, and the basic tenets of the Dharma appear to have been lost somwehere in this wrangle. At the same time, women continue to be initiated into the *kaupīnadhārī* group and do not accept anyone other than Bhima Bhoi as the writer of Mahimā Dharma literature. Women argue that since Krupasindhu Baba had conferred the *bāṇa* to Subarna Mata, there is no bar on women's initiation into Mahimā Dharma.[21] On the other hand, *balkaladhārī sannyāsīs* taking recourse to the Vedas, Vedāntas, Śāstras and Purāṇas, praise orthodox Hindu *sannyāsa* tradition. They regard Biswanath Baba's *Mahimā Dharma Pratipādaka* and *Mahimā Darśana* as the supreme books on Mahimā Dharma.

Conclusion

The controversy on whether Bhima Bhoi was married or not reveals interesting facts. We see how Bhima Bhoi does not fit into the canonical picture of a saint who lives his life in devotion to God and practices celibacy. Bhima Bhoi probably had sexual relation with more than one woman. He also wrote *Cautiśa Madhu Cakra* which includes a lot of erotic poems. There are further 'heretical' stories about Bhima Bhoi being a 'lady killer' in his youth. We came to listen to narratives about him as being fair with a strong, muscular and hairless body, in other words, being 'sexy'. He contested the ascetic ideal promoted by the monastic order of Jorandā though this protest only partly survived.

It was our aim to explore the most interesting circulating stories we came across in our research. These stories tell us about religious values, power, hierarchies and authority. The stories promoted by the monastic order of Jorandā culminate in declaring Bhima Bhoi a heretic while rejecting violently Bhima Bhoi's attitude towards women. Other stories narrated among the followers of Bhima Bhoi in Khaliapali attribute Bhima Bhoi as well as his women a quasi-divine character. Being god, Bhima Bhoi can emanate children, stay with women together without touching them. We also have seen that his companions are conceptualized as goddesses.

Let us recapitulate. Starting with the narratives about Bhima Bhoi's life we tried to explore the little historic reports and testimonies, which we possess today. What clearly came out of this enquiry is that at the end of the nineteenth century Mahimā Dharma was objected to by many. For us this strong reaction indicates provocative ideas and a spirit of revolt. Since its reformative potential should indeed not be underestimated, one could consider Mahimā Dharma as important as the Ārya Samāj or Brāhmo Samāj for Orissa. But there is no point to speculate why Mahimā Swāmī did not become so famous like Dayananda Saraswati or Rammohun Roy. One of the major differences between Mahimā Dharma and the other reform movements is its non-intellectual basis. The voices heard at that time lamented that only lowly and uncivilized people followed Mahimā Dharma and that therefore the glory of this religion could not last. In the language of *Utkal Deepika* these people were nudes, drug addicts, fools and barbarians. The then intelligentsia of Orissa, which was in contact with Western education and civilization had no courage to listen to the rebellious voice of the low castes and tribes. Mahimā Dharma was a challenge to them and needed through its Brahmanized appearance in Jorandā to be domesticated (see Beltz, 2006).

What remains? The *balkaladhārī sannyāsīs* completely prohibited women from Mahimā Dharma and Nrusingha Baba's *āśrama* in Mahulpada is now an abandoned crematory ground and this revolutionary spirit of Mahimā Dharma is difficult to trace nowadays. Even in Bhima Bhoi's *āśrama* at Khaliapali only a few *sannyāsins* live, though outside the actual compound of the monastery. Only the Satya Svādhīn Mahimā group, a recent offspring based in the Kardulla village near Chipilima of Sambalpur district continued Bhima Bhoi's tradition of giving rights to women. This branch went even one step further in demanding that all *babas* have to be married. It is said that because Bhima Bhoi was a *gṛhastha*, all have to be *gṛhasthas*. In other words, Mahimā Dharma is seen as a lay religion or a *gārhasthya dharma*. At present, its leadership is taken up by a Mata Jyanendri Das, a Scheduled Caste woman of more than 80 years of age. Being the widow of Satya Narayan Baba, the founder of that sect, she explained that she only initiates those devotees who lead a family life. According to her, the one who lives with his family is the real *sannyāsī*. In fact, Mahimā Dharma is the religion of the mother. That is why women get initiated first. We were also told that Mataji is considered as the *ādiśakti* (arch-mother). Interestingly, the Svādhīn Mahimā Dharmīs justify their stand by arguing that they alone are the true followers of Bhima Bhoi. Satya Narayan Baba is seen as an incarnation of Bhima Bhoi and Jyanendri Das represents herself as the incarnation of Annapurna. Devotees worship this Scheduled Caste woman as the embodiment of the primal energy of Mahimā Dharma, the *gurumata* and *brahmavidya*. Hundreds of devotees from Orissa, Chhattisgarh and Andhra Pradesh assemble here every year.

Notes

1. Proverb, popular saying in western Orissa.
2. The Mahimā Dharmīs of the *garhjats* of western Orissa gave Bhima Bhoi the status of a guru. This was confirmed by Chandra Baba in an interview at Lachhipur, a village near Sonepur in March 2000.
3. Interview with Rabindra Nath Rana, Malbiharpur, March 2001.
4. From the A.S.P. in-charge of Pooree District to the Magistrate of Pooree, 11 March 1881, Board of Revenue, Orissa, document no. 438/2.
5. Samantary (1976: 21) states that Sumedha's father Mohan Das was attracted towards the Mahimā cult. He came from a Vaiṣṇava family of the village Ragapali of the present Bolangir district. Daya Sagar Das from Khaliapali confirms that when Bhima Bhoi was staying at the village Bhrusrapali, Mohan Das offered him *pūjā*, as if he was his *guru*. He also offered his daughter Sumedha, who was only seven years old, to Bhima Bhoi. She would have to serve him, providing *sevā* to the *guru*. It is reported that Sumedha later cooked for the inmates of the *āśrama*.
6. According to Ramesh Samantary (1976: 22), Narayana Das of the village Kudasingha (Bolangir district), the brother-in-law of Mohan Das, was the *śreṣṭha mahimā upāsaka* (greatest devotee of the Dharma). In other words, like his brother-in-law, he was very attracted towards Mahimā Dharma. Narayana Das stayed in the Bhrusrapali *āśrama*. Though he was a householder, he temporarily adopted an ascetic lifestyle. From time to time he went home to his village to see his wife. With the blessings of Bhima Bhoi, he had a daughter whom he called Rohini. When she grew up and did not want to marry, her father gave Rohini as a present to his guru Bhima Bhoi.
7. The notion of *sevā* or venerated service is crucial in the relation between the guru and his disciple. It is the disciple who serves the guru at his feet.
8. Mazumdar (1911) confirms that story by saying that Bhima Bhoi left Dhenkanal, moved around preaching the new faith, and finally settled with his followers in the village Khaliapali around the year 1877.
9. *Jīva parama vihāra ye sama gati, eka āsanare vasi ye veni mūrti*, quoted from Bhima Bhoi's *Ādi-Anta Gītā* (Sahu, 1992: 2); see also his *Stuticintāmaṇi*, verse 67, pp. 10–20 and verse 73, pp. 6–7.
10. Daya Sagara Das, interview in Khaliapali in March 2001.
11. Interview with Baishya Charan Thakur, Sonepur.
12. Daya Sagara Das, interview in Khaliapali in March 2001.
13. An interesting reference is given by the *Brahmanirūpaṇa Gītā*: '*Śatṛ bhagāri ekānta vasibe ye mitra. Gurasta bhārijā hoijibe mātā putra*' (The enemies will become friends and the husband and wife will become mother and son), quoted from Sahu's edition (1992: 11).
14. Pancasakhās stands for 'Five Friends', the five mystics of Orissa of whom Achyutananda Das was one of the most important representatives.

15. They are called so because they wear nothing but a *balkalabana*, a piece of bark from the Kumbhi tree.
16. *Antaryāmī* means omniscient or designates the one who regulates the soul or internal feelings, the Supreme Spirit as guiding and regulating mankind, or the one who knows everything.
17. He claims, for example, that Bhima Bhoi was born at Jorandā, a contention that is absurd and confusing because it is generally accepted that he originates from an area situated between Rairakhol and Sonepur.
18. However, a little information has indirectly been gives about the 'Brahmopāsikas' at page 204 of *Mahimā Dharmara Itihāsa*.
19. This text narrates about Mahimā Dharma through the description of man and woman, their physical relationship and the imagery of body culture.
20. The latter are also designated after their clothing, which consists of *kaupīnabana*, a piece of loin cloth.
21. Interview with Dasarathi Das Baba of the *kaupīnadhārī āśrama* from Julunda, Sonepur and Madan Das Baba of Jorandā.

References

Banerjee-Dube, Ishita (1993), 'Religion and Society in Orissa: Mahimā Dharma in the Nineteenth and Twentieth Centuries', Ph.D. thesis, University of Calcutta.

——— (2001), 'Issues of Faith, Enactments of Contest: The Founding of Mahimā Dharma in Nineteenth Century Orissa', in Hermann Kulke and Burkhard Schnepel (eds.), *Jagannath Revisited: Studying Society, Religion and the State in Orissa*, New Delhi: Manohar, pp. 149–77.

Beltz, Johannes (2001), 'Healing Practices and Mahimā Dharma: A Short Note from Recent Fieldwork in Western Orissa', *Adivasi*, vols. 40 and 41, pp. 92–102.

——— (2003), 'Bhima Bhoi: The Making of a Modern Saint', in A. Copley (ed.), *Hindu Nationalism and Religious Reform Movements*, New Delhi: Oxford University Press, pp. 230–53.

——— (2004), 'Devotion, Poetry and Healing: Exploring Bhima Bhoi's Stuticintamani', in Johannes Beltz, Angelika Malinar and Heiko Frese (eds.), *Text and Context in Orissa*, New Delhi: Manohar, pp. 143–73.

——— (2006), 'Contested Authorities, Disputed Centers, and Rejected Norms: Situating Mahimā Dharma in its Regional Diversity', in G. Pfeffer (ed.), *Periphery and Centre: Studies in Orissan History, Religion and Authsopology*, New Delhi: Manohar, pp. 79-104.

Biswanath Baba, (1954), *An Exposition of Satya Mahimā Religion*, Cuttack: L.N. Press.

——— (1971), *Mahimā Dharma Pradīpa*, Cuttack: Dharmagrantha Store.

——— (1935), *Satya Mahimā Dharmara Itihāsa* (Oriya), revised edn. Mahimagadi Dhenkanal: Mahimadharma Granthakosa Samiti (1991).

Bouez, Serge (ed.) (1992), *Ascèse et renoncement en Inde ou la solitude bien ordonnèe*, Paris: Editions Harmattan.

Callewaert, Winand M. and Rupert Snell (eds.) (1994), *According to Tradition: Hagiographical Writing in India*, Wiesbaden: Harassowitz.

Eschmann, Anncharlott (1975), 'Spread, Organization and Cult of Mahimā Dharma', in Nilamani Senapati (ed.), *Mahimā Dharma*, Cuttack, Dharmagrantha Store, pp. 9-22.

——— (1978), 'Mahima Dharma: An Autochthonous Hindu Reform Movement', in Anncharlott Eschmann, Hermann Kulke and G.C. Tripathy (eds.), *The Cult of Jagannath and the Regional Tradition of Orissa*, New Delhi: Manohar, pp. 375–410.

Gross, Robert Lewis (1992), *The Sadhus of India*, New Delhi: Rawat Publications.

Guzy, Lidia (1998), 'Brahma-Kumaris—Weibliche Askese und Globale Reform: Oder wie aus dem Tod des Weiblichen ein transzendenter Feminismus entsteht', in Manfred Hutter (ed.), *Die Rolle des Weiblichen in der indischen und buddhistischen Kulturgeschichte*, Graz: Leykam, pp. 56–74.

——— (2000), ' "On the Road with the Babas": Some Insights into Local Features of Mahimā Dharma', in *Journal of Social Sciences*, 4 (4), pp. 323–30.

——— (2001–2), 'Voices of Gods: Ecstatic Alekhs and Local Configurations of Mahimā Dharma', in *Adivasi*, vols. 40–1, pp. 61–70.

Hallstrom, Lisa Lassell (1999), *Mother of Bliss, Anandamayi Ma (1896–1982)*, Oxford: Oxford University Press.

Mahapatra, Sitakant (1983), *Bhima Bhoi*, New Delhi: Sahitya Akademi.

Mazumdar, B.C. (1911), *Sonepur in Sambalpur Tract*, Calcutta: Brahmo Mission Press.

Mishra, Bibhuti Bhusan (1998), *Religious Reform Movements in Orissa*, Jaipur: Publication Scheme.

Mahapatra, G.C. (1994), *Selected Extracts from Poems of Bhim Bhoi: From Original Oriya*, Bhubaneswar: Huru Hourange Press.

Nath, Satrughna (1990), *Mahimā Dharmadhara*, Bhubaneswar: Hemalata Nath.

Nayak, P.M. (2001), *The Voice of Silence: Sonepur Durbar and Indian Cultural Traditions*, Bhubaneswar: Orissa Sahitya Akademi.

Nepak, Bhagirathi (1997), *Bhima Bhoi: The Adivasi Poet Philosopher*, Bhubaneswar: Bhagiratha Prakashan.

——— (1999), *Bhima Bhoi*, Bhubaneswar: Bhagiratha Prakashan.

——— (ed.) (2001), *Bhima Bhoi: The Greatest Adivasi Poet Prophet*, Bhubaneswar: Bhagiratha Prakashan.

O'Malley, L.S.S. (1909), *Bengal District Gazetter: Sambhalpur*, Calcutta: The Bengal Secretariat Book Depot.

Pati, Biswamoy (2001), *Situating Social History, Orissa (1800-97)*, New Delhi: Orient Longman.

Sahoo, Dhirendra Kumar (2000), 'Bhima Bhoi's Concept of Sunya', unpublished Ph.D. thesis, Bhubaneswar: Utkal University, Department of Philosophy.

Sahu, Karunakara (ed.) (1992), *Bhaktakavi Bhīmabhoi Granthāvalī*, Cuttack: Dharmagrantha Store.

Samantary, Ramesh (1976), *Odiya Sahityare Bhima Bhoi* (Oriya), Cuttack: Dharmagrantha Store.

Sharma, S.P. (1942), *Three Years in Orissa*, Calcutta: Thacker, Spink & Co.

Vasu, Nagendra Nath (1911), *The Modern Buddhism and its Followers in Orissa*, Calcutta: U.N. Bhattacharyya, Hare Press.

Other Sources Cited

Journal of the Asiatic Society of Bengal, January 1882.

Mukura, December 1907–January 1908.

Utkala Sahitya, 6 September 1883, pp. 66–7.

Utkal Deepika, 20 and 26 August 1871; 'Kumbhiapata Babaji', 19 November 1911.

CHAPTER 8

*Tantric Elements in Bhima Bhoi's Oeuvre**

BETTINA BÄUMER

In the nameless realm
ascend the ladder
to the peak of the Void.

Bhima Bhoi, the poet-philosopher and preacher *par excellence* of Mahimā Dharma, imbibed the religious currents of his time, but his works are nevertheless remarkably original. The relation between influences and original thought and experience is an important theme in interpreting his texts. Since his works reflect many streams of religious traditions of Orissa, they are open to multiple interpretations, depending on the preferences and focus of the reader. Therefore, in spite of considerable research on Bhima Bhoi's oeuvre, it is difficult to generically characterize it. Considering the richness and diversity of spiritual traditions which he absorbed and transformed, and with which he played freely, can we discover a core to his own *sādhanā*? And how does it relate to the religious currents such as the Pancasakhās, the Nātha and Sahajīya *sampradāyas*, besides the more remote Upaniṣadic and Buddhist influences?

In the light of the Vedantization of Mahimā Dharma by Bishwanath Baba and his followers of the Jorandā branch of the Dharma, some important aspects of Bhima Bhoi's spirituality have been almost ignored. The more philosophical and *bhakti*-oriented aspects of his work are generally accepted, but the strong tantric current of his spirituality has generally been suppressed.

This tendency to make unorthodox traditions conform to the

Vedantic mainstream can be observed in many instances. To mention only two from different times and areas: the Srividya tradition, which has been 'de-tantricized' and 'Vedantized' in south India (cf. Padoux, 1998: 16f.), and Sri Ramakrishna Paramahamsa, a worshipper of Kālī who practised tantric *sādhanā,* which was carried forward by his disciple Vivekananda into a neo-Vedanta movement. These phenomena show a kind of 'taming' of the pagan aspects of tantric practice and beliefs.

In the 1970s, Anncharlott Eschmann noted that 'Vishvanath Baba rejects all the tantric elements of Bhima Bhoi's teaching . . .'[1] later, defending Bishwanath Baba's re-interpretation, she rightly stated, mainly with reference to the medieval Pancasakhās, that the tenets of Mahimā Dharma, as propounded by Bhoi, represented the finest examples of medieval secret doctrines.

But first of all, one needs to answer the difficult question of what 'tantric' means. André Padoux has analysed this issue critically and some of his observations are of relevance to our discussion here. For instance, with regard to tantric themes or phenomena, he observes that 'there are no "tantric" texts where you find all of them (that is, tantric themes), whereas not a few of the same features—ideas as well as ritual practices—are to be found in texts and traditions that cannot properly be called tantric' (Padoux, 1998: 11). Certainly, Bhima Bhoi's works, and Mahimā Dharma in general, cannot be called 'tantric', and yet there are many important elements in his texts, which do contain such elements. An important related question is whether the Nāthas are to be defined as tantric as well (ibid.). We may agree with Padoux's general remark: 'But whatever term we use, we must admit the fact that the tantric phenomenon, so special yet so difficult to characterize, is both pervasive and elusive' (Padoux, 1998: 13).

The negative associations of the tantric phenomenon are the reasons that Bhima Bhoi's most mysterious, esoteric and tantric text *Ādi-Anta Gītā* is practically never recited or quoted by the Mahimā Dharma followers. Several reasons can be given: the first is the difficulty of the text itself, the second is the secrecy of its teachings, which are accessible only to initiates in tantric yoga, and third is the eroticism in the verses.[2]

In this paper, I want to draw attention to the tantric elements in Bhima Bhoi's works which complement other aspects of his thought and spiritualism. The popular conception of tantra is associated with magic, sexual practices and symbolism, and also with rituals of healing. This is not absent in Bhima's texts, as for example, the *bolis* (chants) 71 to 77 from *Stuticintāmaṇi* used for healing. Other references can be found to more specific tantric traditions and traits, as we shall see.

Buddhist and Hindu tantra are both part of the religious heritage of Western Orissa. The archaeological monuments of Baudh and Ranipur–Jharial point to Buddhist and Śaiva–Śākta tantric practices, with the important role played by *yoginīs*. Ram Prasad Mishra has stated in an article: 'It appears that these tantric *siddhas* (i.e. Indrabhuti and Lakshmikara) of Kosaliya -Oddiyana or the ancient Western Orissa had profound influence on the creativities [*sic*] of Bhima Bhoi ...' (Mishra, 2001: 26). It is significant that in the account of Govinda Baba's initiation by Mahimā Svāmī, which Bhima Bhoi provides in *Nirvedasādhanā*, Mahimā Svāmī sends his disciple to Baudh, to the village Balasingha.[3] He tells him: 'That is my original place. There I have kept all the treasures of spiritual perfection (*sarvasiddhi*). Inside there is also a temple. That land is for the accomplishment of spiritual perfection (*siddhabhūmi*, or the land of tantric *siddhas*), where Brahma will be realized...'.[4]

There is no doubt that Mahimā Svāmī and his direct disciples were ontologically associated with the *siddhas* and to the Nātha Yogis.[5] I cannot go into a historical proof of this connection, but only refer to some of the tantric elements found in Bhima Bhoi's texts, many of which he derived from the Parcasakhā literature.[6]

The Theory of *Piṇḍa-Brahmāṇḍa*

It is generally accepted that Bhima Bhoi's *Piṇḍa-Brahmāṇḍa* theory has been influenced by the Pancasakhās, that is the connection and correspondence between the universe and the human body, or macro and microcosm. Though its origins can be traced back to the Puruṣasūkta (*Ṛgveda,* 10, 90), to the Viśvarūpa of the *Bhagavad-gītā* (11), to the *Bhāgavata Purāṇa,* its tantric origins cannot be denied in the form in which Bhima Bhoi uses the concept. It has to do with the basic idea that the elements of the universe, all the forefathers, including the ancient *ṛṣis*, as well as the sacred sites of pilgrimage can be found within one's own body. Detailed descriptions of this internal landscape can be found in many texts of Bhima Bhoi. What this means for *sādhanā* is, first, the importance of the body which is the real place and instrument to achieve realization of the Supreme Reality, and hence is an interiorization of not only the external world, but even of the mythical and religious worlds. If Mahimā Dharma criticizes external practices of pilgrimages and temple worship, it is precisely to emphasize that all this can be found in one's own body, the true *tīrtha*. And by relating *Piṇḍa* and *Brahmāṇḍa,* the devotee achieves an integration, which is not a negation of the world. Tantric *sādhanā* aims precisely at such an integration of the outer and the inner spheres, where the body is the link.

Sexual Symbolism

What is generally believed to be the most obvious tantric trait is the sexual symbolism which reaches out from the metaphysical level to the role of sexuality in *sādhanā*, and hence to the role of women. This is certainly not the only element of tantra, as we shall see, but it plays an important role in Bhima Bhoi's thought and life. Let us take the *Ādi-Anta Gītā* as the chief example of his use of tantric sexual symbolism. This text, whose title could be translated as 'The song related to the beginning and the end', consists of a dialogue between *jīva* and *parama*, the soul and the Supreme, but there are three levels of understanding: *jīva* is symbolized as a *yuvatī*, a young girl, and *parama* as a man. At the same time, *jīva* stands for the disciple, Bhima Bhoi himself, and *parama* for the guru, Mahimā Svāmī. Thus, the sexual symbolism expressed in the text in minute details has always to be understood in terms of three levels of union: union of both sexes, union of the soul and the Supreme, and union of disciple and guru. This multilayered symbolism is also a typical tantric method. The theme of the union of *jīva* and *parama* is of course found in many other texts of Bhima Bhoi, but with less emphasis on the sexual symbolism. In *Bhajanamālā*, for example, it is the mystical dimension, which is of importance:

O good people, do not fall prey to delusion and be sad. Go to the Amana temple ('beyond the mind'). There is a passage to Alekha ('the Inexpressible'). Here the soul (*jīva*) and the Supreme (*parama*) meet.[7]

The context of the *Ādi-Anta Gītā* can be summarized as *śarīrabheda*, that is, the body as an instrument of *sādhanā*, the body as the locus where everything is to be found and integrated. This can be related to the *kāyasādhanā* of the Nātha Yogis (Dasgupta, 1969). In both cases, it is a question of making the body immortal:

Durlabha janama piṇḍa go kṣaya nāhīn
akṣaya amara nāma go achi vahi.

This birth is difficult to attain. The body will not be destroyed, it is called indestructible and immortal.[8]

That Bhima was aware of the Nātha Sampradāya is clear in the way he identifies the *ṛṣis* who are placed within the body. Apart from the well-known Vedic *ṛṣis*, he lists Matsyendranāth and Gorakhanāth, as well as the Oriya Sahajayāna poets Tantipā (Tantripāda) and Haripā (*Ādi-Anta Gītā* 3, 18). We may look at some examples from the extremely difficult text of *Ādi-Anta Gītā*. One of the main principles of tantra is the continuity and interrelation of the physical, the sensual and the divine. Bhima expresses this in a short verse:

Bhūmi rasa jihva rasa go stirī rasa
Hari rasa sangatare gotie prakāśa.

The *rasa* of the earth element, the sense of taste, the sexual enjoyment—if they are united with the divine *rasa*, they become a single light.[9]

The term *rasa* itself contains all these levels, but he uses it here consciously to link them in the one *rasa* of the Divine which contains all else. A clear tantric reference is found in his placing of all the 18 *siddhis* or spiritual perfections inside the body. Obviously, this knowledge is the secret of the micro-macrocosmic relationship or *Piṇḍa-Brahmāṇḍa*, which only the saints can realize. The sexual and metaphysical images find expression in the question of the *jīva*:

Puruṣa aṅgaku grāse je stirī aṅga
brahmāṇḍa ku gilideva je śakti aṅga.

As the female sexual organ swallows the male organ,
so the organ of śakti swallows the cosmos.[10]

The importance of śakti in relation to the universe is clearly expressed here. The discussion on the *parama* goes into details of yogic-sexual symbolism, starting from the lowest *cakras* situated in the region of the male and female sexual organs: *guhyacakra* and *padmacakra*.[11] The well-known terminology of tantric *yoga* is found throughout the text, with the *cakras*, *padma* and *dvāra* inside the body. We will come to this topic presently. The aim of the *Ādi-Anta Gītā*, with its occasionally crude sexual symbolism is precisely the union of *jīva* and *parama* in terms of the union of man and woman.

The Theory of *Cakras*

Bhima Bhoi was familiar with the yogic *cakras* and in his characteristic way, took the liberty of playing with the description of the yogic body. We find a mix of ascent and descent through the *cakras*. Only a systematic analysis of the relevant passages and allusions could show whether this apparently haphazard treatment corresponds to his personal experience or if it is just an expression of his poetic freedom. Apart from referring to these subtle centres in the body, there are mysterious passages which seem to reflect his personal experience. Though the interpretation is difficult, I may give at least one example.

In the *Ādi-Anta Gītā*, he compares the body to a mountain (*deha go giri sthala*), implying on the one hand that the backbone is called *merudaṇḍa*, the central cosmic mountain, and on the other the idea of ascent and descent. There is a door at the centre of the palate (*tāluka dvāra siri go lagiachi*) through which the vein passes like a thread, connecting with the *mūlādhāra* below. Passing through the *merudaṇḍa*, it goes to the secret organ in two ways. This may, in descending order, hint at the two *nāḍīs* or veins (though the terms *iḍā* and *piṅgalā* are not used). After touching the lower *cakra*, the power again rises upwards forcefully (*ūrdhve go uṭhijae*) through the central vein, where this force is heated and smoke is produced, speech is liquefied and becomes the *rasa* of the heart (*tālukāre tāti dhūma go prakāśa, taraḷa huai gira go hṛd rasa*). Then it is filled with water and air and when it comes in contact with fire, it overflows. Bhima Bhoi compares this experience with the boiling of milk which overflows due to the excessive heat of fire. In the same way, the *brahmabindu* overflows in the *padma maṇḍala*. A clear expression of an ecstatic experience is that due to inner heat, the poet is not able to contain himself.[12]

This passage is extremely difficult to interpret, and it also lacks the usual terms like *kuṇḍalinī*, but it can be understood in the light of tantric yoga where we find first a descent of the inner energy, followed by an ascent which Bhima describes in terms of an inner fire, making the inner *rasa* boil over. It reflects a passionate spiritual experience which he consciously couches in a secret language. In another complex passage (ibid.: 2), a similar descent through the *cakras* is described:

śūnya maṇḍala	(*brahmarandhra*)
lalāṭacakra	(forehead)
kaṇṭha	(throat)
hṛdaya	(heart)
nābhikamala	(navel)
mūlaliṅgacakra.	(*mūlādhāra*)

In agreement with Buddhist tantric yoga, Bhima Bhoi also says that the light of Alekha rises from the navel (*nābhi maṇḍala*).[13]

Tantric Yoga

Tantric yoga involves many methods of which we find traces and allusions in several works of Bhima Bhoi. One such instance is the association of the yogic *cakras* with *akṣaras* or letters of the alphabet. This is referred to in a complex metaphor of the body being the land of Vrindāvana or Gopabhūmi, where Krishna plays with *gopīs*. Here we find a combination of the inner sacred land-scape with the yogic *cakras*, combined with a symbolic number of *akṣaras*. This description ends with the suggestion: 'Put your hand on the heart and see that it is constantly beating'.

Deha hṛdayare hasta go māri dekha,
sadā sarvadā karuchi go dhapa dhapa.[14]

It is a kind of invitation to experience everything in one's heart and body. An important method of yogic *sādhanā* is referred to by Bhima Bhoi, which is a result of both his own experience and the instruction he has received from his guru. It is significant that he describes this practice in *Nirvedasādhanā* in the context of the initiation of Govinda Baba by Mahimā Svāmī. In the translation of A. Das:

This is the initiation into Brahma without uttering letters. Control your mind and the air, and do meditate. If you will be acquainted with it, you will get salvation. Make both of them one in your heart. If this is accomplished with satisfaction you will be immortal, in all the ages. Many have said this but they did not know.[15]

Then he says: *kevala mātra eka saṅga, mana pavana dhyāna-yoga* (You will have only one companion, that is, the yogic medi-tation on mind and breath.). Govinda asks for an elaboration of this practice, which the Anādi Guru gives in the following way:

I am speaking about the mind and the air. The mind is said to be a mendicant and it is bound by the air; the name of God will act as *dhāraṇā*, the sound of Brahmā will be there.[16]

The word *dhāraṇā* is a technical term used in both Hindu and Buddhist tantra as a method of meditation or concentration (not in the sense of the *Yogasūtra*). That this very practice or *dhāraṇā* was also Bhima Bhoi's own can be seen in a verse of *Stuticintāmaṇi*:

I have controlled my breath and restrained my nature and I am in deep meditation every moment. O Lord of the helpless, if you show kindness to me, I will get bliss.[17]

What is described here is not simply yogic *prāṇāyāma*, but a method of unifying mind and breath. This comes closer to the Śaiva idea which is quoted repeatedly in all the works of Kashmiri Śaivism or Trika: *prāk saṃvit prāṇe pariṇatā* ('Consciousness was first transformed into breath', ascribed to Kallaṭa).[18] This is the metaphysical basis for *prāṇa* (*pavana* in the case of Bhima Bhoi) being the most excellent means for controlling the mind. Controlling here does not imply suppression, but rather a unification of mind and breath, an integration of consciousness and body.

The Higher Stages of Tantric *Sādhanā*

Generally, frequently used terms like *śūnyabrahman, śūnyadehī, anākāra*, etc., are understood in an Upaniṣadic–Vedāntic or Buddhist sense, taking into account the influence of the Panca-sakhās. The consideration of these apparently negative terms from the tantric perspective reveals, however, that they belong to the higher stages of tantric *sādhanā*.

A frequent epithet used for the formless Brāhmaṇ is *śūnyadehī*, which occurs in the famous *boli* of *Stuticintāmaṇi* (53, 1): *rūpa-rekhā nahīn he śūnya dehī* ... (He has no shape and form, the one whose body is void).[19] One whose body is void, that is, the ultimate Reality, can only be reached through a meditation which requires clearing the mind and body of all attributes. This is clearly related to Upaniṣadic and Buddhist meditative methods, but is not exactly identical. In Śaiva tantra, especially in the *Vijñāna Bhairava*, we find *dhāraṇās* or meditative practices that require imagining one's own body to be void.[20]

The same *boli* speaks of the path leading to the formless Absolute as *asādhanā mārga*, 'a path without any means', a pathless path.[21] This is very much in tune with the highest means described in the *advayavāda* of Kashmiri Śaivism: *anupāya*. According to the *Mālinīvijaya Tantra* and its elaborate exegesis by Abhinavagupta in his *Tantrāloka*, there are essentially three ways or means (*upāya*) to reach identification with the Divine, and beyond every method lies the pathless path of *anupāya*, at the very highest level of the Absolute Reality.[22] In Bhima Bhoi's famous *boli*, there is a mysterious expression following the verse mentioning *asādhanā mārga*: *pati patnī karanti yugala* . . . (53, 6). Is this an allusion to Śiva–Śakti in their inseparable union as *ardhanārīśvara*? One cannot be certain, but since Bhima shifts immediately from the pair (*yugala*) to the one Lord (*prabhu*), the allusion is not improbable.

In this connection, another method of higher tantric *sādhanā* should be mentioned; this is the spontaneous recitation of the *ajapā* mantra. Thus, the guru instructs the disciple: 'Recite the name called *ajapā*'.[23] This corresponds to the *haṃsamantra* of tantric *sādhanā*.[24] Let us look at another term which occurs frequently in the context of the highest, nameless experience:

Parace hoi pārile aṇa ākāre
niścaya bheṭa pāiba amana pure.

If you concentrate on his formlessness,
you will surely meet him in the realm beyond the mind.[25]

Other expressions are *amana maṇḍala* or *amana mandira* (*Bhajanamālā*, 11), similar to *Śūnya-Mandira*; hence, 'the temple of thoughtlessness' and 'the realm beyond the mind'. These expressions correspond exactly to the highest stage in the tantric yogi's ascent through the *cakras* and through the stages of *oṃ*, beyond the *sahasrāra*. The last two levels above the head are called *samanā*, 'with the mind', where a trace of the mind still exists, and '*unmanā*, beyond the mind', where the bondage of thought has ceased completely (Padoux, 1990; Silburn, 1988). *Amana* and *unmanā* correspond to the same stages of tantric yoga. In the words of Bhima Bhoi:

Anādi (the Beginningless One) is sitting on the seat of the Void,
and he reveals himself without words in the mindless realm.[26]

Expressed in terms of space, it is the highest level of ascent of the yogi. Bhima says: 'in the nameless realm, ascend the ladder to the peak of the Void (*śūnya śikhare*)'.[27]

Conclusion

In the end I want to return to one of the basic elements of tantra: the overcoming and the integration of opposite, or rather, complementary realities. The union of the two sexes is the most obvious example, but it stands for an entire metaphysics and yoga of complementary opposites. The aim of tantric *sādhanā* is not only *mokṣa* (liberation), but also *bhoga* (enjoyment). Bhima Bhoi expresses this basic insight in his *Stuticintāmaṇi*:

Yoga bhoga duhen samāna aṭanti kāhāra pakṣareyiba,
biṣa amṛta benibhāga karichi kebaṇa bhāgaku neba.
sādhu sujñajana nyāya kara tumbhe beni pakṣaku vicāri,
beni bhāgajāka ekaṭhābe achi jāhāguṇa jeun pari.
beni bhāga guṇa toḷi napāriṇa paḍiachi sandhi madhye,
dhari gurupāda bhaṇe bhīma kandha ṣoḍadaśa śatapade.

Yoga and pleasure, both are one.
Towards which should you be biased?
He has made two parts, one nectar,
one poison. Which will you choose?

Oh wise and pious,
consider these two.
Both parts co-exist,
each with its own qualities.

Unable to weigh their attributes,
I am caught between the two.
Thus says Bhima Kandha in the sixteen-hundredth stanza,
clutching the feet of the Guru.[28]

This 'centre' between *yoga* and *bhoga* is what is to be attained in tantric *sādhanā*. To quote only one example: 'One's mind should neither be engrossed in suffering nor in pleasure. O Bhairavi! You should know the middle state (between them)—then the Reality alone remains.'[29] In fact, I would like to emphasize, again, that Bhima Bhoi's works cannot be understood without considering the strong tantric elements of his thought and experience, which, albeit not his invention, have nevertheless come to him through his guru, Mahimā Svāmī, and have been enriched by his own philosophy and experience. Discovering such correspondences with tantric yoga, among others, does not diminish his originality, but they are essential for any exegesis of the texts of this mystical poet.

Notes

* I thank Shri Kedar Mishra for his assistance in collecting material for this paper. All quotations from Bhima Bhoi are taken from K. Sahu's (1992) edition.

1. See the posthumously published paper by Eschmann in the present volume.
2. The editor of the Dharmagrantha Store edition of the *Ādi-Anta Gītā* cautions in the preface: 'This *Adi-Anta Gita* manuscript is collected from Bhakta Daitari Charana Singh of Khandapada and published with his kind permission. Here sexual acts of wives and husbands are narrated in "Sarira Bheda" way according to Tantra and Kāmaśāstra. This text is prescribed for *grhastha* devotees. But for Niskama devotees, Brahmachari and Sanyasi's this is not admissible. Still the last chapter is open for all' (Sahu, 1992: Preface).
3. Balasingha is the original seat of Govinda Baba, the first disciple of Mahimā Svāmī. It is located on the bank of Mahanadi, between Sonepur and Baudh.
4. *Nirvedasādhanā*, Chapter 3, quoted from the English translation by A. Das, South Asia Institute Heidelberg, MSS no. 854. The citation is from page 16, the verse number is not given. The Oriya text has been published by Sahu (1992).
5. The history of the Nāthas in western Orissa has to be taken into account to understand their influence on Bhima Bhoi. It is significant that there is a *ghāṭ* on the Mahanadi in Sonepur called *Matsyendra-ghāṭ*.
6. Ishita Banerjee-Dube, 1993, Chapter 2, pp. 6–7.
7. *Bhajanamālā* 179, 1; in the manuscript of Khaliapali, the order of *bhajanas* is different, and this is the third *bhajana*.
8. *Ādi-Anta Gītā*, 13.
9. Ibid., 12.
10. Ibid., 22.
11. These terms for the male and female organs also occur in other texts, *Bhajanamālā* 178, 2.
12. *Na rahi parai bhande go agni trase*, *Ādi-Anta Gītā*, pp. 23–4.
13. *Stuticintāmaṇi*, 89, 12
14. *Ādi-Anta Gītā*, 61.
15. *Nirvedasādhaṇā*, Chapter 3, quoted from A. Das' translation, p. 14.; for further details see n. 4.
16. Ibid., p. 15, see n. 4 for further details.
17. *Stuticintāmaṇi* 12, 4. The Oriya says: *Pavanaku bandhi prakṛti ku chandi anukṣaṇe dhyānayoga anāthara nātha karuṇā kale mūmabhibaimukha bhoga*.
18. Kallata is a master in the tradition of Spanda whose works have not survived, except in fragments like this one which is quoted frequently, without any surviving text as a source. He lived probably during the ninth century. For a detailed description of different Śaiva systems see Sanderson, 1988.

19. Mahapatra, 1983, pp. 56–9.
20. 'One should contemplate on one's body as void even for a moment, free from thoughts, then one is liberated from thought . . .' (Singh, 1979, verses 46 and 47–8).
21. [*A*]*sādhanā mārge pai he*, *Bhajanamālā* 53; the same *asādhanā* is praised in *Brahma Nirūpaṇa Gītā*, Chapter 5, pp. 89–95.
22. Abhinavagupta's *Tantrāloka* (1918–38), *āhnika* 2; Bäumer, 1997: 3–22.
23. *Bhajanamālā* 258, 6.
24. Cf. *Vijñāna Bhairava*, ed. Lakshman Joo, 2002, verses 156–7.
25. *Bhajanamālā* 9, 1.
26. [*B*]*asi achanti anādi śūnya āsana sampadi ana śabade prakāśa amana dāṇḍe*, *Bhajanamālā* 10, 3.
27. *Bhajanamālā*, 9, 6.
28. *Stuticintāmaṇi* 80, 18–20, tr. B. Bäumer, Johannes Beltz and Sadananda Das.
29. Lakshman Joo, 2002. 103.

References

Abhinavagupta, *Tantrāloka of Abhinavagupta with Rajanaka Jayaratha's Commentary*, ed. M. Kaula, 12 vols., Srinagar, Kashmiri Series of Texts and Studies; new edition in 8 volumes in 1987, New Delhi: Motilal Banarsidass.

Bäumer, Bettina (1997), 'The Four Spiritual Ways (Upāya) in the Kashmir Śaiva Tradition', in K.R. Sundararajan and B. Mukerji (eds.), *Hindu Spirituality* (*World Spirituality Series*, vol. 7), New York: Crossroad Publishing Co., pp. 3–22.

Banerjee-Dube, Ishita (1993), 'Religion and Society in Orissa: Mahimā Dharma in the Nineteenth and Twentieth Centuries', Ph. D. thesis, University of Calcutta.

Dasgupta, S.B. (1969), *Obscure Religious Cults*, Calcutta: Sanskrit College.

Lakshman Joo, (ed.) (2002), *Vijñāna Bhairava: The Practice of Centring Awareness*, Varanasi: Indica.

Mahapatra, Sitakant (1983), *Bhima Bhoi*, New Delhi: Sahitya Akademi.

Mishra, Ramaprasad (2001), 'Samvalaka Tantra-Rajarsi Indrabhuti and his Influence on Culture of Western Orissa', in *Souvenir, Lok Mahotsav 2001*, Sambalpur: DCC, pp. 125–33.

Padoux, André (1990), *Vāc: The Concept of the Word in Selected Hindu Tantras*, Albany: State University of New York Press.

——— (1998), 'Concerning Tantric Traditions', in G. Oberhammer (ed.), *Studies in Hinduism II: Miscellanea to the Phenomenon of Tantras*, Vienna: Österreichische Akademie der Wissenschaften (Austrian Academy of Sciences), pp. 9–20.

Sanderson, Alexis (1988), 'Saivism and the Tantric Traditions', in S. Sutherland (ed.), *The World's Religions*, London: Routledge & Kegan Paul, pp. 660–704.

Sahu, Karunakara (ed.) (1992), *Bhaktakavi Bhīmabhoi Granthāvalī*, Cuttack: Dharmagrantha Store.

Silburn, L. (1988), *Kuṇḍalinī. The Energy of the Depths*, Albany: State University of New York Press.

Singh, Jaideva (1979), *Vijnanabhairava or Divine Consciousness*, Delhi: Motilal Banarsidass.

CHAPTER 9

Institutionalization of Mahimā Samāja

FANINDAM DEO

Introduction

The aim of this paper is to analyse how socio-cultural ideas and values affected the formation of and became embedded in the organizational structures of Mahimā Dharma. 'Institutionalization', in this paper, denotes a course of action by which norms and rules are made working and undeviating amongst a set of followers who, in their turn, make the transgression of these norms punishable. From this angle, Mahimā temples (*Śūnya Mandira, Samādhi Mandira, Dhuni Mandira*)[1] and the priests (*niti bābās*) who offer ritual services there would not be considered institutions just by virtue of their presence or by the services rendered everyday. Institutionalization has to be seen in the meanings and expectations generated in the process of elaborating ritual services and how these get reinforced by those who share, assist, look after and guide these services. Joseph T. O'Connell raised this point in a different way:

> . . . Institutionalization is not a once-for-all matter (of simply getting from a first charismatic generation to a second institutionalized generation of a movement), but an ongoing process, subject to changing historical circumstances that are ever in tension with the received 'value orientation' of a movement or community. It is also clear that, in the process of institutionalization, explicitly religious motivation and meaning are inextricably bound up with mundane constraints and interests.
>
> (O'Connell, 1999: 9)

Mahimā Dharma began in the nineteenth century (Das, 1952; Eschmann, 1978). Emerging from a fluid and unsettled formative phase, it gradually came to acquire a definite and established form (Deo, 1999a). This entailed a changeover from a stance of newness—that attempted to cause disruption in the Brāhmaṇ–Kṣatriya manoeuvred Oriya socio-cultural *status quo*—to a new position more or less pleasing the followers of the faith and acceptable to Oriya society.

There are many dimensions in this journey; one that had an uncertain beginning in the mid-nineteenth century, passed through a phase of institutionalization in the last quarter of the nineteenth century, and took new shape in the twentieth—a journey in which ideas and institutions were passed from one generation to another and got transformed in the process. Mahimā Dharma was initiated by Mahimā Svāmī, a charismatic personality, in the mid-nineteenth century. It was consolidated by other leaders like Govinda Baba, Nrusingha Baba and Bhima Bhoi. After the death of Mahimā Svāmī there was a crisis. The leading disciples of the faith were not certain of how to ensure the continuity of the teachings and the popularity of its founder who had not recognized the institution of *guru-paramparā* (lineage of masters) and therefore not nominated a successor.

There was also neither an elite core group nor a coherent community of followers of the religion. Hence, it was decided to construct a *samādhi* (memorial) for the founder—a concrete structure that would symbolize his authority—and other dwelling places and places of worship (ibid.). In other words, in the process of institutionalization, the first step was to identify the sacred topography, the dwelling places of the founder; and the second to have control over these places. In the next phase, the need was to formulate a mode of worship, rituals and festivals according to the local calendar. This gave rise to the framing of rules for daily, monthly and yearly rituals and the rules concerning the lifestyle of priests and *bhaktas* (devotees). These were crucial modes of institutionalization in the case of Mahimā Dharma.

Complementary to this was the composition and compilation of devotional lyrics of prayer like *bhajanas, jānānas, cautisās* in praise of the Creator, Alekha Brahma, and the founder. These lyrical compositions have over time come to acquire the place of sacred literature, almost equivalent to sacred scripture, of Mahimā Dharma. The dissemination of the main tenets of Mahimā Dharma amongst literate and illiterate *bhaktas* was made possible through these devotional songs. Here it may be recalled that in nineteenth-century Orissa, oral tradition was very strong. Collective singing and recitation of the verses was a powerful mode of emphasizing the values advocated by the new faith upon its followers. In the process, the commitment of the *bhaktas* to the faith was ensured. Thus, it was a useful means which reiterated and perpetrated the crucial duties of the followers and institutionalized them in the course of time.

The Social Context

Conditions in nineteenth-century Orissa were such that they generated restlessness among different groups of people (Deo, 1999b). British rule began in Orissa at the start of the century. The *garhjat* rajas (rulers of the tributary states), *zamindars* (landlords), Brāhmaṇs and moneylenders established a nexus with colonial rulers. The gradual transformation of what had been gifts into dues, monetization of the economy and commutation of feudal dues and services into cash had their impact on society, thereby affecting the social structure, economic and agrarian institutions and the political system. The *garhjat* rajas, now in closer contact with areas under direct British administration, entered into competition with the chiefs and princes of these areas. In order to enhance their status and political position, they started constructing palaces and temples. Each *garhjat* chief, *zamindar* and even some *gautia/thekedar* (village headman) started building temples, palaces and other grand structures. The subjects had to bear an additional burden of *beṭh-begār* or forced labour. For the temples the chiefs needed Brāhmaṇs and for both temple and Brāhmaṇs they needed land. The rulers began to reclaim and redistribute land at the expense of the peasants. In most places the *garhjat* rajas imposed tax on everything that could be taxed.

In the nineteenth century, the cult of Jagannātha, the principal deity of Hinduism in Orissa, had come under the iron grip of the raja–Brāhmaṇ nexus. The sabara *devatā* (tribal god) had been hijacked by the ruling classes of Orissa from the *adivasis* and was being used as a tool to exercise their authority over the latter (Kulke, 1978 and 1993). *Dīnabandhu* (friend of the downtrodden, another epithet of Jagannātha) had been Brahmanized as *Baḍaṭhakura* (great lord) and had gone beyond the reach of the downtrodden. *Sabaras*, being bird eaters, were not even allowed to enter the temple dedicated to their god (Banerjee-Dube, 1993). All this went against the basic principle of universality that the cult of Jagannātha represented.

The *adivasis* and people of lower castes, who formed the bulk of the agricultural population in the tributary states of Orissa, considered the orthodox Jagannātha cult and the raja–Brāhmaṇ nexus as being responsible for the loss of cultivable areas that had traditionally belonged to them. The resultant antagonism was intensified by the cultural differences between the *adivasi*–peasant and Brāhmaṇ–Kṣatriya, which was accentuated by the latter's ideas of purity, pollution, dietary restrictions and rigid caste distinction. All this converged with the great famine of Orissa in 1865–6, which took a toll on millions of people (Jena 1978). A section of people started thinking that the famine was a result of the *pāpa* or sin committed by the ruling classes. Some saw the raja–Brāhmaṇ combine and their associates as the cause of their miseries, and Lord Jagannātha as the protector of the former.

However, it would be wrong to assume that all social groups revolted *en masse* against the oppressor. As a matter of fact, we find that the reaction of each group in Orissa was conditioned by its own historical context. The meaning a group gives to a circumstance or an event is out of a range of meanings and options available to them at the time of their particular experience of that entity or event. Thus, while the lower orders of the society in Orissa, bristled under the unequal system, the measures they adopted to deal with it varied. While in some areas they accepted a low position, in others they tried to be a part of the *garhjat* estates in the hope of improving their condition. Yet other groups, unable to cope with external pressure, withdrew to inaccessible areas and at times revolted against exploitation.

It has been observed by David Lorenzen (1995), Schomer and McLeod (1987) and many others that religious ideas, and particularly within the *bhakti* tradition, have long been the language of protest, innovation and expression of individual and separate identities. These ideas provide vast scope for reinterpretation that helps legitimize the aspiration of various sections of the population and justifies changes in existing social relationships. Mahimā Svāmī, drawing inspiration from various available options, provided a separate new identity for downtrodden people. The scope for *mukti* (emancipation) was extended to all human beings in Mahimā Dharma irrespective of their social position. The idea of emancipation from birth in an unjust world was opened even to the lowest stratum of the hierarchical caste society.

Initiation and Dissemination

Mahimā Svāmī, the founder of Mahimā Dharma, was an historic personality who believed in and preached the meaninglessness of idol-worship, ritualism and Brahmanical interpretation of *dharma*. He propounded the worship of the one and only invisible almighty Creator, Alekha Parama Brahma. His eloquent and convincing sermon appealed to and created a deep impression on the mind of the father of Oriya nationalism Madhusudan Rao, who saw Mahimā Svāmī in 1874 at Patia. Madhusudan later remarked that if he had met the Svāmī before his conversion to Christianity, his course of life would have been different. 'If Svāmī had been born in Bengal or Punjab he would have become a world figure.'

In addition to Mahimā Svāmī, his *dharma* is linked with the names of Govinda Baba, Nrusingha Baba and Bhima Bhoi. They were the earliest and foremost disciples of the founder and were influential in making the teaching of Mahimā Dharma available to all. Under their guidance, Mahimā Dharma matured into a meaningful and organized religious campaign in the 1860s and 1870s. By the end of the century, it had attracted 30,000 people of Orissa as followers (Pattnaik, 1961). It had mustered enough strength and power to question the socio-ritual dominance of the kings and priests and their associates, and the Brahmanical interpretation of the Jagannātha cult. The followers of Mahimā Dharma were forbidden to accept anything from the raja–Brāhmaṇ combine and their associates. They were also prohibited from taking the *prasāda* (graced leftover) of Jagannātha, worshipping idols, and from taking part in traditional rituals. Bhima Bhoi went a step ahead and preached that 'the final deliverer' had already appeared in Orissa in the form of Mahimā Svāmī. Upon seeing this, God Jagannātha of Puri, he said, had left his temple and become his disciple.

Mahimā Svāmī travelled widely in the *garhjats* of Orissa preaching his message in the second half of the nineteenth century. He set up *tuṅgīs* in different places (Asiatic Society of Bengal, 1881–2).[2] A *tuṅgī* is a hut of special purity for the ascetics of Mahimā Dharma. He also established a mud altar and lit a sacred fire at its centre. This was the only mode of worshipping Alekha Brahma. He ordained two categories of *sannyāsīs* (ascetic disciples), called *kaupīnadhārī* (wearer of waist-cloth) and *kumbhīpaṭadhārī* or *balkaladhārī* (wearer of the bark of the *kumbhī* tree) (Biswanath Baba, 1935; Nepak, 1974; Pal, 1994). He emphasized that ascetics should not strive to attain only personal salvation. They had to work for the good of the *bhagatas* (Mahimā followers) and *jagata* (Mahimā universe). Those who became *sannyāsīs* were instructed to travel and spread the *mahimā* or glory of Alekha Brahma. The *sannyāsīs* were enjoined not to stay more than a day in a village. To become a *sannyāsī* and not work for the *bhagatas* and *jagata* was a fundamental breach of the principle of Mahimā Dharma. It was an itinerant, active *dharma*. Self-perfection and social interaction were at its core (Deo, 1999a: 140). The faith thus blended individual pursuit of wisdom with fellow-feeling.

Mahimā Svāmī was against performing miracles. According to him, such acts testified to an incomplete spiritual development. After attaining *siddhi* (spiritual realization), a *sannyāsī* had to work for the emancipation of the laity instead of displaying his powers of *siddhi* to them. Apart from his ascetic disciples, the Svāmī also initiated a large number of *gṛhībhaktas* or *āśritas* (householder followers). Mahimā Svāmī left behind no written work; but he had addressed hundreds of formal and informal gatherings of *sannyāsīs* and *bhaktas* over nearly 10 years. In their memories, the latter must have preserved some of the key ideas. Later, these ideas became reflected in their compositions and teachings.

One such person was Bhima Bhoi, who composed not only after the death of Mahima Swami but also during his lifetime. It is widely accepted by Mahimā followers that Bhoi was empowered by the Swami to compose *bhajanas* and *jānānas*.[3] These devotional lyrics contain the essence of Mahimā Svāmī's teachings. Other than Bhima Bhoi, many *sannyāsīs* and *āśritas* with little or no formal education orally transmitted their experiences and encounters to their respective disciples. This gave rise to contrasting interpretation after the death of Mahimā Svāmī. It seems Mahimā Svāmī himself was at the root of this multiplicity of interpretation, in that he avoided a canonization of his teachings, did not choose a successor, and did not specify the relative position of the two orders of the *sannyāsīs* he ordained. His householder and ascetic followers perceived and interpreted his ideas—initially explained by him in Oriya and preached orally—according to their respective understanding. This led to the formation of more than two groups, each with its own rules, ideals, followers and institutions. The shape of the ideals and institutions depended on their different geographical locations and their respective stands on the position of women (Deo, 1999a: 145). At present, there are four such areas: *uttara* (north), *dakṣiṇa* (south), *paścima* (west) and *pūrva* (east).[4] The *sannyāsīs* have their own bands of followers: *kaupīnadhārī sannyāsīs* allow women to become *sannyāsinīs*, but do not allow them to travel. Of late, a *mātā maṭha* has been built in Jorandā for women.

Crisis

Two years before his death in 1876, Mahimā Svāmī denounced all kinds of permanent structures and destroyed some of the important *tuṅgīs* and refused to initiate new *sannyāsīs* (Biswanath Baba, 1935; Pal, 1994).

His first and foremost disciple, Govinda Baba, had died before him. The second important ascetic disciple Nrusingha Baba had been implicated in a murder case at Banki, and had virtually withdrawn unto himself. He was not accepted by the *balkaladhārī sannyāsīs* into their fold. Bhima Bhoi, who popularized Mahimā Dharma through his *bhajana* and *jānāna*, was no longer a celibate, having taken to the life of a householder. Mahimā Svāmī was not supposed to die—his followers had deified him. He was identified with the Creator, who had taken human form of his free will in this *kaliyuga* to establish *satyayuga* and *satya mahimā dharma*. But he did die, and the new *dharma* was left without a leader. There were two categories of *sannyāsīs*: the *kaupīnadhārīs* and *balkaladhārīs*, and their relative positions were not defined. Thus, the situation was open and fluid, as well as susceptible to a variety of interpretations.

There was a crisis in Mahimā Dharma after the founder's death. Many *āśritas* reverted to their earlier faiths; the *āśramas* of Malabiharpur and the *tuṅgī* of Jorandā were sold by the government as intestate property; and the few belongings of Mahimā Svāmī at Banki were auctioned. In this extraordinary situation, *sannyāsīs, bhaktas* and *āśritas* met at a council in Jorandā in 1876. In the absence of the founder and without any consensus about a leader to succeed him, without any scripture or systematic written document to follow, they searched for ways and means to overcome the critical situation. They decided to build one *Samādhi Mandira* of the guru at Jorandā. In the absence of the guru his *Samādhi Mandira*, or *Gadi*, became the focal point. Land and donations from *bhaktas* and sympathizers were sought, and within a year the temple was ready.

This initiated a new phase in the history of Mahimā Dharma. The founder who had fought against rituals and acquisition of landed property and against any permanent structure was interred in concrete. As time rolled on, Mahimā Svāmī became a legendary figure. His *samādhi* became the heart of Mahimā Dharma. Jorandā, the village where it was located, became the pilgrimage centre for Mahimā followers. In addition to the *Samādhi Mandira*, there was a need to accommodate *bhaktas*, sympathisers and others during their visits to the pilgrimage centre. The *bhaktas'* enthusiasm to gain *puṇya* (merit) by contributing to the guru's cause resulted in lavish donations both in cash and kind. *Āśramas* and *tuṅgīs* were built in large numbers at Jorandā. Gradually, all places associated with the life of Mahimā Svāmī were considered sacred and *mandiras* were built and worshipped as *Dhuni Mandira* or *Śūnya Mandira*.[5]

This institutionalization of *āśramas, tuṅgīs* and *mandiras* was the beginning of a semi-sedentary life as opposed to the former itinerant life for every wandering *sannyāsī*. Here was a clear shift of emphasis, which resulted in partial distancing between *sannyāsīs* and *āśritas or bhaktas*. Rather than *sannyāsīs* visiting the *āśritas*, now the *āśritas* were invited to visit the pilgrimage centre at least once annually during *guru purṇimā* (full moon day of *Māgha*, January–February) dedicated to the guru. Perhaps it was because social interaction got confined to a particular place and specific times of a year that framing of rules and regulations became essential.

The permanent structures at Jorandā, landed property and the development and maintenance of *mahimā gadi* (or pilgrim centre), the performance of *sevā pūjā* and *nīti* or daily rituals required rules and regulations. They also needed some semi-sedentary *sannyāsīs* to perform *nīti*. Mahimā Dharmīs had to formulate a set of rules and decide whether *nīti* should be performed by the *balkaladhārīs*. This brought in the additional problems of deciding on how the ritual services were to be performed. Should the ascetics take turns at different times of the year to offer the services, should they be allowed to stay at one place for a length of time in order to perform *nīti* and, finally, who would be the competent authority to formulate these rules—should the decisions be taken by all collectively, or only by the senior *sannyāsīs*?

Organization and Institutionalization

Since *sannyāsīs* were supposed to travel from place to place (though some had to stay back at the *gadi*) and come together just once a year, there was need to convene a *satsaṅga*, or a communal meeting during the annual festival of *Guru Purṇimā*. As there is theoretically no distinction between *sannyāsīs* and *āśritas*, they sit and eat together in this gathering (Banerjee-Dube, 1993; Eschmann, 1978). Before they are allowed to take part in the *satsaṅga*, each aspiring participant has to go through questioning conducted by senior ascetics, confess to any infringement of rules and undergo *prāyaś-citta* (penance) if there have been infringements.[6] Sometimes they have to pay a fine and in case of serious breach of rules have to relinquish Mahimā Dharma. The latter punishment is specially meant for the *sannyāsīs* in case of murder, theft or violation of the rules of celibacy (Biswanath Baba, 1935).

As mentioned earlier, Mahimā Svāmī had initiated two orders of *sannyāsīs* without specifying their relative positions. Relations between the two orders were strained during the lifetime of Mahimā Svāmī, but they had not reached the level of an open conflict. The death of the Svāmī signalled the beginning of the rift. Whereas Jorandā gradually became the centre of a properly regulated monastic order where celibacy was strictly observed, Bhima Bhoi, in the year 1877, built an *āśrama* at Khaliapali, Bolangir, where women were accepted as lay followers of the Dharma. Bhima Bhoi lived with five female companions, three of them spiritual and two worldly. He did not visit Jorandā after he set up his own *āśrama* and started leading the life of a householder, allowing women entry into his *āśrama*.

Let us now turn to the trouble between the two groups of ascetics that arose over their relative position. The *balkaladhārīs* claimed a superior status over *kaupīnadhārīs* on the grounds that the Guru Mahimā Svāmī himself and his first disciple Govinda Baba wore *balkala*. This claim was opposed by *kaupīṇadhārīs* on the ground that they too, like the *balkaladhārīs*, were ordained by the Guru himself. Moreover, in the early stage of his life Mahimā Svāmī wore *kaupīna*, and his second important *śiṣya* Nrusingha Baba also wore the waist cloth. So, according to them, *kaupīna* was the *ādi-bana* (first garment) of the guru.

An important development took place in Mahimā Dharma in 1896, a year after the death of Bhima Bhoi. Up to 1896, no new *sannyāsīs* had been initiated as per the decision taken by Mahimā Svāmī two years before his death. But in 1896, the last of the first line of *balkaladhārīs*, the *siddha* Nanda Baba, received a *śūnya-*

bāṇī (a voice from void) to ordain new *sannyāsīs* amongst the probationers who had joined the order. Accordingly, 200 *sannyāsīs* were initiated over the next 16 years (Biswanath Baba, 1935, 306–7).

In 1912, the same *siddha* received another *śūnyabāṇī* to promote 56 *kaupīnadhārī sannyāsīs* and grant them *kumbhipaṭ*. However, Krupasindhu Baba, another *kumbhīpaṭadhārī siddha*, suspected the claims of Nanda Baba. He opposed the decision of Nanda Baba to award *balkalas* to some *kaupīnadhārī sannyāsīs* and managed to get the support of the raja of Dhenkanal state in this matter. Nanda Baba and his followers were asked to leave the Mahimā *gadi*; but a few years later, another *siddha*, Anama Baba, gave *balkala* to thirty-three *sannyāsīs*. Some followers close to Krupasindhu Baba insisted that he should also award *balkala* to his close followers. In disgust, he gave them *balkala* but left Jorandā. So there emerged within *balkaladhārīs* four groups, called *chapanamūrtis* (fifty-six persons), *tetismūrtis* (thirty-three persons), *kodiamūrtis* (twenty persons), and a fourth which opposed the award of *balkala*. The promotion of *sannyāsīs* gave them new motivation. They took on the duty of propagating the faith with great energy. The guru's teaching was reinterpreted and festivals were celebrated with vigour. New *āśramas* and *maṭhas* were built. Biswanath Baba occupied the centrestage among the new *balkaladhārīs* in all these developments.

Biswanath Baba

The next important phase of Mahimā Dharma's history was marked by the influence of Biswanath Baba. At the age of 13 he received the *kaupīna*, and in 1925, when he was 21 he was initiated as a *kumbhīpaṭia*. In the 1920s and 1930s, he wrote *Mahimā Dharma Pratipādaka* and *Satya Mahimā Dharmara Itihāsa* (published in 1931 and 1935 respectively). For the first time, Sanskrit *śāstras* were quoted to establish Mahimā Svāmī as *Īśwara Puruṣa* and *Prabuddha Avatāra*. The *Itihāsa* states that the first person to locate Mahimā Svāmī while the latter was in *nirbikalpa samādhi* at the top of the Kapilāś hill was Sadananda Sabar. Sadananda saw a seven-headed serpent spreading its hood over the Svāmī and immediately recognized him as *Īśwara Puruṣa*. He was the first to obtain the right to supply fruits for 12 years to the Svāmī during his *sādhanā* (meditation). Here is a clear reflection of the Jagannātha myth as *sabara devatā*. This description is not there in Bhima Bhoi's writing. This is new information added by Biswanath Baba. His *Itihāsa* also displays the *mahimā* of the Svāmī in curing the sick, giving life to the dead and many more miraculous activities.

The *Itihāsa* draws upon symbols embedded in diverse traditions of Orissa to create a mythic tradition for Mahimā Dharma and to give the faith a legitimate past. Mahimā Svāmī evolved from an ordinary *sannyāsī* to become a pure incarnation of *Alekha Parama Brahma, Prabuddha Swāmi* and *Īśwara Puruṣa*. Biswanath Baba deeply influenced the *kumbhīpaṭia* group. As stated before, he re-interpreted the teachings of Mahimā Svāmī, giving preference to Sanskrit texts such as *Vedanta* and *Bhāgavata Purāṇa* as 'spiritual proof'. In the process, the anti-establishment orientation of the early phase gradually subsided. *Brahma-upāsanā*, worship of the Absolute, was declared to be the most important aim of the Dharma. Mahimā Dharma came closer to high Hinduism and its existence became acceptable to 'Oriya–Hindu' society.

The followers of Mahimā Dharma, or *Brahma-upāsakas* as they came to be called, were broadly divided into two categories: the *bābās* (or *abadhūtas,* or ascetics) and the *gṛhīs* (or householders). *Sannyāsīs* were expected to possess such qualities as simplicity, mercy, calmness, pure body and mind, and selflessness. They were placed higher than *gṛhīs*. A *kaupīnadhārī sannyāsī* or an *apara sannyāsī* was one who had renounced the world and material comfort, internalized Mahimā Svāmī's teachings and understood their deep meaning. It was at a later stage that these *sannyāsīs* would become capable of receiving *balkala*. So *apara sannyāsīs* wore *kaupīṇa* and *para sannyāsīs* wore *balkala*.

Thus, a clear distinction was established between *kaupīnadhārīs* and *balkaladhārīs*, placing the latter at a spiritually higher level. This interpretation came along with the construction of new architectural structures and with the expansion of the *Gādi Mandira*.

At the beginning, the *Gādi Mandira* was a simple *samādhi*, open from all sides. Later, a small wall was built over it. In the first decade of the twentieth century, a big temple was built over the smaller one with a boundary wall that had four gates.

According to the information given by Biswanath Baba in his *Itihāsa,* the *mandira* was built according to the desire of the vision of Anama Das Baba, a *balkaladhārī abadhūta*. Nanda Baba offered the first *nīti* or daily rituals at this temple (Biswanath Baba, 1947: 7). The design of the temple, the right to perform *nīti*, the procedure for the offering, the right of entry into the inner sanctum and management of *gadi* were all monopolized by the *balkaladhārīs*. The job of the *kaupīnadhārīs* was to sweep and clean the outer compound (ibid.: 8). The norms and hierarchies of Mahimā Dharma were gradually becoming rigid.

In the year 1929, Krupasindhu Baba returned to Jorandā. He refused to join the *balkaladhārīs* and built a small *tuṅgī* near the *Gādi Mandira* (ibid.: 151). Now *kaupīnadhārīs* and the dissatisfied *sannyāsīs* who had been denied *balkala* started rallying behind Krupasindhu Baba. His *tuṅgī* became the pivot of a separate order—the *Kaupīnadhārī Samāja*. Krupasindhu Baba took the help of the king of Dhenkanal and was able to shift the *akhaṇḍabati* (eternal flame) of the guru to a place of his choice.

The *balkaladhārīs* treated all these developments with contempt. They did not like the emergence of a rival order at the nerve centre; that is, the guru's *gadi*. They lost faith in the traditional way of solving disputes and finally, in 1930, took the case to the court of law. They sued Krupasindhu Baba for building *tuṅgīs, āśramas* and a *Dhuni Mandira* within the *gadi* compound. They appealed for the demolition of the structures built by Krupasindhu and to issue an injunction against any new construction. This created the final breach between the *balkaladhārī*s and *kaupīnadhārīs* and led to the establishment of two rival *samājas* to mobilize resources and gather strength for the legal battle. These *samājas,* over time, organized themselves with their own sets of rules and ways of interpreting the guru's teachings. The requirements of law compelled each to explain its own views and standpoint. They had to form managing committees and, in order to mobilize public support, had to produce texts and counter-texts. Thus, we see proliferation of Mahimā literature. Now each *samāja* has its own *paricālana samitis* (management committees) to supervise its work, with *adhyakṣas* (officials) and *sampādakas* (secretaries) and with definite rules and regulations.

Conclusion

At present, followers of Mahimā Dharma are to be found in every district of Orissa; but it is impossible to ascertain their exact number because the census does not enumerate them separately. They are also spread in the neighbouring states such as Chhattisgarh, Jharkhand, Bihar, Bengal, Madhya Pradesh, Andhra Pradesh and Assam. Moreover, *āśramas* and *tuṅgīs* of the faith number over 2,000 in Orissa. These not only provide shelter to the ever-mobile Mahimā ascetics, but also function as organs for the propagation of Mahimā Dharma. Therefore, these shelters, which were in an obscure state during the lifetime of Mahimā Svāmī, achieved an important status later. With the spread of Mahimā Dharma, these *tuṅgīs* and *āśramas* became important centres of activity and received patronage from followers. In the 1870s, there were hardly five such shelters in Orissa. According to a survey conducted by Eschmann in the 1970s (Eschmann, 1978: 387), the number had increased to 1,372, and our survey in 1994 recorded 2,157 *tuṅgīs* and *āśramas* in Orissa (Deo, 1999a: 142).

To sum up, Mahimā Dharma initially became popular among the lower segments of caste society and *ādivāsis* in the nineteenth century because of its anti-establishment, iconoclastic and radical orientation that mainly derived from the teachings of Mahimā Svāmī and his followers. However, it later managed to institutionalize its own sectarian organizational structures. Regardless of the pull and pressure of competing *samājas* and their sub-groups, Mahimā Dharma spread widely throughout Orissa and its neighbouring states in the twentieth century and has remained alive to the present day. The faith has adapted, and continues to adapt, to the changing historical circumstances. Therefore, its institutionalization remains an ongoing process.

Notes

1. On the spot where Mahimā Svāmī, the founder of Mahimā Dharma, breathed his last, a temple called *Śūnya Mandira* was built, which is completely empty. The *Dhuni Mandira* serves as one of the sacred temples of Mahimā followers. It contains a sacred fire which is ever-burning. According to popular belief, Mahimā Svāmī lit the *anāhata dhuni* or inextinguishable fire. The ashes of the fire are also considered sacred. The *Samādhi Mandira* is also known as *Gādi Mandira*. *Gadi* means seat or throne, but here it has been used as equivalent to the burial place (*samādhi*) of the saint. *Nīti* means daily rituals and *nīti baba* is a *sannyāsī* who performs these rituals.
2. Jagannath Temple Correspondence, Acc. no. 438, 441, 4465, Orissa State Archives.
3. This was informed by the *sannyāsīs and bhaktas* during the author's field study; see also Sahu's (1992) edition of Bhima Bhoi's works.
4. The author collected the information during the *Māgha Pūrṇimā* festival (February–March 1994).
5. Jorandā has several *maṭhas* or monasteries. *Balkaladhārīs* have built two big *maṭhas* called *baḍa maṭha* and *latā āśrama*. These *maṭhas* were built on the boundaries of two villages. This enables the *sannyāsīs* to stay for a longer period without breaking the norms set by Mahimā Svāmī. Within *baḍa maṭha*, there are several *tuṅgīs* for ascetics, rooms for pilgrims, a library, Sanskrit *ṭol* (school), a *bhanḍāra* (granary), a big meeting hall and a storeroom. The northern gate is very large and is called *singhadwāra* (lion gate). Near *Gadi Mandira* the *kaupīnadhārīs* have built their own *Śūnya Mandira* and *Dhuni Mandira*. They have their own *maṭhas*, the most important being the one just in front of the *Gadi Mandira*, known as *Sana Maṭha*. There is also a *Mātā Maṭha*, for women ascetics.
6. The author attended one such *satsaṅga* in 1994 at Jorandā during a field visit.

References

Asiatic Society of Bengal (1881–2), *Proceedings of the Asiatic Society of Bengal*, November 1881, pp. 145–57, January 1882, pp. 2–6.

Banerjee-Dube, Ishita (1993), 'Religion and Society in Orissa: Mahima Dharma in the Nineteenth and Twentieth Centuries', Ph.D. thesis, Calcutta University.

Biswanath Baba (1931), *Mahimā Dharma Pratipādaka* (Oriya), Cuttack: Dharmagrantha Store.

——— (1935), *Mahimā Dharmara Itihāsa* (Oriya), Cuttack: Dharmagrantha Store.

Das, Chittaranjan (1950), 'Studies in Medieval Religion & Literature in Orissa', in *Visva-Bharati Annals*, 3, pp. 107–87.

——— (1952), *Odisāra Mahimā Dharma* (Oriya), Calcutta: Viswabharati.

Deo, Fanindam (1999a), 'Institutionalization and Organizational Aspects of Mahima Dharma', in J.T. O'Connell (ed.), *Organisational and Institutional Aspects of Indian Religious Movements*, New Delhi/ Simla: Manohar/IIAS, pp. 137–51.

——— (1999b), 'Socio-Political Changes in Nineteenth Century Orissa & the Rise of Mahima Dharma', *Studies in Humanities & Social Sciences*, 6, 1, pp. 19–32.

Eschmann, A. (1978), 'Mahima Dharma: An Autochthonous Hindu Reform Movement', in A. Eschmann, H. Kulke and G.C. Tripathi (eds.), *The Cult of Jagannath and the Regional Tradition of Orissa*, New Delhi: South Asia Institute/Manohar, pp. 375–410.

Jena, K.C. (1978), *Socio Economic Condition of Orissa*, New Delhi: Sundeep Prakashan.

Kulke, H. (1978), 'Early Royal Patronage of Jagannath Cult', in A. Eschmann, H. Kulke and G.C. Tripathi (eds.), *The Cult of Jagannath and the Regional Tradition of Orissa,* New Delhi: South Asia Institute/Manohar, pp. 139–55.

——— (1993), *Kings and Cults*, New Delhi: Manohar.

Lorenzen, David N. (ed.) (1995), *Bhakti Religion in North India*, Albany: State University of New York Press.

Nepak, N.B. 1974. *Kabi Bhima Bhoi o Mahimā Dharma Parichaya*, Bhubaneswar: Bhagirathi Prakashan.

O'Connell, J.T. (1999), 'Introduction', in J.T. O'Connel (ed.), *Organisational and Institutional Aspects of Indian Religious Movements*, New Delhi/Simla: Manohar/IIAS, pp. 1–10.

Pal, K. (1994), *Kaupīnadhārī Samāja Dharmadhama Itihāsa*, Bhawanipatna.

Pattnaik, S. (1961), 'Orissa in 1867', *Orissa Historical Research Journal*, 10, 3, pp. 61–73.

Sahu, K. (ed.) (1992), *Bhima Bhoi Granthabali*, Cuttack: Dharmagrantha Store.

Schomer, Karine and W.H. McLeod (eds.) (1987), *The Sants: Studies in a Devotional Tradition of India*, New Delhi: Motilal Banarsidass.

CHAPTER 10

Changing Contours of Mahimā Dharma: Bhima Bhoi and Biswanath Baba

ISHITA BANERJEE-DUBE*

In roughly 140 years of its existence, Mahimā Dharma has undergone mutations as it has evolved and taken shape as a sect. Initiated by Mahima Swami in the 1860s in the tributary states of Orissa, this faith has moved from being a loose body of adherents of a radical, mobile preceptor to a well-coordinated institutionalized religious order with definite rituals and ceremonies and prescribed codes of conduct. This paper will use the words and works of two key figures of Mahimā Dharma—Bhima Bhoi and Biswanath Baba—as a prism to understand, on the one hand, the interface between the works of the two leaders and their interpretation by the followers; and on the other, between their practices and the shifts in emphases within Mahimā Dharma.

Marginality and militancy characterized Mahimā Dharma in its initial phase. Appearing in Puri, Mahimā Svāmī toured the areas under direct British administration before deciding on Kapilāś in the tributary state of Dhenkanal as his place of meditation. The far-flung territories of the *garhjats* (tributary states under Oriya rulers) were also the regions where he moved and preached the new faith from 1862 until his death in 1875–6.[1] His message was simple yet significant: worship of stone and wooden images of gods was meaningless; the real object of veneration was a formless, all-powerful, indescribable (*alekha*) Absolute who had created the world out of his *mahimā* (radiance/glory). Anyone could have access to the Absolute through pure devotion. There was no need for priests and pilgrimage; hierarchy among human beings was artificial and superfluous.

The founder's disregard for property, authority, establishment and discrimination was articulated in his practices. He was constantly on the move; he neither constructed any permanent structure as his place of residence nor acquired property. He slept on bare ground, ate only one meal a day received as *bhikṣā* in a broken earthen pot, and forbade his disciples to accept anything but cooked rice as alms, thereby rooting out any tendency to accumulate. Cooked rice was to be accepted from every household without regard for caste; only the Brāhmaṇ, the raja, the barber and the washerman were denied the privilege of granting alms to the ascetics of Mahimā Dharma. Mahimā Svāmī nominated no successor and left no written records of his own. Instead, he endowed Bhima Bhoi, his tribal devotee, with the gift of knowledge and poetry and entrusted him with the task of propagation of the faith through his inspired utterances. Bhima Bhoi played a crucial role in the two decades that spanned the death of the founder till his own death in 1895.

Reading Bhima Bhoi

Bhima Bhoi is a colourful figure, an iconoclastic poet difficult to be defined only in relation to the dictates of a single faith. Believed to have been born blind to poor Khond parents, Bhima had a difficult childhood and never received any formal education.[2] He had, however, recourse to 'traditional' modes of education and imbibed a great deal by listening to the readings, recitations and interpretations of the epics and popular religious texts at communal gatherings in the village. *Bhajanas* (devotional songs) and songs recounting the love of Rādhā and Kṛṣṇa opened for him the doors to Vaiṣṇava and Bhakti philosophy. The influence of various religious traditions, apprehended aurally and orally, crucially shaped Bhima Bhoi's thought and ideas. Throughout his life he remained rooted in the rich oral tradition of Orissa, a tradition he drew upon and enriched.

By stressing Bhima Bhoi's lack of formal education and his

integral association with the oral tradition, I do not intend to reinforce the dubious dichotomy between orality and writing that translates as illiteracy and literacy, with writing being accorded a privileged and an elevated position. Rather, my purpose is to underscore the complex relation between reading and writing, orality and literacy that occasions the creation of new texts in the process of dissemination through joint renderings. This is particularly true of Bhima Bhoi, a poet-devotee, who has over the course of the twentieth century risen to the status of a saint, and who, like the Pancasakhās (Five Friends)—the five medieval mystics—has had texts composed in his name.

A blend of the oral and the written inheres in the composition and diffusion of Bhima Bhoi's works. Bhima Bhoi, the ardent poet, sang out his praises to the Lord. Four scribes wrote down these inspired utterances, which were then sung at common gatherings of the devotees. The contents of the numerous *stutis, jaṇānas,* and *bhajanas*, inflected with the intensity of personal communication with the Master of the world, who was also the poet's own guru, made Bhima Bhoi and his works immensely accessible and variously appropriable.[3] Reflecting an ingenious combination of the precepts of Mahimā Svāmī and different religious-philosophical traditions of Orissa, these works speak of an *alekha* (beyond writing/indescribable), all-pervading, *nirguṇa* (beyond attributes) Absolute—the Creator of the world—as the only object of devotion. Pure devotion makes this distant and difficult-to-comprehend Supreme attainable by all.

High philosophy was thus transformed into a popular message of hope that denounced social discrimination, idol-worship and the mediation of Brāhmaṇs between the deity and devotees. Bhima Bhoi stayed with the followers and 'readers' all along, at times speaking passionately of his own woes and sorrows, trials and triumphs as a devotee; at others, guiding other devotees along the path of *nirveda sādhanā* (meditation/worship not outlined in the Vedas), which if followed properly and sincerely would lead to salvation. Moreover, Bhima Bhoi impressed on the followers the urgency of taking recourse to the true faith by speaking repeatedly about the perils of the evil era of *kali*, which had cast an iron grip over the world. This preponderance of the everyday concept-metaphor of *kaliyuga* aligned Bhima Bhoi's works to the ever-present and ever-popular *mālikās* and made them amenable to diverse perceptions and understandings. *Mālikās*, apocryphal texts that speak of the vileness of *kaliyuga* and the assured end of the evils of the age at the hands of an incarnation of Viṣṇu, have been a part of the Oriya popular (Vaiṣṇavite) tradition since the sixteenth century. Comprising prophesies of a vague and general nature and lacking a strong authorial voice, *mālikās* are reinterpreted as they make their appearance in different times of stress. At the same time, their authorship is ascribed to the Pancasakhās, a fact that lends credibility to the prophecies, demonstrating the hold of the medieval mystics over Oriya popular imagination. Bhima Bhoi, whose works bear a close resemblance to that of the Pancasakhās, and whose simple message of salvation in *kaliyuga* through devotion to the Supreme holds a wide appeal for subordinate groups of men and women, became a true successor of the Five Friends in the veneration he commanded.

Bhima Bhoi's colourful life added to the mystique and charisma that surrounded him. After Mahimā Svāmī's death, the poet severed association with ascetics who sought to keep the faith together by constructing a memorial for the guru at Jorandā in Dhenkanal. Bhima set up his own *āśrama* (sanctuary) at Khaliapali in Sonepur, cohabited with more than one woman, and went beyond his preceptor's tenets by allowing women into the monastic order. If this incensed the renouncers at Jorandā and caused confusion among some of his followers, it also generated a stock of legends and stories about the enigmatic poet, who came to take the place of the founder among the adherents of western Orissa.[4] Stories of his birth and his deep devotion leading to his initiation into Mahimā Dharma by Mahimā Svāmī increased in number and attained new dimensions, becoming the stuff of legend soon after his death. Bhima Bhoi's elevation to the status of a saint began.

The vernacular literature was the first to record this beatification. In 1908, a senior official of the court of Sonepur wrote an essay entitled 'Bhima Bhoi's Acquisition of Knowledge'. In parenthesis, he called it 'A Legend'. Published in the Oriya literary magazine *Mukura*, the essay strived to make Bhima Bhoi and 'his religion' known to readers (cited in Dash, 1997). In a very interesting turn of events, Bhima Bhoi's fall into the well, an incident widely believed to have occurred during Mahimā Svāmī's time, indeed a marker of Bhima Bhoi's devotion that induced Mahimā Svāmī to initiate him, was stated to have happened after the disappearance of Mahimā Svāmī. Distressed by the pitiful state of the faith, a distraught Bhima called out to the formless Alekha and jumped into a well. He heard a voice near the well asking Bhima to hold his hand and climb out of the well to avoid death. But the thought of death was not what troubled the earnest devotee. Indeed, death was much less painful than the pang of witnessing the erasure of the name of Alekha from the world.

The number of Alekha's devotees was painfully small and it was dwindling day by day. There was no written text to help people concentrate on the worship of Alekha and gain solace. 'Were all the efforts of the guru going to be in vain?' Hearing Bhima Bhoi's words, the voice asked him why he, a fervent follower, was blaming others instead of making the effort to put the guru's deeds in writing. But for Bhima Bhoi it was an impossible task to carry out. He was ignorant, with no knowledge of the letters, and blind. How could he write about the glories of Alekha that the guru had preached, which was difficult for even learned men to understand? At that, the owner of the voice lifted Bhima Bhoi out of the well, set him on the right path and addressed him as the 'guru of the *bhaktas* (devotees)'. The vision of truth was conferred on Bhima. The precepts of 'Mahima Das' and the essence of his faith were to blossom in Bhima's heart in the form of *prakruta* songs. He needed only to utter, scribes were to commit them to writing. Mahimā Dharma would gain fame and popularity through Bhima who would spend the remainder of his life serving at the feet of the Lord.

The 'legend' published in the Oriya magazine added distinct emphases to the tale of Bhima Bhoi and Mahimā Dharma. The absence of written texts was taken to be the main cause for the crisis of the faith. Bhima Bhoi was the person selected to deal with the crisis. He was granted inner sight by dint of which the essence of the teachings of Mahima Das were to burst forth from him in the form of *prakruta* songs. Indicating a shift from the oral to the written, the essay nevertheless underscored the spontaneity of Bhima Bhoi's creations. It also brought to focus the importance Bhima Bhoi had come to acquire among the followers in western Orissa. Within a few years of Mahimā Svāmī's death, he had become the key figure in the propagation of Mahimā Dharma, the real 'guru of the *bhaktas*'. Mahima Das had preached it no doubt, but it was Bhima Bhoi who saved the faith from extinction, and aided the interpretation and proliferation of its message in a way as to become its real leader.

This essay was soon followed by N.N. Vasu's (1911) influential text in English[5] that sought to establish Mahimā Dharma as a neo-Buddhist sect and Bhima Bhoi as its main proponent who in 1881 had led the march of some lay followers of Mahimā Dharma to the temple of Jagannātha in Puri to destroy the idols. Official reports of the incident of 1881 do not, in any way, associate Bhima Bhoi with the 'attack'.[6] Present-day adherents of Mahimā Dharma vigorously deny any connection of Bhima Bhoi with the incident.[7] At the same time, Vasu's text, written within 15 years of Bhima Bhoi's death, bears testimony not only to the poet's hold on the minds of the adherents, but also to the way his works had been perceived and comprehended. The link between Bhima Bhoi's declaration that Jagannātha had left Puri to become Mahimā Svāmī's first disciple[8] and the long march of a small group of anonymous men and women from western Orissa to the temple to destroy the lifeless image ensconced there and demonstrate that Jagannātha had indeed left Puri, is after all, not tenuous. The dramatic incident revealed at once the spread and reach of Bhima Bhoi's compositions and the force of particular readings that armed ordinary, marginal men and women with the strength to carry out an audacious and almost unimaginable task. A divine command communicated through a dream convinced them of the necessity of the difficult task they had to undertake in order to counter the setback to the faith caused by the death of the founder.

The appeal and influence of Bhima Bhoi's works were highlighted again in the first half of the twentieth century, when *mālikās* in the name of Bhima Bhoi made their appearance.[9] Mahimā Dharma had survived the death of Mahimā Svāmī through the presence of the powerful personality of Bhima Bhoi and also through the construction of a memorial for the guru at Jorandā. In the 1920s, the faith was threatened by dissension among the ascetics at the helm of affairs in Jorandā. The crisis within the faith coincided with a very enthusiastic phase of the nationalist struggle against colonial rule under the leadership of Gandhi.[10] Stories about the 'Mahātmā' blended with the teachings of Bhima Bhoi to give rise to apocryphal texts that prophesied the reappearance of Mahimā Svāmī as Gandhi and Kalki to root out the forces of *kali* (the British) and re-establish *satya dharma.* An ingenious amalgam of myth and history, orality and writing, linear and cyclical notions of time, these *mālikās* brought together gods and saints, legendary heroes and political leaders as soldiers of the Absolute to fight the *mahābhārata* (epic) war of *kaliyuga* and bring to an end the era of evil by annihilating its forces—the resourceful, manipulative and exploitative British—as well as the 'fake' followers of Mahimā Dharma who were threatening the true faith with their divisive tendencies.

Bhima Bhoi did not compose the *mālikās* that mention twentieth-century personalities and also vary significantly in style and content from his works. But they seize upon an important component of the creations of Bhima Bhoi—the perils of the pervasive *kaliyuga,* and the call to all human beings to seek shelter in Mahimā Dharma without delay to avoid destruction. Combining the concern of the humanist poet-devotee with the prophecies of apocryphal texts, these *mālikas* at once urged the adherents of Mahimā Dharma to remain steadfast unto their faith and provided them with hope by promising a bright future. The crisis in the faith and the difficulties of the present were to be resolved by the reappearance of Mahimā Svāmī.

The appearance of *mālikās* over four decades after the incident of 1881 underscore the continued accessibility and efficacy of Bhima Bhoi's precepts and promulgations. The presence of thoughts and ideas drawn from popular religious traditions of Orissa and the use of the quotidian metaphor of *kaliyuga* made it easy for these difficult compositions to be easily apprehended and diversely deployed. The fact that they were first spoken, then written down and further disseminated through collective singing, lent them a unique force. They got reworked through different readings as they spread.[11] Bhima Bhoi became the poet-philosopher of ordinary, subordinate groups of men and women, whose message—responsive to different appropriations—remained a source of solace, support and strength for the marginal people. In spite of going beyond his guru's teachings, Bhima Bhoi maintained the preceptor's emphases in important ways.

Voices from the Periphery

Mahimā Svāmī had shunned property, authority and establishment. He had moved away from Puri, the centre of religio-political power, and preached his faith in the remote areas of the tributary states among the poor and common folk who predominantly came from the lower castes and tribes. Indeed, the Svāmī had refused to take alms from Brāhmaṇs, rajas, barbers and washermen, displaying his disdain for the repositories of power and their human instruments for the exercise of control. His constant mobility, complemented by total detachment, was a powerful statement against establishment.[12] It is not surprising then that Mahimā Svāmī left no written records of his own and entrusted the task to a blind, tribal person without any formal education, whom he graced both with the 'eye of knowledge' and with the gift of poetry. The blind devotee's inspired utterances were to be noted down, but they were to spread not through writing, but through collective reading and performance.

It was this stress on the oral, the everyday, the ordinary and the peripheral, and the challenge and interrogation inherent in them, that Bhima Bhoi's compositions preserved and carried forward. Although he set up his own *āśrama* and settled there permanently, and produced compositions that contained difficult philosophical concepts, Bhima Bhoi did not get 'sedentarized'. The combination of oral forms and written modes in the construction and dissemination of his works, the radical force of his message, and the surfeit of meanings and understandings it generated, kept Bhima Bhoi very close to the lay disciples of western Orissa, who turned to him again and again for comfort and consolation, encouragement and action. The location of Bhima Bhoi's *āśrama* in Khaliapali, Sonepur, at the edge of western Orissa, and its geographical distance both from Jorandā in Dhenkanal, which over the twentieth century emerged as the headquarters of Mahimā Dharma, and from the seats of ritual-political power, served to underline Bhima Bhoi's distance from the centre and establishment governed by rigid rules, and his proximity to the margins of society. Despite being canonized by the Oriya literati in the twentieth century, Bhima Bhoi has defied categorization. He has retained an inherent sense of the unexpected and the unbound that has preserved his hold over popular imagination and let his works be drawn upon in distinct and diverse contexts.

Writing History: Biswanath Baba

Let us now turn to Biswanath Baba, a leading ascetic who dominated the affairs of Mahimā Dharma at Jorandā from the late 1920s to the early 1990s. To a large extent, Biswanth Baba, a rigorous renouncer in the mould of the founder, typifies the shift in Mahimā Dharma. Like Bhima Bhoi, he took on the important task of ensuring the continuity of the faith and brought about significant changes in the process. Biswanath came to prominence at a critical moment in the life of Mahimā Dharma: when the faith was threatened by dissension and division.

Mahimā Svāmī had initiated two groups of ascetics into the monastic order. He had given *kumbhipata* (the bark of the *kumbhi* tree, which is what he wore) to some and *kaupīna* (waist-cloth) to others while initiating them. Although there is some indication that there was occasional conflict between the wearers of *balkala* (bark) and those of *kaupīna*, it did not assume any significant proportion during the lifetime of the founder. The relative position of the two groups did not become a major issue. The crisis produced by the death of the deified guru aggravated tensions, but the more pressing problem of the survival of the faith made the two groups of ascetics work together to first construct the *samādhi* (memorial) of the preceptor and then to turn it into the repository of the guru's authority. The memorial was intended to compensate for the absence of a nominated successor or a universally accepted leader.

It was precisely the importance acquired by the *samādhi* over time that brought the two groups of renouncers again into conflict. The wearers of *balkala* (*balkaladhārīs*), by virtue of the fact that the founder wore *balkala* and made it the garb of his first disciple, claimed superiority over the wearers of *kaupīna* (*kaupīnadhārīs*) and sought to monopolize control over the conduct of services and ceremonies at the *samādhi*, the *gadi* (seat) of the faith. The *kaupīnadhārīs* challenged this claim by arguing that the guru, who was opposed to all kinds of discrimination, had never introduced any gradation among his disciples. The disagreement reached a climax when Nanda Baba, a prominent *balkaladhārī*, promoted 56 of his disciples from the status of the wearers of *kaupīna* to the wearers of *balkala*, underlining the inferior status of *kaupīnadhārīs*.[13] The act was said to have been based on the command of the guru. But it was challenged by another eminent *balkaladhārī sannyāsī*, Krupasindhu Baba, who ordered the new wearers of *balkala* to move out of the inner compound of the *gadi*.

This was the beginning of a long story of friction and conflict that eventually involved the mediation of law and turned the two groups of ascetics into contending litigants and permanent opponents, a process I have discussed elsewhere (Banerjee-Dube, 1999). Here I mention this only to trace the immediate background of Biswanath's rise to prominence within Mahimā Dharma. Still in his twenties, he was the most outstanding of the 56 *sannyāsīs* granted *balkala* by Nanda Baba. Born to Mahimā Dharmī parents, Biswanath had come into the fold of the faith at a young age and he had also made his mark as a scholar. He was the best suited to lead the new group threatened with expulsion by a direct disciple of Mahimā Svāmī. He performed his job well.

Krupasindhu was forced to leave Jorandā and go on a long tour. At the same time, as a person devoted to the faith, the young ascetic was concerned not only with consolidating his position and that of the newly ordained *balkaladhārīs*, but also with mitigating the danger posed to the faith by disharmony among the *sannyāsīs*. It became more severe once Krupasindhu returned to Jorandā and formed the nucleus of a rival order, as several disaffected *kaupīnadhārī sannyāsīs* gathered around him. The new leaders of the *balkaladhārīs* adopted several measures to counter the threat to the faith: they sought to widen the social base of the Mahimā Dharma faith among the urban middle classes: they moved to the law court to settle the dispute, and tried to prove their claim to be the sole interpreters of the guru's teachings through a display of their scholarship. Biswanath Baba again took the lead in this regard. He had acquired a reputation as a scholar among the renouncers. What was required was a demonstration of that scholarship. The guru himself directed the new leader. Biswanath Baba's *Mahimā Dharma Pratipādaka* owed its publication 'to the grace of Mahima Mahaprabhu' (Nath, 1977: 4).[14]

Mahimā Dharma Pratipādaka (Biswanath Baba, 1931), as the name suggests, was geared towards an exposition of the teachings of Mahimā Svāmī and the main tenets of the faith. The exposition addressed scholars and people of intellect—the ones capable of judging the efficacy of the faith by testing it against reason and truth (ibid.: 2). Consequently, the proof of each statement was sought to be corroborated by citations from scriptures and texts of Indian philosophy. Mahimā Svāmī, described as *prabuddha avatāra* and *īśwara puruṣa*, was shown to have the special features of *avatāras* and *īśwara puruṣas* outlined in Hindu scriptures. Quotations from the *śāstras* were profusely used, and citations were followed by translations. The author's mastery of Sanskrit was displayed along with his understanding of the *śāstras*. The discussion of the founder's *svarūpa* was followed by an eclectic interpretation of the terms *mahimā* and *dharma*. The next six chapters elaborated the teachings of the Dharma and their implications for the various categories of *bhaktas*. Brahma *Upāsanā* (worship of the indescribable Absolute) was declared to be the highest form of worship and the primary principle of the Dharma. Prayers and supplication to gods and goddesses and their idols, it was argued with the help of the *śāstras*, were inferior modes of worship.

The initiates in the path of Brahmā *Upāsanā* were divided into two categories: the *gruhīs* (lay disciples) and *avadhūtāśrama sannyāsīs* (renouncers who would eventually become *avadhūtas*, the highest form of being). *Sannyāsīs* were again of two orders: lower and higher; the *apara* and the *para*. *Apara sannyāsīs* rose to the status of *para sannyāsīs* only when they attained self-realization. This realization dawned—very much in the Advaita Vedantic tradition of Śankaracharya—with the consciousness of attaining or being Brahma (Biswanath Baba, 1931). It was the culmination of *Brahma-jñāna-bhakti yoga*. The *apara sannyāsīs* wore *kaupīna*, while the *para sannyāsīs* had the distinction of wearing *balkala*. The spiritually higher status of the *balkaladhārīs* was established as a fact, and there was no hint of any tussle, of clearly drawn battle lines. This was hardly surprising. Biswanath Baba could not afford any ambivalence about the matter. The *balkaladhārīs*' credentials as the leaders of the faith were at stake.

The *Pratipādaka* was followed by *Satya Mahimā Dharmara Itihāsa* (Biswanath Baba, 1935), the first formal, official history of the sect. Composed partly as a response to the law court's requirement of written records as evidence, the *Itihāsa* provided the followers of Mahimā Dharma with an 'authentic' past in the mode of Western rational historiography and granted the guru the dignity of chronology and temporality. At the same time, it freely drew upon Purāṇic traditions of *itihāsa* to establish the divinity of the preceptor.[15] Mahimā Svāmī was situated within tradition but beyond history. Extending the concerns of the *Pratipādaka*, the *Itihāsa* discussed the self-willed *līlā* (sport) of the divine guru in a chronological sequence, explained the essence of the faith he preached, codified his teachings and demarcated the norms and rules he had laid down for the different categories of followers. Gradation among the *sannyāsīs* became an established fact, and the right of *balkaladhārīs* to conduct the services at the *gadi* and guide all adherents of the faith became a norm set by the founder. The attempt by *kaupīnadhārīs* to create a rival *samāja* was decried as an act that went against the teachings of Mahimā Svāmī. Through all this, Mahimā Dharma was brought close to high

Hinduism and declared to be *sanātana* Hindu Dharma, pristine Hinduism as it had existed prior to the advent of *kaliyuga*.

The *Pratipādaka*, *Itihāsa* and several others that followed not only made Biswanath Baba the leader of the *balkaladhārīs*, the group that commanded affairs at Jorandā; they also reflected and perpetrated mutations and shifts in emphases within Mahimā Dharma. Indeed, it is through these changes set in motion by processes in the twentieth century that Mahimā Dharma evolved as a sect, an institutionalized religious order. I now turn to these shifts and draw out their implications through a comparison between Bhima Bhoi and Biswanath Baba.

Critical Comparisons: Bhima Bhoi and Biswanath Baba

Bhima Bhoi and Biswanath Baba took on the leadership of the faith at moments of crisis. Both explained and interpreted the teachings of Mahimā Svāmī for the benefit of the followers. They also agreed on the basic tenets—belief in the one and only formless, indescribable Absolute as the sole redeemer of humanity, abandoning of the worship of gods and goddesses and rejection of the rules of caste—which find a prominent place in their writings. Both were ordained by the preceptor for the job. This is where the similarities end.

To begin with, Bhima Bhoi, a poor tribal without formal education, is widely believed by Mahimā Dharmīs to have been entrusted with the task of propagation of the faith by Mahimā Svāmī. The claim is made on behalf of Biswanath Baba by his middle-class sympathizers. Bhima Bhoi, as stated before, was a radical, passionate poet who defied categorization. Emotion is the key feature of his numerous *stutis*, *jānānas* and *bhajanas* that evoke a sense of complete devotion and total surrender, of utter abandon of an ardent devotee pouring his heart out to his master. There is no display of scholarship, no conscious effort to assume the prestigious role of the disseminator of the master's teachings. Sung out spontaneously by the poet, these devotional poems and songs circulated orally through group incantation of primarily non-literate followers. The emotive lyrical compositions drew upon a common stock of knowledge prevalent in popular religious traditions, and lent themselves to diverse interpretations and reworking. As his message was variously drawn upon, the poet's life became a source of legends. Bhima Bhoi the poet-philosopher became a saint in spite of leading the life of a householder. In life and legend, he remained on the threshold, leaning toward the marginal. Himself blessed by the guru, the poet continued to guide subordinate groups of men and women through pleasure and pain, happiness and sorrow.

In Biswanath Baba we encounter an adherent of an entirely different kind. Separated from Bhima Bhoi by a generation, he did not have the privilege of being initiated by Mahimā Svāmī. He was, however, born in a family of followers of the faith, and was attracted to the monastic order at a very early age. Biswanath, we are informed in the foreword of the *Pratipādaka,* wanted to renounce the world when he was only eight years old, but was refused permission by his parents. Disappointed, he persisted in his dedicated learning of Hindu scriptures till the age of eleven, when he was afflicted by a painful and incurable disease. Biswanath told his parents that the cure lay in his renunciation of the world. His parents were forced to grant him permission (Das, 1931). We have here the makings of a new kind of leader, who was both a devoted ascetic and a dedicated scholar. At the same time, his life had the touch of the magical. His initiation into the monastic order was divinely ordained. The blessing and direction of the divine master were to accompany all his subsequent ventures, most importantly, the publication of his texts. By composing these written texts, Biswanath Baba provided a signal service to his faith. He answered the need felt sorely both by the self-realized ascetics of Mahimā Dharma and its sympathizers among the Oriya literati, for authoritative treatises that would make 'the movement meaningful, provide an intellectual base and maintain stable continuity of the principles' (Nath, 1977: 2–3).

Biswanath Baba's scholarship was informed by a privileging of the written over the oral. He was no ardent poet, schooled in the informal modes of 'collective' education, but a serious scholar in the classical mould whose command of Sanskrit was the first step towards his mastery of Hindu scriptures. And it was this command and mastery that his texts displayed. The table of contents of *Mahimā Dharma Pratipādaka* carried a list of 185 *śrutis*, *śāstras* and other works cited in the text, works that supplemented, substantiated and justified Biswanath Baba's arguments at each step by providing the crucial *pramāṇa*, evidence held as important by schools of Indian philosophy. The text, of course, is not meant for memorized recitation by groups of non-literate devotees. It is aimed at people of intellect, capable of reading and reflecting in private, of using their power of reasoning to judge the truth of the statements in accordance with *pramāṇa* (Biswanath Baba, 1931: 2). The *Pratipādaka* underscores the venture of a detached scholar guiding formally educated followers along the path of salvation, laying down standards they should strive to attain, and inscribing the milestones on the path of self-realization. *Brahma-jñāna-bhakti* replaces Bhima Bhoi's *bhakti*; ascetics are ranked in accordance with the spiritual standard they have attained, and promotion comes as a reward for the attainment of spiritual superiority—gradation therefore becomes an integral part of the monastic order.

Bhima Bhoi and Biswanath Baba attended to different needs and performed different functions within Mahimā Dharma. Jorandā, the centre from its inception dominated by ascetics, held no attraction for Bhima Bhoi, a non-conformist poet of tribal descent who took to the life of a householder. Bhima Bhoi dissociated himself from the *Mahimā gadi*, aligned himself with the margin and became a very powerful force for lay followers, who respected him as their divine master and 'read' and used his works to great advantage.

Biswanath Baba, on the other hand, directed all his efforts to provide the faith with a strong centre. A learned scholar in Sanskrit and Hindu philosophy, he firmly believed in the efficacy of written texts and the necessity of spreading the faith among the middle classes, particularly those residing in Cuttack and Bhubaneswar, seats of intellectual and political power. His written texts were intended to impress, to teach by establishing the intellectual superiority of the author. *Śrutis* and *śāstras* were drawn upon profusely, both to substantiate Biswanath's arguments and to highlight his mastery of Hindu scriptures. Needless to say, this reliance on scriptures stood in marked contrast to Bhima Bhoi's writings, which criticized, ridiculed and dismissed the societal norms and rules laid down in the *śrutis* and *śāstras* and instead advocated *nirvedasādhana*. Biswanath, it bears pointing out, did not prescribe the reading of *śāstras* as a means to achieve self-realization. Indeed, knowledge acquired from the *śāstras* was declared to be useless once *ātmajñāna* (self-knowledge) and *brahmajñāna* (knowledge of Brahma) had been achieved. But the scriptures had to be studied, if only to realize their uselessness. *Jñāna* (knowledge) thus came to constitute a necessary and at times the more important companion of *bhakti* (devotion) in the attainment of salvation.

Biswanath Baba, the rigid ascetic and the rigorous intellectual, symbolized the centre, the institution and the establishment. It is not surprising then that it was mainly through his efforts and those of his compatriots that a *sthāvara* (static) memorial replaced a *jaṅgama* (mobile) founder as the nucleus of power, and the observance of rules and norms became the crucial mode of preserving order. There was a return from the *vana* (forest) to the *kṣetra* (field/society), from the liminal to the clear, from the border to the centre.[16] The precedence accorded to the written over the oral, and to reason over emotion was a corollary to this. These shifts underwrote the evolution of Mahimā Dharma as an institutionalized religious order in the twentieth century, a faith that rearticulated its relationship with Hinduism. Biswanath Baba, the scholar and the teacher, in the course of providing a reasoned explication of his faith, aligned it to high Hinduism, eventually calling it *viśuddhādvaitavāda*—pure non-dualism with 'supporting evidence from Vedanta and other Shrutisastras'.[17]

Conclusion

Biswanath Baba died in 1992. His death was mentioned in Oriya newspapers, memorial meetings were held in Cuttack, and commemorative volumes published.[18] His life did not give rise to legends, but to written texts—biographies and expositions of his life and philosophy.[19] The position of the head of the organizing committee of the Dharma, left vacant by the Baba's death, was filled by four *balkaladhārī* ascetics, while some dissenting sub-groups sorted out their differences with the main group. The affairs of the *balkaladhārīs* at Jorandā continue to be guided by the standards laid down by Biswanath Baba, who is spoken of reverently by renouncers and householders. Mahimā Dharmīs take recourse to the works of Bhima Bhoi and Biswanath Baba, move between and negotiate contrary tenets to hold onto their faith, and at times, assert their independence and distinct identity. Mahimā Dharma lives on as a faith that symbolizes dissent and resistance, incorporation and restraint.

Notes

* I thank Johannes Beltz first for inviting me to the conference on Mahimā Dharma held in Bhubaneswar in 2001, then for asking me to contribute a paper to the volume once I failed to attend the conference and, finally, for the generous offer to co-edit this volume. I thank him also for intellectual feedback and support extended over the past four years.

1. For an exploration of the life and teachings of Mahimā Svāmī and an analysis of their implications, see Banerjee-Dube (2001, 2007).
2. The notion of Bhima Bhoi's blindness has increasingly been challenged since the 1970s, in particular by scholars from western Orissa. However, there is general agreement that Bhima Bhoi had had no formal education. See the works of Bhagirathi Nepak (1973, 1976, 1987 and 1998) and Debendra Kumar Dash (1997). For a different analysis of Bhima Bhoi's blindness, see Beltz (*forthcoming*).
3. *Janāṇa* is a couplet where the tone is of dialogue/conversation with the Guru/Lord. The huge corpus of *bhajanas*—the *Bhajanamālā*, the autobiographical *Stuticintāmaṇi* and *Nirvedasādhanā* are among the most important and popular of Bhima Bhoi's numerous compositions.
4. This is evident in the formal and informal interviews I have conducted with many lay disciples who live in or near Khaliapali and the Sonepur–Barpali region. The fieldwork of Johannes Beltz carried out in the region in 2000–1 confirms the picture.
5. His long section on Mahimā Dharma was subsequently published in 1911 as a separate text entitled *The Modern Buddhism and its Followers in Orissa*.
6. Reports on the incident and on the faith in general written by police officers and local officials of the colonial government like the *tahsildars* of Angul

and Banki and the manager of Dhenkanal, in response to the thorough enquiry ordered by the commissioner of Orissa on behalf of the Government of Bengal, were incorporated in the *Proceedings of the Asiatic Society of Bengal 1882*, as a long feature entitled 'On the Origin and Growth of the Sect of Hindu Dissenters who Profess to be the Followers of Alekh'.

7. A detailed examination of the incident is given by Banerjee-Dube (2001 and 2007).
8. *Nirvedasādhanā*, one of Bhima Bhoi's most well-known compositions, identifies Govinda Das, the first initiate of Mahimā Svāmī, with Jagannātha. The text declares that Visnu in the form of Jagannātha had left Puri to become the Swami's disciple in order to purge himself of the impurities incurred in his several descents. This belief and identification persist till today (Bhima Bhoi, 1992, Chapter 1).
9. I found translations of two *mālikās* of Bhima Bhoi in the Eschmann *Nachlass* at the South Asia Institute, Heidelberg. The Oriya text of the longer of the two *mālikās*, *Bhima Bhoi Malika ba Padmakalpa*, was also among the Eschmann papers, which I later came across in Orissa. I have not been able to locate the other text.
10. For insightful analyses of Gandhi's impact on peasant consciousness, see Amin (1984) and Sarkar (1984).
11. An exploration of the interface of orality and writing in Bhima Bhoi's works, its connection with the appearance of *mālikās* in Bhima Bhoi's name, and a thorough analysis of *Bhima Bhoi Malika ba Padmakalpa* is contained in Banerjee-Dube (2003); see also the paper by Johannes Beltz in this volume.
12. A.K. Ramanujan (1973) gives a penetrating analysis of the use of mobility/movement (*jaṅgama*) by Vīraśaiva ascetics as a mode of questioning establishment (*sthābara*).
13. It is difficult to ascertain the exact date of this incident but the reading of materials, discussions with adherents of Mahimā Dharma, biographical details of Biswanath Baba's life that can be culled, court records and the dates of Biswanath Baba's publications all indicate that it most certainly happened in the 1920s. This is also the time when the *mālikās* of Bhima Bhoi appeared. Fanindam Deo, however, places the incident a little earlier. See his paper in this volume.
14. Satrughna Nath, a retired teacher, is a prominent lay disciple of Mahimā Dharma and was a close associate of Biswanath Baba.
15. See Banerjee-Dube (1999) for a detailed and critical analysis of the *Itihāsa*.
16. An interesting discussion of the concepts of *vana* (*araṇya*) and *kṣetra* (*grāma*), and their particular characteristics in Vedic times is contained in Malamoud (1996). For an examination of the concepts, see also Sontheimer (1987).
17. See Nath (1974: iv) in Biswanath Baba, *Philosophy of Mahima Dharma*, a

published version of the speech Biswanath Baba delivered at a religious conference held at Puri in 1974. A detailed discussion of the philosophy of Mahimā Dharma is contained in Biswanath Baba's *magnum opus*, *Sarva Veda Vedānta Sāratattva Śiromaṇi, Alekha Paramabrahmā Darśanam*, written with the help of Ananta Charan Baba in 1968 and 1973. The first volume was translated into English as *The Philosophy of Mahima Dharma (Philosophy of Unalloyed Non-Dual Supreme Being)* in 1987 (Cuttack: Mahima Dharmalochana Samiti).

18. The Mahima Dharmalochana Parishad of the Alekhtungi in Chandni Chowk, Cuttack, where Biswanath Baba lived most of the time, brought out a special issue entitled *Samarpan*, in honour of Biswanath Baba.
19. Nath (1992) provides details of Biswanath Baba's life, and dwells at length on his philosophy and efforts to spread the faith. I also located a handwritten biography of Biswanath Baba among the Eschmann Papers, in Heidelberg. According to Satrughna Nath, it never got the 'Baba's' permission to be published. This is one indication of the very strict codes Biswanath kept for himself.

References

Amin, Shahid (1984), 'Gandhi as Mahatma: Gorakhpur District, Eastern UP, 1921–22', in Ranajit Guha (ed.), *Subaltern Studies II: Writings on South Asian History and Society*, New Delhi: Oxford University Press, pp. 1–62.

Banerjee-Dube, Ishita (1999), 'Taming Traditions: Legalities and Histories in Twentieth-Century Orissa', in Gautam Bhadra, Gyan Prakash and Susie Tharu (eds.), *Subaltern Studies X: Writings on South Asian History and Society,* New Delhi: Oxford University Press, pp. 98–125.

——— (2001), 'Issues of Faith, Enactments of Contest: The Founding of Mahima Dharma in Nineteenth-Century Orissa', in Hermann Kulke and Burkhard Schnepel (eds.), *Jagannath Revisited: Studying Society, Religion and the State in Orissa*, New Delhi: Manohar, pp. 149–77.

——— (2003), 'Reading Time: Texts and Pasts in Colonial Eastern India', *Studies in History* (n.s.), vol. 19 (1), pp. 1–17.

——— (2007), *Religion, Law and Power: Tales of Time in Eastern India, 1860–2000,* London: Anthem Press.

Beltz, Johannes (2006). 'Contested Authorities, Disputed Centers, and Rejected Norms: Situating Mahimā Dharma in its Regional Diversity', in Georg Pfeffer (ed.) *Periphery and Centre: Studies in Orissan History, Religion and Authropology,* New Delhi: Manohar, pp. 79-104.

Bhima Bhoi (1925), *Stuticintāmaṇi*, ed. Artaballabh Mahanti, Cuttack: Prachee Samiti.

——— (1971), *Bhima Bhoi Mālikā ba Padmakalpa*, Cuttack: Dharmagrantha Store.

——— (1992), 'Nirveda Sādhanā', in Karunakar Sahu (ed.), *Bhaktakabi Bhīma Bhoi Granthābalī*, Cuttack: Dharmagrantha Store.

Biswanath Baba (1931), *Mahimā Dharma Pratipādaka,* Bhubaneswar: Satya Mahima Dharmalochana Samiti.

——— (1935), *Satya Mahimā Dharma Itihāsa*, Cuttack: Satya Mahima Dharmalochana Samiti.

——— (with Ananta Charan Baba) (1968), *Sarva Veda Vedānta Sāratattva Śiromani, Alekha Paramabrahmā Darśanam*, vol. 1, Bhubaneswar: Utkal University.

——— (with Ananta Charan Baba) (1973), *Sarva Veda Vedānta Sāratattva Śiromani, Alekha Paramabrahmā Darśanam*, vol. 2, Cuttack: Satya Mahima Dhramalochana Samiti.

——— (1974), *The Philosophy of Mahimā Dharma*, Cuttack: Satya Mahima Dharmalochana Samiti.

Das, Ghanashyam (1931), 'Foreword' to Biswanath Baba's *Mahimā Dharma Pratipādaka,* Bhubaneswar: Satya Mahima Dharmalochana Samiti.

Dash, Debendra Kumar (1997), 'Bhima Bhoi o Mahima Dharma', *Eshana*, vol. 34, pp. 120–52.

Malamoud, Charles (1996), *Cooking the World: Ritual and Thought in Ancient India* (trans. David White), New Delhi: Oxford University Press, pp. 74–91.

Nath, Satrughna (1974), 'Introduction', in Biswanath Baba's *The Philosophy of Mahima Dharma*, Cuttack: Satya Mahima Dharmalochana Samiti, pp. i-iv.

——— (1977), *A Saint Self-realised in Mahima Faith: Biswanath Baba*, Cuttack: Dharmagrantha Store.

——— (1992), *Mahima Bhakti Rasamruta*, Cuttack: Mahima Dharmlochana Parishad.

Nepak, Bhagirathi (1973), *Bhima Bhoi: Chinta, Chetana, Jiban*, Bhubaneswar: Publication Committee.

——— (1976), *Odiya Sahityara Tini Bhima,* Bhubaneswar: Bhagirath Prakashan.

——— (1987), *Bhima Bhoi: The Adivasi Poet Philosopher*, Bhubaneswar: Publication Committee.

——— (1998), *Bhima Bhoi: His Life and Works*, Lachhipur: Bhima Bhoi Sanskrutik Sansad.

Ramanujan, A.K. (1973), *Speaking of Siva,* Harmondsworth: Penguin.

Sarkar, Sumit (1984), 'The Conditions and Nature of Subaltern Militancy: Bengal from Swadeshi to Non-Cooperation', in Ranajit Guha (ed.), *Subaltern Studies II: Writings on South Asian History and Society*, New Delhi: Oxford University Press, pp. 271–320.

Sontheimer, Günther-Deitz (1987), 'The *Vana* and the *Ksetra*: The Tribal Background of Some Famous Cults', in G.C. Tripathi and H. Kulke (eds.), *Religion and Society in Eastern India: Anncharlott Eschmann Memorial Lectures, 1978–1986*, vol. 1, Bhubaneswar: Utkal University, pp. 117–64.

Vasu, N.N. (1911), *Modern Buddhism and its Followers in Orissa*, Calcutta: U.N. Bhattacharyya, Hare Press.

——— (1981), *The Archeological Survey of Mayurbhanja*, New Delhi: Rare Reprints.

APPENDIX I

My First Encounter with Biswanath Baba[1]

ANNCHARLOTT ESCHMANN

Dear Mom,

Thank you for your long letter. I was so delighted (...) My expedition (to Joranda) was very successful although it had a dramatic start. Just as I was about to set out, distraught servants reported that the Stietencrons in the neighbouring house had been broken into. There was absolutely no one there, everyone had gone to Puri to the beach for the weekend, while I was still fighting the flu. So I had to fetch the police, not that this would do any good, but rather because the servants would have otherwise lost face. I insisted upon a two-star officer—your average Joe on the street, however, is more eloquent. Here, it is not the watchman who writes the report for the complainant, but rather it is the complainant who writes the report for the watchman, in English and three times, and he only reads through it and with a nod of his head he reaches for his pith helmet. . . .

Because of this, we didn't arrive in 'my' village until later in the afternoon. It is a very beautiful place, an expansive plateau with mountains along the edge, quite abrupt, just like in the miniatures; between palms and rice fields, a street of straw-covered houses leads to a square with the temple structures. The jeep squeezed on to the vaulted bridge and through the opening in the wall of one of the cloisters, the sun was beginning to set, and the Baba we had brought with us, disappeared behind the hedgerow. After a fairly long time, the head of the entire sect suddenly appeared, behind him the five highest Wise Ones. The Para-sannyāsī—'complete Holy Ones'— wear only a loincloth of bark, two strips of bark over their shoulders and carry a staff. When one explains it like this, it sounds primitive, but they have an enormously impressive effect and exude imperturbable dignity. The 'Abbot', Biswanath Baba, is very fair with a white beard and white hair, the wise ones behind him are almost black in contrast. This is how they approached me. I wanted to walk towards them, but I was held back and Biswanath Baba remained standing at some distance observing me.

Two minutes is a long time when one is standing there like this, abandoned and barefoot in the twilight, without a bag, since one is not allowed to have any leather on one's person. I really thought, now he's going to kick me out. Finally, one of my assistants said that I'd come from Germany to do research here, to which Biswanath Baba somewhat ambiguously said that it is certainly desirable that the only true religion spread itself across the world. After that, I stepped in and explained in Oriya that in Germany and England I had already heard of this religion and its followers, and that I had then come to learn more about it. At that, Biswanath Baba suddenly laughed, radiant, through thousands of little wrinkles—in addition to all his wisdom, he is extremely charming, and this charm just burst out all at once. And as I then, this time myself, in correct Oriya, excused myself for my previous lack of language skills, he asked me to sit down near him on the steps. This is, as it became clear to me only later, a tremendous honour. Strictly speaking, women are not allowed to step in the cloister district and their shadows are not allowed to fall on the Wise One. As far as 'my people' see it, Buddhism has been ruined only because it allowed women to become nuns. But everything I had feared in Germany appeared not to be relevant for me here. As I was leaving, Biswanath Baba blessed me and explained that without a doubt 'Alekha', the invisible, sole God himself, had sent me from such a distance and they wanted to accept this gratefully, but that I should also prove myself honourable of the mission.

Perhaps it was the new Punjabi dress I had chosen after long consideration that helped; an orange coat decorated with dark blue batik and blue pants, the basic colours corresponding with the saffron colour of the traditional monk's dress. Also, the bark that the highest Wise Ones wear takes on this orange colour after a while. I fit in great—and therefore my frequent trips to the tailor are now treated as important business errands.

After this grand entrance, which could indeed have gone awry, all doors were opened to me; the next day Baba himself showed us the library and some of the grounds and buildings, and spoke with us three times for three hours. It was lovely to stroll through these gardens where everything forms a procession: Baba at the front, behind him the frond carrier, then us, followed by servant brothers, and on the edge of the path the laymen, who touch the ground with their foreheads before Baba. Everything there is very primitive, but yet great—it's very difficult to describe.

Also very lovely was the stately guest-house—much nicer than the one in the little city where I was supposed to stay at first—the only place in the town with a toilet, even if it's not a WC. This problem kept my companions quite preoccupied; during the entire trip they kept telling me how there was indeed a High School but no 'Latin'. I reassured them numerous times that it's not bad at all if no one there knows Latin, until I realised that they were talking about 'latrines' and about the school as a building. The bungalow staff was in a fit of excitement; six months ago, the last tax inspector was there, and now me. They said that for skin as light as mine, one should better boil all of the bath water in buckets, just like it comes from the draw well. They were very worried about whether I could eat their rice, and our meals were the attraction of the town. Relieved, they got confirmed that people also eat with their fingers in Germany.

It really is nice in the evenings when people come strolling at night holding oil lamps amidst the chirping crickets, to hear the latest news, for example, who had become the 'king' of Germany after Hitler. One servant with a completely sharp-edged, emaciated face didn't believe in the Alekha religion and assured me that there were also blackguards among the followers. Both of my 'assistants', deeply impressed by Baba's 'Yogic personality' and by the ambience of the *āśrama* (sanctuary), repeatedly tried to silence him, but the soft, grumbling voice of doubt could not be quieted. (. . .) Just as our jeep was departing, a jeep from the state was coming towards us. The street is supposed to be extended through the temple grounds and Baba is preparing himself for expropriation negotiations. (. . .)

Great big hugs from your Anncharlott.
Bhubaneswar,
14 November 1970

Note

1. A copy of this letter was kept in the Orissa Archive at Heidelberg's South Asia Institute. Since it gives an authentic and simultaneously moving report of Eschmann's first encounter with Biswanath Baba in Jorandā, the editors decided to get it translated into English and publish excerpts of it. It should be added here that Bishwanath Baba deeply influenced Eschmann's perception of Mahimā Dharma.

APPENDIX 2

Bhima Bhoi, Stuticintāmaṇi, Boli *27*

This *boli* is probably one of the most popular poems composed by Bhima Bhoi. When the Sahitya Akademi in New Delhi asked for a poem in each of the 14 Indian languages, an extract from this *boli* was chosen to represent Oriya. It is the seventh strophe where Bhima Bhoi asks his Guru to redeem the world, even if he should go to hell in exchange. We present here a joint translation by Bettina Bäumer, Johannes Beltz, Sadananda Das, Kalidas Mishra, Kedar Mishra and Sanjeeb Nayak.[1]

You commanded me to establish the sacred fire,
and to tell others of its worth.
But, having made me your servant,
why did you let me down, abandoning me half way? (1)

I have neither courage nor hope.
Tell me what to do.
Bear your own burden! Protect your devotees!
Take care of the world! (2)

See, the endless sorrow of the devout
has been put at your feet.
Bundle up their miseries,
carry this burden on your own shoulder. (3)

Both fortune and calamity,
both salvation and suffering are created by you.
Who will bear the burdens of sin and sorrow?
Let them lie at your feet. (4)

Your presence is manifest,
so why don't you care? How can I escape?
Having earned the burden of my sins,
I'll make a bundle and place it at your feet. (5)

Desiring shelter at your feet,
the pious cry out, they roll upon the ground.
Forgive them their flaws, my Lord,
be vigilant, protect them. (6)

Endless are the agonies and sorrows of the living.
Who can bear to be witness?
Condemn my life to hell,
but let the world be uplifted. (7)

Oh, most subtle, endless Lord,
with all my devotion I say to thee
that within these three worlds
every creature is your devotee. (8)

The nine hundred thousand stars,
every region, Surāṭa, Virāṭa, Dhruba,
and all the rest, even up to the Sense Void,[2]
all take shelter at your feet. (9)

Beyond the dense Void,
nothing can be seen.
The eternal Brahman pervades like an ocean,
without name, without form. (10)

Be they wicked or saintly, servant or master,
insect or bird, you pervade all.
I see you equally in all beings,
nowhere less than in another. (11)

Who is present in earth, in stones, in wood,
trees and grass, and in every lifeless thing?

My intellect knows that there is only one,
the one known as Śabdabrahman.[3] (12)

I, an ignorant poet, follow a hidden path.[4]
Because of your compassion
I see all things as equal, I cannot discriminate.
Satyadharma is my witness. (13)

Every creature of the three worlds
has a different name, its own identity,
yet I know them all to have the same soul.
I make no distinction among them. (14)

As water is contained equally
in a metal or a wooden bowl,
so the supreme unites with the life of every creature.
I see this clearly. (15)

When there be words of blame, of profit and loss,
when there be arguments, quarrels and assault,
I feel these things pierce through my skin
bringing pain to my life. I grow sorrowful. (16)

The edicts of the five elements
are felt to boil in the heart
like grains of rice,
in a pot on the hearth-fire. (17)

Life is but a shard of bone,
a drop of blood and a slice of flesh.
I know this well, and so
I cannot bear the people's woes. (18)

In the Mahabharata war, five to ten heads
fall as one, from a single stroke of a sword.
As for me, if you kick my leg,
it is my other limb which suffers. (19)

Let a bolt of lightning strike my head
if my devotion bears any flaw.
Use the curse of Brahma to burn my body.
Thus says Bhima Bhoi. (20)

Notes

1. The translation is based on a paper manuscript kept in the archives of the Bhima Bhoi Samadhi Pitha Trust at Khaliapali, Orissa. The entire manuscript is accessible under www.mahimadharma.de. This translation is part of an anthology prepared by the same group of scholars. The book is entitled 'Verses from the Void' and will be published as one of the next volumes in the series 'Studies in Orissan Society, Culture and History'.
2. *Ṭhulaśūnya*; here it designates a region in between the starry sky and that which is beyond (cf. the Aristotelian Spheres, empty and void, yet still solid and impassible).
3. *Śabdabrahman*; the Brahman who/that is sound or Word.
4. *Bheda marga*, possibly 'a path of dualism'.

APPENDIX 3

Historic Documents

This part of the appendix presents a few texts, which we consider crucial for understanding the development of Mahima Dharma. Some are published, others were identified and copied by Gourang Charan Dash, and then translated by Sanjeeb Nayak and Kedar Mishra.

Kumbhipatias

Bengal District Gazetteer, Sambalpur, 1909

The Kumbhipatias are a sect peculiar to Sambalpur to whom attention was first drawn in 1880 when a party of fanatics went to Puri with the object of burning the idol of Jagannath. They were residents of Sambalpur and stated that they were induced to come to Puri in consequence of one of their co-religionists having been commanded by their guru—invisible being without shape or form—to bring the images of Jagannath, Balaram and Subhadra out of the temple and burn them on the road. In obedience to what they believed to be divine command a body of men and women left their homes in Sambalpur. Within a few miles of Puri, 12 men and 3 women separated themselves from the main body and preceded them to the temple. These 15 persons who were almost in a state of nudity came up to the temple shouting 'Alekh, Alekh'. Having forced their way into the building they proceeded to break down the door of the *Bhogamandap*, the building in which the offerings of the worshippers are usually displayed. They then made their way into the great hall of the temple in front of the shrine but found the door called Jay-Bijay shut. On this they went out into the enclosure and rushed about like madmen endeavouring to find an entrance in some other direction. In the struggle which took place one of them fell or was pushed on to the stone pavement. He was lifted up by some of his companions and was assisted out of the temple and a little later he expired.

The rioters being inhabitants of Sambalpur, the Chief Commissioner of the Central Provinces was asked to furnish particulars of the sect and its tenets and in compliance with this request he gave the following information. There is a peculiar sect of Hindu dissenters in the Sambalpur district known as the *Kumbhipatias*. The word *Kumbhipatia* is derived from *Kumbhi* the name of a tree and *pat*, the bark of a tree, the sect is so-called because its followers make ropes from the bark of the *Kumbhi* tree and wear them round their waists. The religion is also known as that of Alekh and its followers claim revelation as its foundation. Alekha Swami, the god incarnate used, it is said, to reside in the Himalayas but about the year 1864 he came to Malbiharpur in Banki in Cuttack district and there revealed a new religion to 64 persons, the principal of whom was Govinda Das. It was chiefly owing to the exertions of the disciples that the religion was propagated. Alekha Swami (which signifies the Lord whose attributes cannot be described in writing) removed to Dhenkanal, a feudatory state, where for three years immediately preceding his death he led the life of a mendicant and wanderer. Although the religion originated in Cuttack it spread more rapidly in the district of Sambalpur and men of all classes and castes except the Oriya Brahmans were freely embracing it. It was not so much the peculiarity of the rules of any particular caste or sect that tended to increase the number of converts as the position in the life of the *converts* themselves, for example in Khinda the people of a whole village embraced the *Kumbhipatia* religion because the *gaontia* had done so. The names of some 30 villages are given as ones in which the *Kumbhipatias* chiefly reside.

Further details are given in the Central Provinces Census Report of 1881 where the following account of the *Kumbhipatias* is quoted from the Census Report of Sambalpur: 'Their religion also known as Alekh appears to have originated in Angul, a Dhenkanal feudatory state, about the year 1866. The name of the founder of the religion appears unknown and its followers state that he is a spiritual being without form who lives in heaven. His elder disciple Govinda Das is dead; another known as Narasingha Das has erected his *matha* (temple) in Banki. The *Kumbhipatias* have another temple in Malbihar in Banki. They have a book called *Malika* which contains predictions. They are divided into three sects the *Kumbhipatia Gosains*, the *Kanapatia Gosains*, and *Ashritas*. The two former sects have renounced the world; the followers of one do not eat with those of the others. They appear to be of dirty habits, not washing after easing themselves and not bathing at all. The third sect called *Ashritas* do not renounce the world nor deem celibacy essential nor are they turned out of caste. They look up to the other two sects as their gurus or spiritual guides and follow their religion. They bathe in the early morning and all three sects turn their faces towards the sun at time of rising and setting and prostrate themselves five or seven times. They do not eat after sunset. Each sect has a separate temple or place of prayer. They recognize the *Bhagavata* as one of the Hindu religious books but interpret it differently from the Hindus. They do not respect the images of the Hindu gods arguing that as no one has ever seen the Supreme Being it is impossible to form his images. They believe in the existence of thirty-three crores of Hindu gods and goddesses but do not obey them asserting that it is not necessary to obey the servant but only the master. Their worship consists of prayer and praise to the immaterial being whom they call Alekha.

Babu Bijay Chandra Mazumdar of Sambalpur has furnished further information regarding the sect which conflicts in some respects with that given above. He states that the leader under whose instructions the *Kumbhipatias* sought to destroy the idol of Jagannath was one Bhima Bhoi, a blind and illiterate man possessed however of considerable mental power. This Bhima Bhoi had his seat at Khaliapali in the Sonepur feudatory state and Khaliapali is still the principal *guru duar* or hierarchical seat of the *Kumbhipatias*. Bhima Bhoi gave new life to the *Kumbhipatia* doctrine and made the cult popular throughout Sambalpur. Some Brahmans indeed openly embraced the religion by throwing away their Brahmanical threads. They worship no god, prayer is never offered and the temples are merely *mathas*. All the religious books of the Hindus, not only the *Bhagavata*, are interpreted in a fanciful manner, according to the Alekha doctrine. Formerly no garment was used, and at times the bark of trees only covered their shame. The lay *Kumbhipatias* observe the customary system, but the specially initiated do not. It is difficult to obtain much reliable information regarding the *Kumbhipatias* owing to the fact that they do not disclose their secret doctrines to the uninitiated.

Origin and Growth of the Sect of the Hindu Dissenters who Profess to be the Followers of Alekha

Proceedings of the Asiatic Society of Bengal, January 1882

The Commissioner of the Orissa Division writes: The founder of the sect is said to have been one Mukunda Das. He lived for a long time in Puri as an Achari Vaishnava, and was known as the Dhula Babaji from the fact of his daubing his body with ashes.

About thirty years ago he left Puri and came to Dhenkanal, one of the Tributary States of Cuttack, where he selected as his dwelling place the Kapilas hills near a shrine of Mahadev. During the first twelve years of his residence at Kapilas, Mukunda Das lived on fruits and accordingly was known as the *Phalahari Babaji*. The next twelve years were passed on milk and water, which secured him the cognomen of *Kshira-Nira-Payi*.

During his sojourn at Kapilas, he was known to be a devout worshipper of the local idol, and took much pains in improving the place by cutting the jungle, making gardens, looking after the *bhog* or sacred food of the idol, and taking care of the pilgrims who visit the hills periodically. This procured him the respect of the mother of the late Maharaja of Dhenkanal, who supplied his food. He gradually succeeded in securing the respect of the people of the surrounding villages and the popular belief was that he was in secret communion with the idol and could successfully intercede with it on behalf of its votaries. The currency of this belief was further facilitated by the fact of his taking special care of the sick people who resorted to Kapilas for the benefit of their health, and very generally succeeded in getting it restored, and his visiting the temple at the dead of night while every one had retired to rest.

After thus remaining at Kapilas for several years, and finding that he had sufficiently established his reputation and secured the respect of the people Mukunda Das left the place and began to preach that Mahadev and other idols worshipped by the Hindus were nothing else but stone and wood, and that the worship of these destructible articles was useless and of no avail, that the Creator of the Universe was Alekha or Mahima (which literally means 'glorious'), a spiritual being without form, omnipresent and omniscient, and that he alone could hold communion with Him and get his prayer granted. He eschewed his *kaupin* (waist cloth) and *kanthi* (wooden beads worn round the neck), the two distinctive features in the raiment of a Vaishnava, and wore *kumbhipat* (the bark of a tree called *Kumbhi*) to cover his nakedness.

From Kapilas, Mukunda Das went to Puri, where he remained for some time in a hut on the sands near the temple of Lokanath Mahadev. He next came to Darutheng in the Government state of Khurda in Puri where he built a *tungi* (a place of worship), and commenced to propagate the new doctrine. It was at this place that Mukunda Das was deified and began to be addressed as Mahima Gosain. It appears that one Govinda Das was his first, and Narsing Das his second disciple. Others followed their example, and in course of time all these followers dispersed on all sides for propagation of the new doctrine, shortly after a place of worship was established at Malbiharpur in Kellah Banky; other places were opened in some of the remaining Tributary States as well as in Sambalpur, Puri and Cuttack. At some of these places of worship the Mahima Gosain gave large feasts, which were numerously attended. In 1875 in the month of *Kartika* on the day of full moon, a fair was held at Jacka in Dhenkanal, where a large number of the followers of the Gosain assembled with rich presents including valuable clothes, silver utensils (. . .). It is said that the Babaji, or Swami as he was also addressed, offered these presents to the late Maharaja of Dhenkanal, and on his declining to accept them they were openly burnt in the fire of the sacred Dhuni (fire kept up by religious mendicants). Thus in a few years the Mahima Gosain succeeded in making many disciples and followers, and on the days of the full moon thousands of men and women from distant parts of the country might have been seen wending their way to the *tungis*, with loads of *ghee*, sugar and other valuable presents. It is said that at present the new faith is more popular in Sambalpur than in any other district. It is confined mostly to the ignorant and illiterate people of the lower classes of the Hindu community, who were it is said, induced to adopt the new religion by hopes of enjoyment if they followed, and threats of perdition if they did not follow its precepts.

The disciples of the Mahima Swami inculcate self-denial and resignation to God as the sources of salvation they do not aspire after worldly greatness or pleasure, extreme humility is one of their characteristics. They have no prescribed mode of worship except praise of god and prayer for his mercy. They recognize the *Bhagavata*, one of the religious books of the Hindus, but interpret it in a different way from the Hindus. They have a *Malika*, or book of predictions, which treats of the incarnation of Alekha in the shape of Mahima Swami to redeem the world from sin and to indicate the way to salvation. Besides this they have got another book containing songs and dialogues interpreting the truth of Alekha. Most of these songs are said to have been composed by Bhima Bhoi, a Kandha, who is said to have been born blind, and afterwards endowed with sight by the Mahima Swami.

The following extract from the reports of the Manager of Dhenkanal throws some light on the real sentiments of the Swami:

> The man who was at first called the Phalahari Gosain was afterwards designated Mahima Gosain, and was believed to be an incarnation of the almighty God. In the year 1874, while I was on tour in the interior of Dhenkanal, the founder of the Mahima or Alekha religion went with me from place to place and was with me about a week, and I also saw him on several other occasions, but I never heard from him that he professed to be the Creator of the world as his disciples and followers believed him to be. From what I heard from him, I concluded that he believed that the Creator of the world was a spiritual Being, omnipresent and omniscient, without any form, whom he called Mahima and also Alekha Prabhu, and that he alone could communicate with the Alekha Prabhu and get done what he wished. He believed in the existence of the Hindu gods and goddesses, but said that they were under his commands, and that they were to obey whatever he wished them to do.

The followers of the Alekha Swami are divided into three sects: (i) the Kumbhipatias, (ii) the Kanapatias and (iii) the Ashritas. The first two have renounced the world and deem celibacy essential. The males are called 'Babas' and the females 'Matas'. The difference between these two sects is that a Kumbhipatia wears the bark of the Kumbhi tree, and Kanapatia pieces of rag. They beg from door to door, have no distinction of caste, and take their food only during the day-time at an open place beside a public road. They eat food cooked by people of any caste except the raja, a Brahman and a washerman, whom they consider as sinful beings in this world, the raja as he is responsible for the sins committed in his state, the Brahman as he accepts all sorts of gifts from sinful persons, and the washerman as he washes sinful people's dirty clothes. They are not accustomed to live at any one place for more than a day, or to beg twice from the same house. They wear long matted hair, and do not bathe. They turn their head towards the sun at the time of rising and setting and prostrate themselves several times to beg shelter and mercy of the Alekha Swami. The Ashritas do not forsake the world nor do they deem celibacy essential, they bathe generally early in the morning, and clean their teeth with cow dung. They do not wear long hair nor do they use *kumbhipata* or *kanapata* like their confrères, but use *geru basan* or cloth coloured with *geru* or red earth, like Brahmacharis of the Hindus; they do not observe any Hindu ceremony or festival, neither do they respect the gods of the Hindus. They perform their marriage ceremony in a very simple way by the side of a public road or thoroughfare, the bride puts a garland of flowers around the neck of the bridegroom in token of offering herself to him, and the friends and relatives of both loudly call upon their Alekh Swami to protect the new pair in their career through life. Polygamy is prohibited among the Ashritas. For any misconduct an offender is made to do penance by drinking a solution of cow dung. The Ashritas consider the other two sects as their gurus or spiritual guides. The Tahasildar of Anugul reports that the new faith of Mahima has brought a change for the better among the Pans of that killah, who are notorious for their thieving proclivities. Those who have accepted the new faith regard theft with abhorrence.

In 1875, Mahima Swami, who was believed to be immortal died at Joranda in Dhenkanal, and the *tungis*, together with the gods and chattels they contained, were sold as intestate property. Most of the followers of the new faith, finding that the Swami was no better than an ordinary mortal, disbelieved what he had inculcated and reverted to Hinduism. Those of his disciples and followers who had left their homes and friends and had been out-casted continued to practise the new faith they had embraced.

At present there are only two places of worship in Dhenkanal, one at Joranda where Mahima Swami died and was interred and another at Mahalpara (Mahalpada) where Narsing Das now lives. The Kumbhipatias resort the former and the Kanapatias to the latter of these places: they are reported not to be on good terms with each other. During the lifetime of Mahima Swami, the Kumbhipatias and Kanapatias were not regarded as distinct sects. Any person who wished to adopt the new religion first became an Ashrita, which literally means protected. He was not required to leave his house and friends; afterwards if he wished to forsake the world he was required to eat with every person without distinction of caste and to remain at one of the places of worship called *tungis*. In this novitiate, he was allowed to wear cloth and was therefore called Kanapatia. If after trial any of the Kanapatias was considered fit to be a Kumbhipatia, Mahima Swami favoured him with a *kumbhipata* (bark of the Kumbhi tree) and from that time he was prohibited to wear cloth.

The followers of Mahima Swami appear to have had no leader since his death; they are scattered throughout the *garjhats/gadjats* of Orissa, in the Chhattisgarh division of the Central Provinces, in the regulation districts of Orissa and in Ganjam, the adjoining district of the Madras Presidency. The system has however taken more in Sambalpur than elsewhere.

Mahima Babaji

Utkal Sahitya, *6 September 1873, pp. 66-7*

Our Jajpur reporter writes that nearly four or five hundred people of Dhenkanal, Sukinda and Keonjhar *gadjats* have organized a community named Kumbhipatias. Their other name is Mahima Babajis. Two or four persons of this community, entering into Madhupur, tried to destroy the caste system. The kings have driven them away from his state considering them opposing Hinduism. Two of these Babajis, for nearly the past two months, have been coming to Jajpur. They initiate disciples from Brahmin, Karan and Hadi castes and wander with them. They receive food from all houses except those of kings, brahmins, barbers, Dhobas, Malis and prostitutes. They do not even keep themselves away from Christians. Asking for boiled rice from these houses, which they keep in an earthen pots, the master and the disciples eat the rice together from the same pot in the street and then together break the pot into pieces. Common people respect them and some people tell their sorrows before them. They receive the commands of these ascetics and cherish them in deep devotion. It is known that these ascetics have blessed their devotees with sons. However, seeing their ways of destroying caste system, the Brahmins of Jajpur have held a meeting and decided that the ones who have lost their caste by becoming followers Mahima Babaji, will be socially ostracized and no one will have social contact with them unless they expiate for their sins through penance. Because of such regulations the number of disciples is decreasing and many of those who had become disciples are returning home and trying to expiate for their sins.

The Deputy Magistrate, hearing all this, invites the Babajis to his residence to find out more about the matter. The Babajis told him that they do not honour the authority of Veda or any other scripture. Nor do they worship any God. Their religion is Nirveda and Alekha. They only respect the Mahima. Mahima is the name of the formless Brahma who exists in all beings. Yet they do not have contact with five castes like the Brahmins and Kshatriyas, etc. In their view, member of these castes are all irreligious and they never perform any religious activities. Therefore they are banned. Hearing all this the Deputy Magistrate, refuted their arguments, and asked them to go away and leave the sub-division.

There is one matter of great concern. We have nothing to say about the religion. But the people belonging to this community regard the king as irreligious. What is its implication and who do they mean when they refer to the king? If the king belongs to the *gadjat*, then there is cause to worry. Because the ruler of the *gadjat* is capable of taking necessary steps to prevent them from promulgating their opinions. If king implies the British Government, then there is cause for concern. And the authority should collect extensive reports about this community. It may well be that by calling the British irreligious, they indirectly invite the people to lose their faith in the ruler and rise in rebellion. The people of the *gadjats* are illiterate. A rebellion has already taken place in Keonjhar and there is great faith in the words of Babaji. If common men are told repeatedly that the king is irreligious and shown some imaginary examples, then is there any doubt that when the number of followers of the Babajis increase, some misfortune will occur?

Mahima Dharma

Utkala Deepika, *25 August 1883, p. 267*

The father of a student in Dhenkanal is a Mahima Dharmi. The Headmaster punished the student for telling a lie. He commanded him to stand on the bench. The father has told the headmaster: 'Beware of this boy. He is Alekha. It means that he is the grandson of Lord Mahima. He will not pay you any money. Don't punish him, I will give money as much as you need.' The teacher asked: 'How is Lord Mahima?' The old man said: 'He takes up different incarnations in different Yugas. He delightfully travels in the human world. Let me tell you of his incarnation one by one. First he takes on a fair-complexioned body, has matted hair on his head, and a necklace of *akshyas*, on his chest. He wears a bark round his waist and has four hands. He holds a *kamandalu* in one of his hands. This is the form of god, whom all *sadhus* worship.' The teacher said: 'He is only a swindler, a cheat, who lives on cheating people. His body was moth-eaten. How can he be God?' The old man replied: 'Who have no faith in the religion, will succumb in their own way, the Lord will not be guilty of it. I will not send my son to study here any more. Strike out his name.' This religion had first become influential. But because of the efforts made by the former Commissioner Sahib, its prominence had diminished. Now again it gradually spreads. We should keep our eyes on it.

Attack on Sri Jagannath Temple at Puri

Utkala Deepika, *12 March 1881, p. 42*

A rumour has broken out here that for the last two weeks that a gang of gypsy-like men and women, bringing with them rice-boiling earthen pots, forcibly entered into Sri Jagannath temple at Puri. At that time the sacred food for the Lord was being carried. The guards of the temple prevented them. But they disobeyed and tried to approach the idol of Lord Jagannath. Then a combat took place with the guards in which one of the attacking gang died all of a sudden. Others, throwing rice from their pots, making the sacred food of the Lord unholy, threatening that they would burn the wooden idol of Lord Jagannath and paste the ashes on their body, came out of the temple. A lot of criminal activities occurred there in a moment. But the rumour does not say whether they are arrested by the police or any case has been filed in the court against them. And we do not know if any government report has come out by now. If there is any truth in this event, then there is danger for Lord Jagannath and no follower of Jagannath has come out to save Him. This is quite a wonderful thing that Kalipada Babu has not even gone to Puri to rescue Lord Jagannath from the attack, nor any other preventive measure has been taken yet. We hope that we will be able to communicate the truth in the coming week.

Kumbhipatia Babaji

Utkala Deepika, *19 November 1881*

We have already communicated the news of a few Kumbhipatias of Sambalpur being punished by the court for attacking on Jagannath temple. Readers must have remembered it. After this news came to the knowledge of the government, the Chief Commissioner of Madhya Pradesh has, by the request of the government, sent a document on the Kumbhipatia community. Since this document is published in the *Calcutta Gazette*, newspapers have cited this fact and because it is an interesting subject to know, we too communicate a little on them to our readers.

That (Kumbhipatia) community exists in Sambalpur district. As they wear the bark of a tree called Kumbhi, they call themselves Kumbhipatias. Sometimes, some of them come to this district and wander in the rural areas. People call them Kumbhipata babajis and like them much. The name of their religion is 'Alekha'. They regard Lord Alekha as the incarnation of god. Lord Alekha was residing amidst the Himalaya mountains. In 1864, he came to Malbiharpur of Banki district, expounded Alekhism and initiated 64 disciples. This religion was propagated by those disciples. Lord Alekha went to Dhenkanal from Banki, he went through 'Vikshyashram' for three years and finally died there.

Though this religion was first expounded in Banki district, very soon it spread to Sambalpur district and there, except the brahmins, people belonging to all other castes followed this religion. At present this religion has already been established in thirty villages of that district. Kumbhipatias are divided into three sects (1) Real or original, (2) Kanapitias and (3) Grihasthas. The followers of the first two sects are 'Niangi' and homeless. (They have left their homes for good.)

Kumbhipatias accept one God only. Truthfulness, receiving of guru's advice and faith are the main principles of that religion. They do not accept caste differences and they eat the food from the hands of people belonging to any caste. But they never receive food from the hands of kings, Brahmins, Dhobas and Hadis. Because a king collects money by corruption, Brahmin eats the rice taken from obsequies and Dhobas and Hadis do many heinous works. They accept the thirty-three crores of Hindu gods and goddesses, but they never worship their idols or images. They tell that no one has ever seen god, hence how can his idol be rightly made? Therefore, they do not worship gods and goddesses and they have ill feelings towards the symbols of Hinduism. Because Hindus consider Tulsi leaves to be sacred, Kumbhipatias never touch them. There are many other such things. Kumbhipatias worship in the morning and evening and eat only during the day not touching food at night. They drink water to quench their hunger and thirst at night. They do not take medicine and rely on god to be cured from disease.

Kumbhipatias have been divided into two sects since last two years. A man named Bhima Khond is their leader. He is blind from his birth but highly intelligent. He is illiterate, but has been able to compose verse by only listening to the *Mahabharata* and the *Bhagavata* written by others. He has composed some rare pieces of songs and hymns in praise God which are not even possible by many highly educated persons. Since he made a woman pregnant developing illicit love with her, Kumbhipatias got irritated with him. Then he deceived them saying that Arjuna, getting birth through that woman would kill the ones who disbelieve in Alekhism. The followers waited for the birth of Arjuna, but a daughter was born. Then Bhima Khond told that God had commanded him that a divine nymph would be born from that woman and would kill the disbelivers by the might of Mahima. But the daughter died after a few days. Bhima then told that the celestial nymph, abhorring the sinful world, went back to heaven. At this, those who had even a little bit of intelligence, separated themselves into a different sect. The rest, sticking to Bhima's sect, are worshipping him. Daily Bhima sits in the morning on an altar with his wife and his disciples, circumambulating around them, washing their feet in milk, drinking the milk as a sacred nectar. The other reason of segregation into two sects is that Bhima Khond had identified himself to be the incarnation of god. Those who attacked Jagannath temple are inhabitants of Chandrapur and Dasaram was their leader. Dasaram had come to Puri with a few Kumbhipatias with the intention that if Jagannath would be burnt down Hindus would understand the temporariness of Hinduism and all would follow Alekhism, but finally Dasaram lost his life in an awful riot there.

If a Kumbhipatia tells lie or commits crime, he is ex-communicated. If someone wants to receive initiation to this religion, he has to appear for a test first. There were some Panas (low caste people) in Anugul who were hardcore criminals. As the

Tahasildar initiated them to Alekhism, they are now away from crimes and peace now prevails in Anugul. As such, this religion is really beneficial, but it is told that the leader of the Kumbhipatias tells lies and practices adultery. And not all the people belonging to a caste or religion behave honestly.

A Letter Regarding Mahima Religion

Utkal Deepika, *17 March 1883*

... The followers of this religion (Mahima Dharma) are monotheist and they do not stick to caste discrimination. They do not take food except the duration between the sunrise and the sunset. (Taking food except in day time is prohibited.)

As the Christians believe in the reappearance of Jesus, so the Mahima Dharmees believe in their reunion with the prophet Mahima here in this world. No social development has been achieved by this religion; The majority of the Mahima Dharmees are the low and uncivilized people. The glory and fame (mahima) of this religion did not persist long. Otherwise, like Brahma Dharma, some social development could have been possible by this religion.

The followers of this religion are divided into two groups, the yogis (ascetics) and the bhogis (hedonists). The people of the first group are Kumbhipatias, meaning that they wear *kumbhipata* (the bark of Kumbhi tree). Their *ashrama* or monastery is in Joranda, a village of Dhenkanal. Here lies the *samadhi* of Lord Mahima. There stands near the *samadhi* a doorless temple. This monastery is not as enjoyable as that of Mahulpada.

The followers of the last (second) group are Kanapatias, meaning they wear cloths besmeared with red ochre and *matha*. Their monastery is in the solitary forest near the village Mahulpada, nearly three *krosas* distant from the fort. Here is Narasingh Das, Lord Mahima's first disciple. This monastery reminded me of the *ashrams* described in the past. Seeing this *ashram* all thoughts went away from my mind and there arose wonderful divine feelings. There, through the entrance of the monastery, flows a clear fountain that caters the need of the animals and beasts. There is a high altar at a distance. There are many small houses for the disciples. There is a *shunya griha* built by bricks, a stone house and a fire house. The fire house has four doors on its four sides. Small trees of mango, jackfruit and banana, bending down being fruit laden, express the glory of the place. The dwellers of the *ashram* never eat fruit from their trees. Other people eat them. There is a trench round each trees at the bottom, from which birds drink water, seeing how fearfully the birds drink water from these trenches, one can realize well how much horrifying violence is. Though there were no deer found in the *ashram* yet deer sometimes coming form the forest to beautify the *ashram*. Are creatures swinging down in the speed of wild as if to offer fruits?

A number of smooth terraces, the mind-stealing twitter of the birds, the sweet buzz of bees, those holy sacrifice in the fire-house, the slow blowing fragrant breeze, the peace-giving, mind-enchanting clay altar under the Kadamb trees are adding to the beauty of the *ashram* and filling the minds of the visitors with the ripples of bliss.

Letter to the Honorable Editor of *Utkala Deepika*

Utkala Deepika, *20 August 1871*

Sir,

We shall be obliged if you would like to place the following report (news) in your newspaper. There lives a Vaishnava in our Orissa province since long, who eats only fruits. He is, at present, selecting the dense forest of Dhenkanal and some other *gadjats* as his place of habitation, initiating majority of the population of these areas to his religious cult, enhancing the number of his followers day by day. We can say, at the least of our count, that the number of his followers cannot be less than a thousand. About three hundred of those have already obtained Kumbhipata (bark wear). Though the rest are consecrated institutionally, yet they have not left their home. Within a few days they may wander wearing *kaupina*. It is a matter of grief that being influenced by such a stupid and barbarous man such a large number of people of Orissa would abandon their *grihastha dharma*. Hence we pray that the government would pay attention to it and take necessary steps to abolish this practice.

APPENDIX 4

Mahima Alekh Parambrahmana Saranam[1]

Alarmed by the decline of Satya Dharma (true-faith) in the universe, holy and pious sages and saints, gods and goddesses, came together and earnestly prayed to Jagadisvar Paramātmā (Supreme Being) to save the world by re-establishing Satya Dharma. In answer to this prayer, Mahāmahimā Svāmi, the gracious Lord of the Universe, came down to earth from the Void in the form of Prabuddha Narayana to found true faith. At first, he spent several years in deep self-meditation on the peak of mount Kailas in the Himalayas taking no food, just breathing air. Then he came down from the peak of Kailas and commanded the holy saints: 'Now by the grace of god you go and take birth as human beings. God will preach the true Mahimā Dharma in Utkal Pradesh in the eastern part of India. You will take darsan (vision) of the Lord there, hear the tenets of Satya Dharma and tour the world as ascetics spreading the message of the true faith for the good of humanity.' Instructing the sages thus, Mahimā Svāmi travelled all over India in the hidden form of a 'prabuddha sannyasi' (enlightened ascetic) before manifesting himself in Puri in Utkal in 1233 of the era of the Delhi king, which corresponds to 1826 C.E., in order to establish the 'true, eternal Mahima Dharma'. It is said that the Lord used to sit and sleep in the dirt of *Badadanda*, the grand road in front of the Jagannath temple in Puri. He barely spoke to people. However, if someone wanted his fortune told or conveyed his aspirations to the Lord, the ascetic foretold the future correctly and also got wishes fulfilled. This amazed people so much that they came to look upon the renouncer as a divine incarnation.[2] They named him Dhulia Gosain (an ascetic who covered his body with dirt) and started worshipping him. The ascetic wore a saffron coloured cloth around the waist and had matted locks on his head. He remained immobile in deep self-meditation in a cave close to Puri called Arka Gumphā (Sun cave).

Rules for Householders (Grihasthara Dharmaniti)

Householders should always remember that this *samsāra* (world) is transitory[3] and that only Prabhu Parambrahma is Satya and, therefore, eternal. He is our father and mother, Guru and Prānadātā (giver of life). The duties that you perform as the devotee of that Lord should be carried out in a detached manner with no desire for the result by invoking the master in the beginning. Never be desirous of the result, reward will be given by the mercy of God. Take up an honest livelihood in order to take care of your father, mother, family members and relatives. Do not do your duties with the intention of enjoying svarga (heaven) after death. Be as detached as possible. Never take up a dishonest profession. Dishonesty does not lead to prosperity. Prosperity is the natural reward of noble deeds. The head of the house should induce his wife and children to become initiates of Satya Dharma. It is also a duty of the wife to persuade her husband to follow the path of Satya Dharma. Husband and wife should unite sexually only in order to procreate and the couple should have intercourse on specific days of the month in accordance with the wife's menstrual cycle. The couple should not have sex on other days.

Menstruation and Sexual Life

A menstruating woman (*rajasvalā nārī*) should not cook food or touch anybody, nor massage the feet of her husband till the seventh day. She should perform the morning and evening *darśana* with folded hands in an upright position and take *renu* (holy dust) from the ground. *Sāstanga śarana*[4] should be avoided. The same rule applies to the husband, wife and their relatives during the period of impurity following a birth. The menstruating woman should apply cow dung to her body and bathe seven times in the morning on the seventh day of menstruation. Following this, she should wear a clean, saffron-coloured cloth, drink a holy mixture composed of the excrements of the cow (*pavitra gomaya*) twenty-one times and offer *śarana* and *darśana* in the normal way. Then she will be able to resume her normal duties of cooking for the husband and other members of the family and also massage the feet of her husband. She should take proper care of ascetics and other guests. Married women should never think of any man other than the husband. Similarly, married men should not take any interest in any woman who is not the wife. Everyone should have faith in the precepts of Satya Mahima Dharma and follow them with care and devotion.

Parents should impart good advice to their children and guide them on the path of dharma. The wife should have sexual intercourse with the husband only on the eighth night of her menstrual cycle. On other days, she should only massage the feet of the husband and not embrace him or engage in any sexual act. The couple should not have sex after the birth of a child till the time the child grows teeth. The parents should abstain from sexual life totally once the children become capable of running the household. They should devote themselves to Parambrahma and perform their duties dispassionately in order to be united with the absolute at the end of their lives.

A married follower should cohabit with his wife on the eighth night of the wife's menstrual cycle with the intent of procreation. They should rise before sunrise the following day, apply cow-dung to their bodies and bathe seven times. Then they should change into a clean saffron cloth, drink *gomaya-pabitra*, invoke Alekh and perform *darśana*. They should not make love on other days of the cycle or within the first seven days.

Treatment of Ascetics[5]

All members of the household should respectfully perform *bhumistha śarana* (mode of showing respect by lying prostrate on the ground) to all Abadhuta Sannyasis who become their guests. They should give the ascetics a clean and comfortable place to stay. None of the family members should eat before offering alms to the renouncers. Rice and other food cooked at home should be given as alms. The food should be served either in a new earthen pot or on leaves of trees except the leaves of the Bata (Banyan) tree and leaves of the Aswatha (Pipal) tree. The members of the household should wait for the ascetic to finish his meal and then gladly accept the leftovers as the *prasāda* of the saint.

Disciples of Mahima Dharma should construct tungis (sheds), *asthānas* (seats) and dining places for the renouncers in relatively quiet parts of their village. They should accommodate ascetics who visit them there and offer hospitality to them. After the ascetics have spent a night, lay followers should offer alms to them again the next morning and bid them farewell. Householders should accompany the saints till the end of the village and then return to their houses and resume their normal duties.

Other Duties

The householders will clean the *gurudvara tungis* and *asthanas* everyday morning and evening and offer prayers, saran and *darśana* there. They should pray to the Lord to keep them and their relatives and friends on the right path. At the time of performing *darśana* they should discard expensive garments and use a saffron coloured clean cloth. All householders should strive to keep the noble company of ascetics, learn from them about true religion, give up evil thoughts and company and be a part of an association of good men, *satsanga gosthi*. They should avoid dishonest saints. They should only respect Abadhuta Sannyāsis and keep away from fake renouncers who earn their livelihood by posing to be gurus. They should not offer *bhumistha pranam* to any saint of any religious group except Mahimā Dharma. Lay followers should shed bad company. They should try their best to help the poor and the needy by giving them food and clothes.

Householders should perform *bālya lilā* on the morning of every sukla caturdasi, 14th day of the bright fortnight. On the same day they should clean and purify the *tungi*, the *āsthāna* and their homes with cow dung water and offer the morning and evening prayers together, mediating on Parambrahma. The evening should be spent in singing *bhajanas*. They should light lamps with ghee in the *tungi* and *asthana*. Women should light lamps with ghee in their own houses and stay up the whole night.

Brahma Marriage[6]

When Satya Mahimā Dharma spreads in the country, the followers of the faith will bring unity in society by getting their sons and daughters initiated into the dharma and marrying them in accordance with the rules of Brahma marriage. After boys and girls have completed their education, gained knowledge of the Dharma and have reached a marriageable age, their fathers will speak to other members of Satya Mahimā Dharma in order to arrange the wedding of their respective child. The devotees will select someone from among themselves as the mediator who will enquire both about the character of the future bride and groom as well as their opinion about the proposal. If the bride and the groom express their willingness, the devotee will fix an auspicious date for the marriage.

The father of the bride will invite the groom and other friends and followers to his house a day before the marriage. He will get a *mandapa* (decorated platform) built for the marriage ceremony. On the day of the wedding, the father will bring the bride and the groom, the mediator and all invitees to the *vivāha mandapa* in the morning after the bride and groom have bathed and cleaned themselves. The bride and the groom will wear new clothes and ornaments after first offering them to Paramabrahma. Then they will pray to the Absolute standing erect. Parents of the bride and the groom and all other devotees should also offer their prayers to Paramabrahma.

The parents of the bride will give their daughter to the groom after invoking Paramabrahma as the witness. Thereafter the bride will take a vow in the name of Brahma and accept the groom as her husband. This will be followed by the groom accepting the bride as his wife, once again after taking a vow in the name of Brahma. Then the newly weds, their parents and everyone present at the ceremony will pray to God for a long and prosperous life of the couple. Finally, the mediator will tie the hands of the bride and the groom with a sacred thread and explain to them how they can lead a happy and peaceful life by obeying the principles of Satya Mahimā Dharma. At the end, all present will chant the name of

Paramātma and pray to him for the well-being of the couple before returning to their respective seats.

The father of the bride will arrange a good feast for all the guests, devotees and relatives. Then he will accompany couple to the groom's residence where the groom's father will also offer hospitality to guests and relatives. Before the wedding, lamps should be lit with ghee, *bālya lilā* performed and ascetics of the Dharma invited in the houses of the bride and groom.

Birth of a Child

For the householder, the period of impurity will end on the twenty-first day after the birth of a child. On that day he should light lamps with ghee and sing *bhajans* (devotional songs) along with other devotees through the night. The next morning he should perform *bālya lilā* and invite ascetics and lay followers to be his guests. *Siddha sadhus* (self-realized ascetics) will give a name to the new child and pray to the Absolute so that the child enjoys peace and prosperity in life and he is blessed with true knowledge and devotion. They all will utter the sacred name of Alekha confer blessings on the child for a happy and healthy life. Householders should hold *bālya lilā* on every auspicious occasion, light lamps with ghee and invite ascetics and lay devotees to sing *bhajans* with them. If lay disciples follow the above rules with care and be ever devoted to Parambrahma they will be united with him after death.

Renunciation of Home by an Ascetic

Oh Gobinda! Any person who craves for the company of saints and pious people and whose total devotion to Brahma arouses in him an apathy toward the world and hatred for material things, can leave home in order to be initiated in the path of Abadhuta ashrama. This path of renunciation does not recognize any distinction of caste between brahmins, *kshatriyas*, *vaiśyas*, *śudras*, nor does it discriminate on the basis of childhood, youth and old age.

When a man has the desire to renounce the world he should

invite *siddhas* and *sadhus* as guests to his house and offer them food after taking into account the wishes of his parents, family and friends. He should then accept *bhiksha* (alms) in the presence of his parents or from his relatives in case the parents are dead. He should also invite his co-religionists and offer them food. In the end, he should pay respect to his parents and leave the village along with the ascetics. After this, he will neither return to his village nor accept anything from his relatives.

He will preach the dharma in a different region, roaming from place to place avoiding the area nearby his village. No one can become a renouncer without the permission of the father and the mother. He can do so only if the parents are non-religious and if they prohibit the son to accept the true path (*satpatha*) on account of ignorance or illiteracy. If the son has brothers capable of maintaining the parents and the household, then he can renounce his home when he feels a strong urge for it on account of the results of his deeds in an earlier life.

A married man cannot renounce the world before having a son. He has to wait for the son to grow up and be able to take charge of his mother and the household. Only then can he seek permission from his wife and son, make arrangements for the upkeep of the wife throughout her life and renounce the world in accordance with the principles mentioned above. An ascetic who acquires property, becomes the proprietor of a matha or returns to family life, accumulates sins for his actions. Those who become renouncers while remaining attached to worldly possessions or in order to escape from loans will be born as animals in the next life and thus pay for their sinful deeds. Those who pose to be sannyasis only in order to get food as alms would suffer the same fate. Fake ascetics who acquire property are not worthy of being associated with Mahaprabhu (the great Lord) in any way, not even as his servants. They are to be ostracized from the noble community of abadhuta ascetics.

The one who comes within the fold of Satya Mahima Dharma as a *tyagi* (renouncer) should, in accordance with the commandments of the preceptor, shave his head and discard all mundane paraphernalia such as garlands, sacred thread and worldly clothes.

He should cleanse his body with a bath in the *brahmamuhurta* the following morning, purify himself by drinking *gomaya-pabitra* (a drink made of the excrements of the cow), wear a clean, saffron cloth five yards long after offering it to the Lord and perform *śarana* and *darśana* of the Supreme. This will complete his induction into *satsangha* (community of honest people) and he would lead the life of a detached renouncer foı some time before becoming an *abadhuta*. One can take to this path anytime in life, but it is better to renounce the world at an early age.

The First Meeting of Bhima Bhoi and Mahimā Swami[7]

Toward the end of the time when Mahimā Swami was living only on milk in Kapilas, Govinda Baba came to the Balasingha ashrama. That evening, Mahimā Swami, in order to give *darśana* to Bhima Bhoi, walked through space to Govinda Baba's ashrama in the village Balasingha in the state of Baud and called out the name of Govinda. It was ten o'clock at night. Govinda Baba woke up with a start, came to the Swami fearfully and asked him why he had come to Balasingha and not commanded Govinda to go to Kapilas. He also enquired what had brought the Swami to Balasingha in the middle of the night. The Swami replied: 'I have come here because I want to give *darśana* to Bhima Bhoi. You come with me.' Govinda followed the Swami's order and the master and disciple went in an invisible form to the village Kankanpada in Rairakhol. They stood in front of Bhima Bhoi's door and the Swami called out Bhima's name. A surprised Bhima Bhoi asked: 'Who is calling me in the middle of the night?' The Swami commanded, 'Come out, Bhima, we are here to give you *darśana* on account of your *purva punya* (merit accumulated in an earlier life). Bhima Bhoi said 'I am blind, only if you restore my eyesight would I believe that you are here due to my *purva punya*.' The Swami commanded: 'Be blessed with vision.' And Bhima Bhoi gained sight and came out from his mud hut. He saw the Guru and his *śiṣya* and touched their feet. The Swami said 'I'm an omnipresent God, presently here in a human form. I'm here to end the *kaliyuga*. In order to do this, you will have to come within the fold of true faith.' Having spoken thus he gave *diksha* (initiation) to Bhima Bhoi. Then the Swami clapped three times and blessed Bhima Bhoi with poetic power. Overwhelmed, Bhima Bhoi touched the Swami's feet and said, 'Lord, you have given me the power of vision and I am fortunate enough to see your lotus feet. I have no desire to see mundane things with this divine sight. So kindly bless me to be blind again'. The Swami said 'so be it' and vanished.

Mahimā Swami saves Bhima Bhoi from the Well[8]

Bhima Bhoi was a cowherd. Once, while grazing cows he fell into a well. Villagers came to rescue him but he stopped them saying 'Let the one who threw me into the well come and rescue me! Otherwise, I would sacrifice myself.' In the evening Mahimā Swami came to know of the incident and asked the king of Dhenkanal to give him eight soldiers to accompany him to Rairakhol. The king said, 'Lord, it is almost impossible to cover eighty miles on foot over night. How can you go and rescue Bhima Bhoi?' Mahimā Swami said 'Sunya Prabhu will take care of that. You just give me eight soldiers.' The soldiers followed the Swami. After a few miles they could not see him anymore and came back to the palace to inform the king. The Swami, however, reached the well and stretched his foot down to Bhima Bhoi. The latter came out with the help of the Lord's lotus foot and offered *śarana*. Bhima Bhoi was fortunate to get the Lord's touch and his body dazzled with the Swami's gracious touch. He was a very good looking man.

Mahimā Swami's Conversation with a Christian Pastor[9]

Once, a Christian pastor from Cuttack came to the village Nanda in the present district of Keonjhar in order to meet Mahimā Swami. The Swami was ready to receive the pastor because he had come to know about the arrival of the pastor through his miraculous powers. The pastor talked to the Swami in English. The conversation is the following:

Question	I am aware of your glory and being impressed, I have come to see you here. Why are you spreading your glory here in Orissa?
Answer	My glory is spreading with the dissemination of Mahimā Dharma in Orissa.
Question	Hindu religion believes in Idol worship. Do you?
Answer	No. We don't
Question	Then what do you worship?
Answer	We worship Alekha, the one and only supreme Brahma.
Question	Are you impressed by Christianity? Jesus Christ also believed in the one and only God?
Answer	Any religion which guides its followers to worship the one and supreme Lord is great. In our Mahimā Dharma we believe in Brahma. In future this Dharma would go global.
Question	You believe in a formless god? Than why this *dhuni*?
Answer	We never offer ghee *ahuti* (offering) to any gods or goddesses. That is only for the peace of the world.
Question	Is your miraculous *līla* the result of your *sādhana* or of something else?
Answer	My *līla* is not intended for the performance of miracles. It is just natural. I want to establish Satya Dharma.

The Pastor was moved with the Swami's wisdom. He offered his regards and went away. Then the devotees, who were with the Swami pleaded him to translate the conversation into Oriya. The Swami could talk in any vernacular or foreign language. But usually he spoke in Hindi and Oriya.

Mahimā Swami's Last Days and the Origin of Mahima Gadi[10]

It happened that in the *tungi* of the village Jakā, the Swami told his followers that Queen Victoria wanted to arrest him with gold and iron handcuffs. But how could the Queen touch the Lord who is all-pervasive like the air and the sky? The Swami went back to Mahanityapura in the month of *Phālguna*, on the tenth day of the bright fortnight in 1876.

He said that a *gadi* should be built for the peace of the world in Jorandā. Thus predicting, he came to the *tungi* in Jorandā and sat for *samādhi*. After four days Niladri Bābā got order from *śūnya* that the Swami wished to finish his mundane *līla*. They should start building a *gadi* in Jorandā. The Siddhas and Bhaktas put the Swami's body in the *gadi* and started thinking about the construction of a temple (. . .).

After almost a month, on the twelfth day of the bright fortnight in the month of *Chaitra*, twenty-seven *murti siddhas* sat in the village Jakā to decide on the construction of the *gādi*. In the meeting Siddha Anama Das Bābā announced that he has been ordered by the Swami in a dream to build a temple in Jorandā. The temple should have a seven hooded snake (*saptapheni*) on top and should be flanked by a compound wall with four gates. Siddha Nanda Baba would be the first to offer service there by lighting a lamp. Anama Das's proposal was accepted without objection. Thus the construction of the temple started.

Notes

1. This is an excerpt from the first chapter of the *History of Satya Mahima Dharma* by Biswanath Baba, translated by Aniruddha Das and Sanjeeb Kumar Nayak and revised by Ishita Banerjee-Dube. The content is about the appearance of Prabuddha Guru, that is the enlightened teacher Mahimā Svāmi. Parts have been reformulated to make the reading easier. Often the meaning was not easy to understand since the original style is often very technical and composed in the way of Sanskrit sutras.
2. The term used is here *dharma avatār purusha*.
3. The original term is *anitya*.
4. Expression designating the prostration on the ground with the entire body, that means with all limbs.
5. *Mahima Dharmara Itihāsa*, pp. 21–3.
6. Ibid., pp. 26–8.
7. Ibid., pp. 53–6
8. Ibid., pp. 57–8.
9. Ibid., pp. 184–6.
10. Ibid., pp. 281–90.

Contributors

ISHITA BANERJEE-DUBE is Associate Professor at the Centre for Asian and African Studies, El Colegio de Mexico, Mexico City. She is the author of *Divine Affairs* (Shimla: Indian Institute of Advanced Study, 2001), *Religion, Law and Power* (London: Anthem Press, 2007) and, in Spanish, *Fronteras del Hinduismo* (Mexico: El Colegio de Mexico, forthcoming). Her papers have appeared in several important anthologies and journals including *Subaltern Studies* and *Studies in History*.

BETTINA BÄUMER is at present Fellow at the Indian Institute of Advanced Study, Simla, and Visiting Professor at the University of Vienna. As former Director of the Alice Boner Institute in Varanasi. She did extensive field work in Orissa for 25 years.

JOHANNES BELTZ is currently Curator of Indian Art at the Museum Rietberg in Zürich, Switzerland. Being part of the Orissa Research Project he worked intensively from 1999 to 2004 for the Department of Classical Indology at the South Asia Institute in Heidelberg on Mahimā Dharma, spending several months of field work in Orissa. Since 2004 he teaches introductory courses in Hinduism and Buddhism at the University of Zürich.

SADANANDA DAS studied Sanskrit at the University of Pune, where he submitted his Ph.D. thesis on 'Vedic Theories of Creation with Special Reference to the Atharvaveda' in Sanskrit in 2002. At present he teaches Sanskrit at the Department of Indology at Leipzig University.

GOURANG CHARAN DASH is an eminent folk-culturist, promoter and patron of folk-theatre, particularly Ravanachhaya. He taught Oriya language and literature at the Government College, Angul, for several years and is currently based in Puri.

FANINDAM DEO teaches history at the National College, Nuapara, Orissa. He received his Ph.D. degree from the Jawaharlal Nehru University and has been a Fellow at the Indian Institute of Advanced Study. He has contributed papers to academic journals and books.

ANNCHARLOTT ESCHMANN was born in Munich, Germany, on 24 September 1941. As a member of the first Orissa Research Project, she went to India in 1970 and met Biswanath Baba, a leading proponent of Mahimā Dharma, that same year. She carried on extensive research on Mahimā Dharma till the time of her tragic death in Delhi in 1977.

LIDIA GUZY, born in Katowice, Poland, conducted intensive fieldwork in Orissa focusing on asceticism and Mahimā Dharma as a member of the second Orissa Research Project. She teaches at the Institute for Religious Studies at the Freie Universität, Berlin. Her present research project is on endangered musical traditions of subaltern groups in Orissa.

KEDAR MISHRA is the literary editor of the daily Oriya newspaper *Anupam Bharat.* From 1999 to 2004 he worked as Research Assistant for the Orissa Research Project. Originating from Sonepur he had a lasting relationship with Bhima Bhoi. He has published several poems in local magazines and newspapers and two anthologies of his poetry in Oriya.

SANJEEB KUMAR NAYAK is Lecturer in English at the Department of English, Baudh College, Orissa. As founding member of the Mahanadi Sahitya Sansada he has published several poems in Oriya.

Index